Eastern cuisine

The best in Asian food

R&R PUBLICATIONS MARKETING PTY LTD

Published by:
R&R Publications Marketing Pty Ltd
ABN 78 348 105 138
12 Edward Street
Brunswick Victoria 3056
Australia
Phone: (61 3) 9381 2199
Fax: (61 3) 9381 2689
Australia-wide toll free: 1 800 063 296
E-mail: info@randrpublications.com.au
Web: www.randrpublications.com.au

Eastern cuisine: the best in Asian food
© 2005 Richard Carroll

Publisher: Richard Carroll
Production Manager: Anthony Carroll
Food Photography: Gary Smith, Alfonso Calero (Indian)
Travel Text: Kerry Kenihan
Food Stylists: Janet Lodge, Liz Nolan (Indian)
Assisting Home Economist: Jenny Fanshaw
Recipe Development: Jenny Fanshaw, Ellen Argyriou, Janet Lodge
Creative Director: Aisling Gallagher
Cover Designer: Aisling Gallagher
Text Designers: Paul Simms, Lucy Adams and Elain Loh
Proofreader: LoftCom
US Editor:Diana Luger

The publishers wish to thank the management and staff of the Aya Restaurant for
all of their help and assistance in putting the Japanese section of this book together.
Special thanks to Executive Chef, Kenichi Okumura, and Sushi Chef, Junji Kubohara.

Includes index
ISBN 1 74022 526 0
EAN 9 781740 225 267

This edition printed September 2005
Printed in China by Max Production Printing Limited

Contents

Introduction

You could blame it all on the Venetian explorer Marco Polo. After his acceptance by the royal court in China in about 1275 and his sojourns in that vast land, he brought back China's noodles to his native country of Italy. Thus a taste for Asian food first spread to the West, and Marco Polo became the world's first promoter of Eastern cuisine.

Closed to the outside world until modern times, Japan and her food remained for years free from foreign influence, except for the impact of Chinese, Korean and Indian traders. The opening up of Japan to Western tourism and commerce in the last century precipitated the opening of many Western cuisine outlets in Japan. Yet, the Japanese remain at heart true to their own food heritage. Japanese cuisine is probably the most artistically presented on earth, and one of the healthiest. The use of spices is subtle. The cuisine is rarely hot unless you add wasabi, a native green horseradish paste, which lends a sharp, head-clearing impact to sushi or sashimi.

Vietnam adopted many of its culinary traits from China, its neighbor. China ruled Vietnam for 1,000 years from 111 BC and introduced beef to Vietnam via Mongol herdsmen in the 10th century. Thus resulted the national dish, *pho*, a meaty rice-noodle soup. The French, who ruled Vietnam from 1859 to 1954, had a profound impact on Vietnamese cuisine, not only with their cooking methods and European vegetables, but also with French bread styles, particularly the baguette. The Vietnamese are now among the world's best breadmakers. Traditions and spices have come from Vietnam's border countries: Laos, Cambodia and Thailand. Curries are also much loved by the Vietnamese.

Curry forms the basis of the Indian subcontinent's cuisine. The origins of the term 'curry' are disputed, but the term was adopted by the English during the period of the British Raj, to embrace the huge range of Indian food spicing. More than 25 individual spices are used in various combinations to give rise to a multitude of different dishes. Rice is India's staple, most important in the South, while bread is preferred in the North. Both are frequently accompanied by dhal, a thick lentil puree, the daily fare of the poor. Indian culinary traditions, as elsewhere, are affected by religious belief: Hindus don't eat beef as they consider the cow sacred, and many strict Hindus are also complete vegetarians. Pork is not eaten by strict Muslims or Jews.

Side dishes including yogurt are usually served with hot dishes to cool overheated palates, but not all Indian dishes are hot. Tandoori dishes, and particularly tandoori chicken, which are cooked in a tandoor clay oven, have gained popularity in the West, because of their flavour and mildness. Biryani, an orange-colored rice-based meat dish similar to pilaf, is also mild in flavor. Different regions each have their own variation of biryani. Northern Mogul-influenced dishes, especially in Kashmir, are generally much milder than the fiery southern creations. Goan cuisine has been heavily influenced by the Portuguese as a result of their 400 years of rule until 1961. Excellent seafood is available along India's vast coastline. Snacks like samosas or curried vegetable pastries, are adored throughout India. Indians also enjoy very sweet desserts.

China has a culinary history of more than 5,000 years. Emigrating southern Chinese cooks first ignited interest in Cantonese-style dishes when they opened humble eating places in their adopted new homelands. The dishes were often modified to allow for the unsophisticated palates of diners in Western countries. Yet, now, authentic Asian cuisine flourishes not only in restaurants in the West but also in many homes. The Chinese have 11 distinctive regional cuisines, each of which is well worth investigating.

This book on the foods of China, Japan, Vietnam and India offers Western cooks the opportunity to add an exciting variety to their meals. Each section contains several revered national dishes. Few lamb recipes are included as, apart from in northern China and northern India, sheep and goats are generally not raised for meat in Asia. Land suitable for grazing is generally given over to rice or wheat cultivation. However, you can substitute lamb for beef in most of the meat dishes. If using lamb, mutton or goat in a stir-fry or quickly cooked dish, make sure that the meat is as tender as quality beef by pounding and/or marinating before cooking.

At a celebration dinner I held recently, I selected a variety of dishes from each of these cuisines described in this book, boldly flaunting the Chinese culinary custom of ensuring a balance of hot and cool, sour and sweet, spicy and bland, and yin and yang food at any banquet. The dinner was a great success. With the drinks I served two appetizers: Japanese tofu sushi (page 172) and Indonesian foil-baked fish (foil-baked as I had no banana leaves). The firm flesh of the delicately curried fish was lightly moistened by the coconut milk it had absorbed in the baking. I served the fish cut into cubes on a platter with toothpicks for my guests to transfer to their own appetizer plates.

My guests sat at the table for green jade spinach soup from China (page 104). The entrées were Japanese chicken yakitori (page 193) and sauced Chinese crab meat fritters (page 95). I made the fritters economically with seafood sticks, demonstrating that you can adapt recipes according to the ingredients available or what you can afford. The main course was made up of tandoori lamb cutlets (page 288) from India, raita (a side dish of yogurt with cucumber, see page 248) and bean stir-fry with Indonesian festive yellow rice, served with rich fish-flavoured eggplant (page 150), my favorite Chinese vegetable dish, plus Vietnam's Saigon salad (page 74). Dessert was a coconut flan with caramel (page 79) from Vietnam.

It was a fun dinner for my guests whom I challenged to name each dish's country of origin. I offered both dry white and light red local wines to drink, which were very quaffable, yet not of high quality, as hot spices affect your appreciation of fine vintage wine. The other beverage choices were light beer, soft drinks and Chinese green tea. Indonesian coffee was also enjoyed by the guests.

GINGER CHICKEN WONTON SOUP, PAGE 103

INTRODUCTION

To accommodate those who could not use chopsticks I placed Western cutlery beside my Chinese dinner set, along with extra plates.

In some Asian cultures, all the dishes for a meal are served simultaneously at the table or even while sitting on a mat. Ingredients are bought fresh once or sometimes even twice daily because of the lack of refrigeration in isolated and/or poor communities. Frozen produce is rare, even in households that can afford refrigerators. Food is purchased according to its seasonal availability and price, since most Asian countries don't have the reliable cold-storage transport to move fresh food long distances to markets. This is why some Asian foods, particularly fish, are dried as a means of preservation. Chicken is very popular, since it is the least expensive meat, and can be transported live.

You could enjoy a complete and delicious meal in Asia from the variety of appetizers available from the hawker stalls that crowd the streets and market areas. An idea for inventive cooks is a dinner or weekend lunch featuring many of these appetizers. This would make a stunning Sunday brunch—a type of multicultural dim sum.

All the ingredients listed are available in specialty Asian food stores in major metropolitan cities. Ordinary supermarkets, even in regional areas, are stocking greater amounts of these ingredients as the interest in eating and preparing Asian food grows. In terms of crockery and cutlery, Chinese, Vietnamese and Japanese food is traditionally eaten using rice bowls, small plates and chopsticks, while Indian food can be served with Western crockery and cutlery. The best chopsticks have points so fine that the wielder can pick up a single rice grain. Don't buy thick-tipped chopsticks.

Desserts are rarely served as a finale to lunch or dinner in Asia, but are reserved as special treats between meals. However, for your own dinner parties you can either serve fresh seasonal fruits or one of the irresistible desserts included here after the savory dishes have been enjoyed.

Build your spice collection gradually, but in small quantities, as some spices lose flavors if stored too long. Most Western cooks will already have the necessary equipment. A wok is invaluable, but a big frying-pan will do. You will also need a couple of large casserole dishes with lids, suited to both oven and stovetop cooking, a pot with a frying basket, extra saucepans, long chopsticks or a wooden spoon for stir-frying, an egg-slide and sharp knives. Sushi-makers will need a bamboo mat for the rolling of the rice within the seaweed sheets. A barbecue, no matter how simple, will impart super smoky flavors. If not, an oven griller will suffice.

I couldn't be without my mortar and pestle for blending spices and my food processor/blender. Some friends swear by rice cookers, but I cook rice very successfully in a big saucepan with a lid using the absorption method. Otherwise I cheat, using a microwave-friendly, lidded plastic pot in the microwave. I interrupt the cooking cycle by stirring the rice a few times thoroughly with a wooden spoon. No failures yet.

Eat Eastern food well and adventurously, sharing gladly, even if it's only a fine, filling, but inexpensive one-dish meal. Not every Eastern meal has to be a banquet, and there are plenty of recipes in the pages following for you to choose from.

Kerry Kenihan

CHICKEN SPRING ROLLS, PAGE 92

VIETNAMESE
food

the land AND ITS PEOPLE

Status	People's Socialist Republic
Area	127,246 sq mile
Population	81,098,000
Language	Vietnamese
Religion	Buddhist
Currency	Dong
National Day	2 September

FOOD FOR ALL MOODS

On a cold, blustery morning in a narrow, muddied, unsealed, suburban street in Hanoi, the capital of Vietnam, buyers and sellers of vegetables, fruit and flowers and food hawkers huddle under canvas awnings shading shadowy shops. While it was hot in the country's South, here, in the North, we were sheltered from pelting rain. Suddenly, one of the shopkeepers ignited a huge wad of newspapers. Tossing sections towards the road, she created a mini-inferno.

I wondered if she had gone mad, a modern-day victim of more than 2,000 years in which war-torn Vietnam had struggled to expel foreign demons and cope with its own violent rebellions. My young interpreter, Mai, grasped my hand, reassuring me that 'The seller fans the fire to highlight her vegetables'–a simple but effective marketing technique.

I was in Hanoi to become, I believe, the first Western woman to take a professional crash course in tertiary cooking with Madame Do Minh Thu at the Caoson College of Learning, one of Hanoi's five university campuses. Mai, or her fellow students Tek and Hanh, drove me to the course every day as a motorbike pillion-passenger, weaving expertly through the city's insane traffic.

Mai and Tek bought in large quantities from the flame-thrower and other vendors. Later, at Mai's family's narrow three-story home, designed to give maximum space to the vegetable garden (in the style of many city houses), the girls prepared a host of dishes while squatting on the kitchen floor. Many Vietnamese kitchens are tiny, with negligible bench space, a reason why many Vietnamese cook and eat out on the streets. Three invisible food gods presided over the nervous chefs, who had both learned to cook from their mothers.

Until recently, all Vietnamese girls were expected to prove their culinary skills to a future husband's family before marriage, which they still do in some villages. Mai and Tet would pass these tests with flying colors.

A staple of Vietnam is long-grain rice steamed until fluffy in a rice cooker (a more important appliance in Vietnam than a refrigerator). Sticky or glutinous rice is usually reserved for desserts and special festival food, but is often spiced and served for breakfast, wrapped in banana leaves. The world's biggest exporter of rice, next to America and Thailand, Vietnam has dozens of varieties of rice. Rice (cooked unwashed without salt) is turned into rice flour, food-wrapping paper, powder, noodles, vermicelli, wine and vinegar.

Professional cooking courses are relatively new to Vietnam. In recent years visitors have taken short, rather Westernized courses in the 1901-built grand Metropole Hotel in Hanoi, as well as in other hotels and restaurants in Hanoi and Saigon. You need a course of at least three days to explore the Northern and Southern Vietnamese cooking

styles, which are both very different. A distinctive central region cuisine was developed in the former imperial courts of Hue and in the French-influenced old port of Hoi An.

Dominated by China from 200 BC, Vietnam inherited from the Chinese metal ploughs, irrigation systems, beasts of burden, chopsticks, Buddhism (hence vegetarianism), many recipes, table manners and, most importantly, rice cultivation. Cattle were brought to Vietnam by 10th century Mongol herdsmen. Hanoi gave birth to the wonderful beef noodle soup *pho* (pronounced 'fur'), which is Vietnam's national dish.

Thai traditions filtered into Vietnam at about the time the Portuguese missionaries introduced spices and Christianity to Thailand in the 14th century AD. Coffee and tea came to Vietnam via Cambodia. Coffee plants now cover Vietnam's countryside, which was devastated by bomb blasts during the Vietnam War. The Vietnamese are also fond of curries.

The French occupied Vietnam from 1859 to 1954, and left their imprint on Vietnamese cuisine. The French influence ranges from the introduction of produce such as wine, avocados, tomatoes, asparagus, sweet corn, baguettes, pâté, salads, pastries, café au lait, cakes and ice cream, as well as the cooking method of sautéing.

The result of all these cultural influences is a rich array of tastes and traditions. Vietnamese food is not as spicy as Thais but is crisper. Soy sauce is not used much, unlike in China. Having eaten my way from Hanoi to Ho Chi Minh City, I believe

Vietnamese cuisine to be the most exciting on earth. The secret is in *nuoc cham*, a pungent fish sauce. *Nuoc cham* is to the Vietnamese what soy is to the Chinese and Japanese, shrimp paste to the Indonesians and *nam prik* (chili sauce) is to the Thais. Fermented from anchovies, bottled *nuoc cham* is used instead of salt and combines well with all meats and fish. Add lime juice, garlic, fresh, seeded red chili, and sugar and vinegar to taste, and it becomes Vietnam's favorite dipping sauce, also known as *nuoc cham*, found on every table.

the land AND ITS PEOPLE

IS THERE AN S IN VIETNAM?

S is the shape of the country of Vietnam, which has a population of more than 70 million people, including 54 different ethnic groups. You can picture Vietnam as a street vendor with his head raised, his thin spine curved under the heavy burden of a bamboo pole yoke (*don ganh*) balanced on his frail shoulders with each end of the bamboo pole holding a big basket containing anything from bananas to bricks. His knees are bent. In the far South, including the Mekong Delta, the map resembles a foot, poised ready to repel adversaries into the Gulf of Thailand.

The S-shape also represents the national highway which winds from north to south for about 1,000 miles along the Indochinese Peninsula in an area a bit bigger than the 'boot' of the South of Italy. The national highway is paradoxically, both a good and bad way to traverse Vietnam. In seasons of monsoons and typhoons, the road is subject to flooding and mudslides and is pot-holed and sometimes terrifying. Through bus windows, one sees an endless lake of rice paddies punctuated by the conical hats of women working. Running past shark-toothed mountains, the bus affords views of the Gulf of Tonkin and the South China Sea. There is a train at night, but its passengers miss the stunning beauty of the countryside.

The Vietnamese countryside is dotted with waterfalls, rain forests, lagoons, groves of coconut palms and other tropical fruit trees. Cattle, water buffalo and goats graze in the pastures. There is an intriguing mixture of both prosperous and depressed towns (curiously, all advertising photocopying facilities) and an increasing number of resorts.

The climate in Vietnam is varied, from cold in winter to a hot dry summer in the North, to Southern humidity. The central mountains, where the French built hill stations, provide respite from the summer heat.

Much of Vietnam is sub-tropical and hence there is an astonishing variety of fresh produce. In Dalat, Vietnam's honeymoon capital, the terraced hills are so abundant with vegetables and fruits that many residents are vegetarians. Ho Chi Minh City is lavishly supplied with fresh daily produce, including tea and coffee from surrounding plantations. Local wineries are developing in the lowlands extending from the South China Sea where the climate favors grapes.

Vietnam's 2,000 miles of coastline yield gleaming fish and seafood. Fish are also harvested from the Red, Perfume and Mekong Rivers, as well as in countless canals and ponds.

THE PEOPLE

Whether bent in the fields (80 percent of the Vietnamese toil in agriculture), spinning silk, making lacquerware, copying famous artworks of European masters, manning stalls, endlessly serving food, hobbling along streets burdened by their *don ganh* yokes, or working in offices, the Vietnamese are friendly and hospitable. They don't demonstrate any resentment towards nationalities with whom they have previously been at war. Visitors need only be prepared for the amusing attention from competing owners of *pho* shops seeking customers and from the bargaining drivers of *cyclos* (cycle-cabs for one or two passengers), eager for passengers.

Although belonging to various Asian religions —Christianity and Islam (a minority only)—all Vietnamese people celebrate the seven-day *Tet* festival (Vietnamese New Year) with gusto, eating special foods such as sticky rice, yellow beans and spiced pig fat boiled for six hours in banana leaves. Sweetmeats, dried, sugar and salted fruits are sold *en masse*. *Tet* occurs in the lunar calendar in late

January or early February. Wandering Souls' Day on the 15th day of the seventh month is the second largest festival in Vietnam. Gifts, mainly fruits, are taken to pagodas and sweets to houses as tributes to the souls of the dead.

Food is paramount in the Mid-Autumn festival on the 15th day of the eighth lunar month—a festival filled with bright, noisy, night processions. A January rice-cooking festival in Hanoi also enlivens the lunar calendar.

Vietnam is a bountiful paradise where many live in poverty, yet its proud people don't eat to live. They live to eat.

daily food
IN VIETNAM

LE PETIT DEJEUNER

Just before sunrise in Hanoi's old quarter, courting couples called it a day after conquering the night with their screaming motorcycles. Apart from crowding into Internet cafes or flirting over *pho*, motorcycling seems to be the most popular entertainment for young people. No girls were out wearing *ao dai*, their traditional costume of long white pants and a modest thigh-length, wrist-touching top, along with coolie hats and gloves (to keep their hands untanned).

Street sweepers shuffled slowly. Light filtered through an avenue of leafy trees. An old woman painstakingly arranged eggs in the baskets of her *doh ganh*—white in one basket, brown in the other. Shopkeepers and residents gradually emerged to peruse hawkers' vegetables, fruit, meat and fish. Flower vendors offered bright blooms from the baskets of their bicycles. One soup seller's business was busy with manicurists and pedicurists sitting on small plastic stools. Between attending to their female clients, the beauticians spooned up *chao* (rice porridge) or soup, using chopsticks to fish for their soup noodles.

An aged street barber was massaging the neck of his disabled son who was sitting in a primitive wheelchair. A pre-World War II Citroën stopped by

a large pottery shop where salesgirls were eating *pho* with salad. A woman offered me sticky rice in banana-leaf parcels in French—just to taste, no charge unless I liked it. But I'd had already had my *pho* fix. In plush hotels, French Continental breakfast rolls, croissants and pastries were baking. In the fields, men were drinking tea together and eating rice with fish sauce.

Hanoi's seven million people begin every day like this. Their repasts are on the move as they are everywhere in Vietnam. Baguette bikes tow mobile stalls from dawn until dark.

Children have a choice of either morning or afternoon sessions at school. While children sometimes breakfast at home, they are more likely to eat market food with a parent before school starts at 7.30 am. The second session begins after a lunch at home or at the market.

Although coffee aficionados might disagree, Vietnamese coffee, brewed strong and slowly, is delicious. It is always consumed at breakfast and after dinner, with

daily food
IN VIETNAM

milk or cream and sugar. Tea is drunk everywhere in Vietnam and its serving is elevated to an art form as in China, although tea, I was warned, is far too strong for females in the morning. While black tea is cheap, green tea is expensive. In the central mountains, artichoke tea is popular.

In Dalat, inhabitants eat *chao*, but it is quite unlike the bland rice porridge eaten elsewhere in Vietnam. Dalat *chao* is also favored in the evening as warming fuel for those in the cool mountainous terrain. This thick gruel is pork broth based, with meat or fish chunks, garlic and chili oil added, and topped with cilantro, bean sprouts and black pepper. It makes a filling dinner. In southern Dalat one morning, I grabbed a hot melt-in-the-mouth, pâté-stuffed puffpastry from a patisserie and became instantly hooked on another specialty of this area.

In the Mekong Delta's Cai Rang and on Phu Quoc, one of several islands (and Vietnam's most famous source of nuoc cham), floating marketeers feed early risers. Each fragile vessel carries a speciality—fruits, vegetables, fish, pork, rice, noodles, baguettes, tea, coffee and even breakfast beer.

Starting from Ninh Binh town, my friend Jillian and I glided in a traditional rowboat through Tam Coc (the name means 'three caves') along the Ngo Dong River. This river supplies a canal system for rice irrigation. Its spectacular rock formations are like those in Halong Bay and are reminiscent of China's Guilin and Yangzhou. The sole Western visitors, other than holidaying French people, we were assailed in French by boat folk. These boat vendors would row or pole back a long way to port to fetch *pho*, fish, water, beer, fruit, embroidered napery, hats, film, or even rice hooch, such is their enthusiasm for selling.

Jillian became addicted to Vietnamese smoothies—not the same as Western thick-shakes. Melting ice is blended with sweetened condensed milk, a mint sprig, lime or lemon juice, plus any fruit or, for savory smoothies, with avocado, tomato or pumpkin, or any combination of these, garnished with cilantro. Created for Western budget-backpackers, smoothies have been happily adopted by busy young Vietnamese as healthy breakfast starters and as lunchtime coolers.

DEJEUNER – AH, LUNCH

Markets in cities, towns, villages and on fishing waterfronts are abuzz after first light in Vietnam. Those who can go home for lunch, do, but still the street eateries, cafes, restaurants and markets are crammed with people.

Westerners would recognize much Vietnamese lunch fare as snack food or appetizers: spring rolls and rice paper rolls, cold or hot, and other tasty titbits (see the Appetizers section). On sale for lunch in Vietnam are noodles, rice cakes, baguettes, grilled meats, seafood, *pho* and plain steamed rice with fish sauce. People tend to eat at any time of the day. Desserts are something snacked on, rather than eaten as part of a main meal.

From 11 am to noon and onward, Vietnam lunches. At home, women usually cook, while professional cooks and chefs are mostly men. A typical home meal would be rice with soup plus two to three other dishes, one a salad, or sautéed, fried or boiled vegetables. Weekend, and particularly Sunday lunches are leisurely for those families not working then, who, if they can afford it, add an extra dish or two.

Fish or meat is not usually eaten daily because meat, particularly beef, is more expensive than vegetables. Sheep are not bred in Vietnam. Edible leaves are used to garnish and wrap food in heat packets. You need to be wary of eating salads in Vietnam, as the raw vegetables may have been washed in contaminated water. Frequently combined with meat, poultry or fish, Vietnamese salads are delicious and easy to prepare in your own kitchen (see the Salads section). Monosodium glutamate (MSG) is used in many Vietnamese dishes to enhance flavor. As some people are allergic to MSG, it has been left out of the recipes which follow.

Utensils for Vietnamese cooking are simple: one pot for rice, one for slow cooking, the essential mortar and pestle (or a blender or food processor), and a couple of pans. A wok is unnecessary, but helpful. Some Vietnamese use a coolie-hat-shaped pan, similar to a wok. You will also need both large and small sharp knives, an optional cleaver for chopping poultry, a chopping board, chopsticks, bowls with saucers, small bowls for sauces, serving dishes with spoons and tiny cups for tea.

LE DINER – HOME AT LAST

Dinner is time for hard-working Vietnamese parents to be reunited with their children and elderly relatives. Dinner dishes are similar to home-prepared lunches, centered around the rice bowl and all served simultaneously with soup. Dinner could comprise up to eight dishes on special occasions. Fruit is usually served for dessert.

Before eating, guests in the North should wait until the oldest host is seated and until he or she places something in their bowl. Southerners are more casual. It is customary to leave the last tasty morsel in a serving bowl to be offered to the host. He or she will then offer it back to the guest. Some leftovers should remain in the individual bowls to indicate the family has been generous. But do not leave rice in your bowl. A belief exists that if precious rice, the staple, is wasted on earth, a departed soul could be denied basic sustenance in the other world.

In the countryside, cooking is usually done outdoors over a coal brazier. With no refrigeration, shopping at the market may be done twice daily. Small city kitchens may have only two gas or electric hotplates. Most don't have ovens—hence the method of slow pot-cooking. Other Vietnamese cooking methods include sautéing, stir- and deep-frying, boiling, and grilling

over a brazier. Vietnamese use a garlic-infused oil for frying. To prepare this, heat peanut oil (but do not boil), then remove it from the burner, and add crushed garlic. Kept in a jar, garlic oil lasts about a week when kept in the refrigerator and can be brushed on barbecued meat or fish, noodles, bread and vegetables. The garnishing and decoration of Vietnamese dishes is as important as the flavor and freshness of the ingredients.

Typical drinks include fruit and sugarcane juices, and fizzy soft drinks similar to Western ones. Worth a try is a non-fizzy canned drink called bird's nest. Coconut milk is drunk through straws from punctured fresh coconuts. Few women drink alcohol. Men will imbibe light, refreshing beer with a meal out, but most alcohol is consumed at home where ice cubes are often added to cool the beer! Wine, introduced by the French, is an acceptable accompaniment to Vietnamese food, which is only as fiery as the chili sauce or fresh, chopped chili added by the diner. Moonshine is made

daily food
IN VIETNAM

from fermented sticky rice, husks, water and yeast.

It was once only the tipple of a minority ethnic group (the mountain people) at celebrations, but is now more popular in cities. It is cheap and readily available. Depending on where it was made and how long it has been fermented, the intensity of Vietnamese moonshine varies from bland to knock-out! (You can use vodka as a substitute aperitif at home.) As in Korea and China, 'snake wine' comes with a viper in the bottle. This liquor is very strong, so beware.

EATING OUT IN VIETNAM

In Vietnam, *pho* houses and markets are must-sees. Markets can be smelly, but their overwhelming flower perfumes are glorious. Street food is quite safe if the food is served hot. Noodle-soup stallholders bang together bamboo sections or pieces of metal to advertise their presence. You'll eat cheaply and well in, or in front, of a simple shop. There is no menu, you just point.

Simple eating establishments are called *com* (meaning 'rice'). These are family-run, no-frills places. Some display picture menus if the *com* is a shop rather than a stall. Otherwise, you eat in the street—perfect for people-watching.

Eager to try Hue's legendary seafood-stuffed crêpes (see the Shrimp Crêpe recipe on page 17), I wandered into a *com*. There was no menu, but the place had both indoor and street seating. The intelligent old father was deaf and mute, so I drew a primitive picture. He rushed to his wife and daughter in the miniscule backyard and returned with a selection of canned drinks in his hands. I chose light beer. Soon, I was served by the women who then awaited my appraisal of the crêpes. 'Magnifique', I attested honestly.

Dog, cat, snake, field mice and rats, and embryo ducks from eggs are served in certain restaurants (though these recipes are not included). Do try the eel recipe on page 52 in this book, however.

Many shop or stalls sell desserts, cakes and sweetmeats. Pancake outlets serve savory and sweet pancakes, but differ from Western pancake parlors. Waterfront restaurants, both indoor and out, abound in river and sea ports. Upmarket restaurants are found in major Vietnamese cities. The waiters may not speak English, but a translated menu will give the number of the dish. Vietnamese, or European classical music, mainly French composers, provides a soothing background. In international hotels, the ambience will be French-style with neatly laid tables, good service and Vietnamese/French/English menus. You should visit a hotel like the legendary Rex in Saigon for a drink, a rooftop view or elegant environment, even if you can't afford to dine there. More and more grand French mansions are being restored as high-class restaurants.

In Vietnam, you should offer flowers as a gift to your host. On my last day in Vietnam I bought big bouquets for Mai, Tek, Hanh and Madame Thu. Their ribbons streaked towards the sky as we whirled through suicidal peak traffic on my last motorcycle ride.

'Love our country', they asked me. I do. Even if you never visit Vietnam, I hope you can gain a understanding of this scenically sensational country and its warm people through its delicate yet hearty cuisine, which boasts more than 5,000 dishes. Hue's 19th century emperor Tu Duc demanded 50 dishes in each single meal, and never to be served the same dish more than twice in the same year. The imperial chefs created more than 2,000 dishes during his reign.

Kerry Kenihan

appetizers

Roll on a WRAP

'It's a wrap,' says a film director when a movie scene is finally finished to satisfaction. But a 'wrap' in a Vietnamese kitchen, street market and from a hawker stall means a super snack. At home, a 'wrap' can signify the beginning of a meal or party –cocktail, luncheon or dinner–as so many Vietnamese appetizers come in these tasty parcels.

Wraps may be deep- or shallow-fried, steamed or packed in fresh edible leaves–banana, lettuce, spinach, or cabbage–to be served cool. Wraps are delectable dollops of mixed ingredients folded in rice paper, crêpes, thicker pancakes or omelettes.

Spring rolls are served with nuoc cham dipping sauce. As China has exerted great influence on Vietnamese food, soy sauce is often an ingredient in wraps too. Soy sauce is likely to be on Vietnamese tables as a dipping sauce too and many Westerners prefer it to fish sauce. Use Vietnamese, Thai, Japanese or Chinese soy sauce as American-made sauce is too salty. Finely sliced, small, seeded red chilies are also a good spring roll accompaniment.

Stuffed pancakes (page 16) and seafood on sugar cane skewers (page 23) were both created in the ancient imperial court of Hue and are specialities of Central and South Vietnam.

WHITE SAUCE

Ingredients
1 $^1/_2$ oz butter
3 shallots, chopped
3 tablespoons all-purpose flour
$^1/_5$ cup whole milk
salt and black pepper

Method
1. Heat the butter in a saucepan, then fry the shallots for 5 minutes. Stir in the flour and cook for 2 minutes, stirring. Stir in the milk and cook for 20 minutes, stirring often.

HUE STUFFED PANCAKE

Ingredients
oil for frying
2 oz all-purpose flour, seasoned with salt and pepper
2 eggs, beaten
extra oil for deep frying

Batter
3 oz rice flour
$^1/_2$ cup coconut milk
3 eggs, beaten
pinch salt

Filling
$^1/_2$ tablespoon ginger root, peeled and chopped
1 clove garlic, chopped
1 tablespoon soy sauce
$^1/_2$ cup white sauce (see below left)
5 oz crab meat
3 oz mushrooms, chopped
1 oz scallions, chopped
1 oz bean sprouts
salt and pepper

To serve
lettuce leaves
cilantro, chopped
nuoc cham dipping sauce (see page 17)
1 red chili, seeded and finely sliced

Method
1. To make batter, combine rice flour, coconut milk, eggs and salt. Heat some oil in a 8 inch pan (preferably non-stick) and add enough batter to coat base. Cook for 2 minutes. Repeat with remaining batter. Put all pancakes aside.

2. To make filling, blend ginger, garlic, soy and white sauce. Add crab meat, mushrooms, scallions, and bean sprouts and season to taste. Place a spoonful of the mixture on each pancake. Tuck in ends and roll up so mixture doesn't escape.

3. Carefully roll each pancake in seasoned flour then in beaten egg. Deep-fry until golden. Serve on lettuce leaves, sprinkled with chopped cilantro, accompanied by nuoc cham.

Note: For variation, use thinly rolled puff pastry instead of pancakes. Pancakes can also be filled and served without deep-frying.

Serves 8

SHRIMP CRÊPES

Ingredients

8 oz rice flour

1 teaspoon salt

1$\frac{1}{2}$ teaspoons sugar

1 cup coconut milk

1 cup water

$\frac{1}{2}$ teaspoon ground turmeric

7 oz jumbo shrimp, shelled and deveined

7 oz bean shoots

4 oz pork fillet or chicken

1 onion, sliced

peanut oil (for frying)

nuoc cham dipping sauce (see below)

To garnish

Vietnamese mint leaves

lettuce leaves

Method

1. Mix together rice flour, salt, sugar, coconut milk, water and turmeric until the batter is smooth. Set aside.

2. Wash and dry shrimp and chop roughly. Wash bean shoots and set aside.

3. Dice the pork or chicken.

4. Heat a large frying pan and pour in a little oil. Add pork, onion and shrimp, and cook, stirring constantly, until shrimp change color and pork is cooked through.

5. Pour enough batter over mixture to cover ingredients, top with some bean shoots and cover pan with a lid. Cook for 2 minutes until crisp. Turn over and cook the other side until golden.

To serve: Place a Vietnamese mint leaf on a piece of the crêpe. Enclose in a lettuce leaf and drizzle nuoc cham dipping sauce over. Serve immediately.

Serves 4

NUOC CHAM DIPPING SAUCE

Ingredients

4 oz superfine sugar

1 cup hot water

$\frac{1}{2}$ cup Vietnamese fish sauce

1 tablespoon white rice vinegar

2$\frac{1}{2}$ oz lime juice

2–4 small red or green chilies, finely chopped

3–5 large garlic cloves, finely chopped

Method

1. Put the sugar in a bowl and pour the hot water over it, stirring until it is completely dissolved. Add all the other ingredients, stir well and allow to cool to room temperature.

2. This dipping sauce can be kept in an airtight container in the refrigerator for up to 7 days.

MADAME THU'S STEAMED EGG ROLLS

Ingredients

½ oz dried wood ear mushrooms

2 duck eggs (or 4 standard eggs)

rice wine or dry sherry

oil or pork fat for frying

2 cups water

1 banana leaf or muslin

7 oz ground pork

1 teaspoon sesame seeds

2 cloves garlic, minced

2 pimientos or seeded red chilies,
   finely chopped

4 teaspoons sugar

4 teaspoons fish sauce

pinch black pepper

5 oz field mushrooms

1 piece hot spicy cooked sausage,
   about 6 inches

length of string

nuoc cham dipping sauce

To garnish

slices of cucumber, tomatoes,
   parboiled cauliflower florets
   and fresh parsley sprigs

Method

1. Soak dried mushrooms in hot water for about 30 minutes until soft. Meanwhile, separate eggs into 2 bowls; whites in one, yolks in the other. Beat both, adding a little wine to the whites to reduce the eggy odor and a little to the yolks to make a medium thick consistency.

2. Season a pan with a little pork fat or oil, add some pork to flavor pan. Stir-fry over medium heat, then remove. Add egg white mixture to pan and, when firm, remove pancake and place on a plate. Re-season pan with more pork fat or oil, then pour off excess oil and add beaten yolk and wine mixture.

3. Lower heat. When bubbles form on top of egg, turn off heat and place omelette on another plate. Boil 2 cups water, slip banana leaf in to clean and soften. Strain and place leaf or moistened muslin on a board.

4. Mix pork with sesame seeds, garlic, pimiento or chili, sugar, fish sauce and pepper to taste. Remove stalks from dried mushrooms and discard. Add fresh mushrooms and pound until thin. Heat quickly in pan. Remove.

5. Place yolk omelette on a board. Spread over one quarter raw pork mix with a spatula. Top with mushrooms. Add another layer each of pork and mushrooms, place egg white circle on top then add another pork layer. Carefully press with oiled rolling pin, add single sausage and trim. Gently roll and fill in roll end with pork.

6. Place roll on banana leaf or muslin, tuck in ends and bind with string to hold shape. Steam in a double boiler for about 17 minutes. Remove and cool then refrigerate until cold.

7. Arrange half-moon shapes of cucumber around the edge of a serving plate then, inside the circle of cucumber, arrange tomato slices in a heart shape. Remove leaf or muslin from cold roll, slice to ½ inch thickness and arrange in middle of the plate. Top with parsley sprigs.

Note: These hors d'oeuvres are intended for a Valentine's Day party. Serve with nuoc cham dipping sauce.

Makes 6–7 pieces

PORK SPRING ROLLS

Ingredients

1 oz vermicelli (green bean thread)

3 tablespoons vegetable oil

3 cloves garlic, finely chopped

12 oz half crab meat, half pork

¼ cabbage, cut into fine strips

1 carrot, cut into thin strips

2 scallions, finely chopped

½ teaspoon salt

1 teaspoon sugar

½ teaspoon white pepper

1 tablespoon oyster sauce

20–25 rice-paper wrappers (see page 20)

1 egg, beaten

extra oil for deep frying

To serve

lettuce and mint leaves

nuoc cham dipping sauce (see page 17)

Method

1. Soak vermicelli for 5 minutes in hot water until soft. Drain, cut into 2 inch lengths and reserve.

2. Heat 3 tablespoons oil in wok or pan. Add garlic and crab and pork, and cook for about 8 minutes, stirring so ingredients don't stick to pan. Add cabbage, carrot, scallions and vermicelli and cook on high heat for 3 minutes or until vegetables soften.

3. Turn off heat, add salt, sugar, pepper and oyster sauce. Stir to mix well. When mixture is cool, brush each side of the rice wrappers with water or they will dry and break. Place 1 tablespoon of the mixture into each wrapper, turn sides in first, roll and seal each with beaten egg. Refrigerate until needed.

4. Heat extra oil in wok or pan. Deep-fry rolls until golden. Serve on lettuce leaves garnished with lettuce and mint and serve with bottled sweet chili sauce or nuoc cham dipping sauce.

Makes 20

RICE PAPER ROLLS

Ingredients

3 oz rice flour

3 cups water

salt to taste

oil

Method

1. Make batter with flour, water and salt. Three-quarter fill the base of a double boiler with water and stretch a piece of muslin or cheesecloth firmly over the boiler's top and bind securely with string.

2. Bring water to a boil. Brush fabric with oil and pour a little batter on, using a swirling motion with a spoon to spread it into a circle. Cover with a lid and leave a minute or so until firm. Carefully lift the wrapper with a spatula and set aside. Repeat until all batter is used. Wrappers can be stuffed with pre-cooked filling and served cold or filled and deep fried.

Note: After making rice paper wrappers or opening a bought packet, dip the wrappers in water to soften and cover with a damp tea towel to retain moisture.

Makes about 20

VIETNAMESE HERB SALAD ROLLS WITH HOMEMADE PEANUT SAUCE (opposite)

Ingredients

2 oz cellophane noodles

3 tablespoons rice vinegar

1 tablespoon fish sauce

4 tablespoons roasted peanuts, crushed

12 large shrimp, shelled, deveined, cooked and finely chopped

20 Thai basil leaves, finely sliced

10 Asian mint leaves, finely sliced

$\frac{1}{4}$ cup cilantro, finely chopped

4 leaves of Chinese cabbage or bok choy, finely shredded

2 cabbage leaves, finely shredded

5 scallions, julienned

1 medium carrot, grated

12–16 rice paper wrappers (8 inch)

Peanut sauce

2 tablespoons peanut oil

5 cloves garlic, minced

$\frac{1}{2}$ small red chili, minced

5 tablespoons peanut butter

$1\frac{1}{2}$ tablespoons tomato paste

3 tablespoons Hoisin sauce

1 teaspoon sugar

1 teaspoon fish sauce

$\frac{3}{4}$ cup water

$\frac{1}{4}$ cup peanuts (crushed)

Method

1. Soak the cellophane noodles in a bowl full of hot water for 5–10 minutes or until tender. Drain immediately and rinse with cold water (to halt the cooking). Cut noodles with scissors to about 2 inches long and toss with vinegar, fish sauce, crushed peanuts and shrimp.

2. In a large bowl, mix together herbs, cabbage leaves (both kinds), scallions, noodle mixture and grated carrot and toss thoroughly.

3. Working with 1 wrapper at a time, soak rice wrapper in warm water for 30 seconds and lie it on a flat surface. On each wrapper, place a small quantity of the mixed vegetable/noodle filling. Roll up tightly, folding the sides in to enclose the filling. Continue rolling and folding until all ingredients are used.

4. To make peanut sauce, heat oil and sauté garlic and minced chili until softened (about 2 minutes), then add all remaining ingredients and whisk over moderate heat. Bring to a boil and simmer until thickened slightly (about 3 minutes).

5. To serve, slice each roll on a diagonal, then rest one half over the other. Serve the sauce separately in a small pot for dipping.

Note: As these wrappers do fry successfully, you may like to serve half of them fresh and half of them deep-fried.

Makes 20

SHRIMP BALLS

Ingredients

3 drops rice wine or dry sherry

salt and black pepper, to taste

1 teaspoon sugar

2 oz ground pork fat

8 oz shrimp, shelled and deveined

1 dessertspoon finely ground peppercorns

1 small brown onion, finely chopped

8 oz ground pork

1 dessertspoon fresh dill or parsley, chopped

1 small red chili, seeded
   and finely chopped (optional)

1 chicken bouillon cube

handful breadcrumbs

1 egg, beaten

vegetable oil for deep-frying and handling

To garnish

lettuce leaves, fresh cilantro leaves
   and pared carrot strips

Method

1. Combine drops of wine, pork fat, black pepper, sugar and a little salt in a bowl. Sit bowl in another bowl of hot water to melt the fat.

2. Chop shrimp very finely until mushy. Place in bowl. Add peppercorns and a little extra salt and pepper.

3. Fry onion until transparent, drain oil and add onion to ground pork . Combine, add shrimp and dill or parsley and/or optional chili with shrimps and pork fat.

4. Crush bouillon cube finely and mix with breadcrumbs. Work some oil into your hands, form walnut-sized balls from the shrimp mix and dip each ball in beaten egg and then in breadcrumbs mix. Deep-fry in oil in a wok or pan until golden. Drain on kitchen paper and serve on a plate layered with lettuce. Top with cilantro leaves and strips of pared carrot.

Makes 12–14 balls

SEAFOOD SUGAR CANE SKEWERS

Ingredients

1½ cups shrimp or crab meat, ground
black pepper to taste
1 clove garlic, crushed
½ teaspoon fish sauce
1½ teaspoons sugar
1½ tablespoons vegetable oil
8 sticks sugar cane, 4 inches long

To serve

lettuce leaves and cilantro sprigs
mint
1 red chili, seeded and finely sliced
1 lime, sliced into 8 wedges
1 cup sweet and sour sauce (see page 43)

Method

1. Combine seafood with pepper, garlic, fish sauce and sugar. Pound or blend until combined and refrigerate, covered, for about 8 hours.

2. Oil your hands, divide seafood paste into 8 and mould each portion smoothly around the center of each sugar cane stick.

3. Broil or barbecue over medium heat until golden and crisp, or bake in a moderate oven for 15–20 minutes. Place on serving plates with lettuce, mint, cilantro sprigs, slices of chili and lime slices attractively arranged. Serve with sweet and sour sauce.

Makes 8

SHRIMP IN CARAMEL

Ingredients

1 pound raw shrimp
5 scallions
4½ tablespoons sugar
7 tablespoons water
oil for frying
4 cloves garlic, finely chopped
1 tablespoon fish sauce
1 tablespoon lime or lemon juice
pinch salt
1 tablespoon brown sugar
⅓ green bell pepper, julienned, to garnish

Method

1. Shell and devein shrimp, leaving the tails intact. Finely chop 3 scallions. Cut the remaining 2 into thin strips 1 inch long.

2. In a saucepan, heat sugar until golden, add 3 tablespoons of water and stir until sugar dissolves. Bring to a boil, then simmer gently for about 3 minutes until caramel darkens, but does not burn. Remove pot from heat and add remaining water. Take care caramel does not spatter. Reheat, stirring quickly to remove lumps.

3. Heat oil in heavy pan and fry chopped scallion and garlic over medium heat. Add shrimp for a few minutes until they are pink. Slowly pour fish sauce and warm caramel over shrimp mixture in pan. Cook for 1 minute before adding lime or lemon juice, salt, brown sugar and scallion slivers. Stir together and serve topped with bell pepper strips.

Serves 4

soups

Pho
GOODNESS SAKE

On a short or extended stay in Vietnam, a visitor could exist totally on soup—and yet never become bored or fail to be tantalized.

In Vietnam, soup begins, sustains and ends each day. *Pho* (pronounced 'fur') is the addictive national dish based on a rich, slowly cooked, clear beef consommé with noodles, aromatic with spices, ginger and cinnamon. *Pho* is prepared according to secret family recipes by competitive sellers. These secret ingredients give *pho* subtle variety. Gourmets and food writers have described *pho* as Vietnam in a bowl of soul comfort. The name derives from the French *pot au feu*.

Light as consommé, but chock full of vegetables, meat or fish, with Chinese, Thai and French influences, Vietnamese soups make marvellously hearty lunches when served with crusty bread and, perhaps, a tossed green salad.

Sour fish soup is almost as much an institution as beef *pho*. To really show off, prepare a favorite Tet (New Year) festival first course: cabbage parcels in soup (see page 30). Asparagus and crab meat soup is featured on many Vietnamese menus (see page 28).

For fun at brunch, introduce *chao* or rice porridge to friends. It can contain chicken, duck, fish or oysters combined with pork and at least one green vegetable. You can experiment as the Vietnamese do. Sliced red chili, fish sauce and black pepper should be served in separate small shared bowls for diners to add to their *chao* at liberty.

Soups can be served in individual bowls or a large tureen for self-service at the table. Supply guests with chopsticks as well as soup spoons.

FISH WITH TOMATO AND DILL

Ingredients
3 medium tomatoes
1 ½ pounds freshwater fish fillets
6 cups chicken bouillon
2 tablespoons fresh dill, chopped
salt and pepper
extra fresh dill

Method
1. Chop tomatoes into wedges. Cut fish into large bite-sized chunks. Boil bouillon. Add fish, and turn down to simmer for 6 minutes. Skim surface froth and add tomatoes, dill, and salt and pepper to taste.

2. Simmer a little longer until fish is cooked, but not breaking up. Serve in large bowl or individual bowls and garnish with fresh dill.

Note: This chunky soup is a good starter or as part of a multi-course Vietnamese meal. It also makes a family lunch or dinner when served with fresh baguettes and a salad.

Serves 6

BEEF PHO

Ingredients

8 oz thick steak in one piece

8 oz rice noodles

2 tablespoons fish sauce

1 pound flat, thick dried noodles

$\frac{1}{2}$ cup of bean sprouts

1 white onion, thinly sliced

3 scallions, finely chopped

To serve

$\frac{1}{2}$ cup fresh cilantro, torn into sprigs

$\frac{1}{2}$ cup Vietnamese mint leaves, chopped

1 small red chili, seeded and sliced into rings

2 limes cut into wedges

Bouillon

12 cups water

2 pounds beef shin bones

12 oz gravy beef

1 large white, unpeeled onion, halved

3 medium pieces unpeeled ginger root, sliced

pinch of salt

1 cinnamon stick

6 whole cloves

6 peppercorns

6 coriander seeds

4 whole star anise

2 unpeeled carrots, cut into chunks

Method

1. To make bouillon, pour water into a large pot and add shin bones and gravy beef. Bring to a boil. Skim off foaming scum from surface. Turn heat to medium-low, partly cover and simmer for 2 hours, skimming often. Add remaining bouillon ingredients. Simmer another 90 minutes and remove from heat.

2. Drain bouillon through a fine sieve, then set bouillon aside. Discard bones, carrots, onion and spices. Skim fat from bouillon once cool. Cut gravy beef finely across the grain. Slice steak to paper thin slices and set aside.

3. Soak rice noodles in warm water for about 20 minutes until soft. Drain and set noodles aside.

4. Set bouillon to boil with fish sauce then reduce heat to very low. Fill a separate large pot three-quarters full of water and bring to a boil. Add dried noodles and washed bean sprouts. Continue boiling until noodles are tender, but not mushy. Bean sprouts should retain some crispness.

5. Pour boiling bouillon into 6 serving bowls, add drained noodles, then top equally with gravy beef, raw onion rings, chopped scallions and raw steak slices, and garnish with cilantro and mint leaves.

Note: Diners may help themselves to chili rings and lime wedges.

Serves 6

ASPARAGUS AND CRAB MEAT SOUP

Ingredients

4 cups chicken broth

1 tablespoon plus 2 teaspoons fish sauce

$\frac{1}{2}$ teaspoon sugar

$\frac{1}{4}$ teaspoon salt

1 tablespoon vegetable oil

6 shallots, chopped

2 cloves garlic, chopped

8 oz crab meat

freshly ground black pepper

2 tablespoons cornstarch or arrowroot,
  mixed with 2 tablespoons cold water

1 egg, lightly beaten

15 oz canned white asparagus spears, cut into
  1 inch sections, canning liquid reserved

1 tablespoon cilantro, shredded

1 scallion, thinly sliced

Method

1. Combine broth, 1 tablespoon of fish sauce, sugar and salt in a 6 quart soup pot. Bring to a boil. Reduce heat and simmer.

2. Meanwhile, heat oil in a skillet. Add shallots and garlic and stir-fry until aromatic. Add crab meat, the remaining 2 teaspoons of fish sauce and black pepper to taste.

3. Stir-fry over high heat for 1 minute. Set aside.

4. Bring the soup to a boil. Add cornstarch mixture and stir gently until the soup thickens and is clear. While the soup is actively boiling, add egg and stir gently.

5. Continue to stir for about 1 minute. Add crab meat mixture and asparagus with its canning liquid. Cook gently until heated through.

6. Transfer the soup to a heated tureen. Sprinkle on the cilantro, scallion and freshly ground black pepper.

Note: If white asparagus is unavailable, add frozen or fresh asparagus to the broth in step 1 and cook until tender, before adding the remaining ingredients.

Serves 4–6

HOT AND SOUR FISH SOUP

Ingredients

2 pounds firm-fleshed fish such as red snapper,
1½ tablespoons nuoc cham dipping sauce
  (see page 17)
¼ teaspoon white pepper
1 scallion, chopped
6 cups water
2 stalks lemongrass, cut into 2 inch lengths
  and crushed lightly
2 oz tamarind pulp
¾ cup boiling water
1 tablespoon sugar
¾ cup sliced bamboo shoots
1 cup sliced pineapple
2 tomatoes, cut into wedges
1 cup bean sprouts
mixed fresh Vietnamese herbs such as cilantro,
  bitter herb, Asian basil
deep-fried shallots
lime wedges and sliced chili to serve

Method

1. Remove head, fins and tail from fish and cut into 8–10 large pieces. Combine fish, nuoc cham dipping sauce, pepper and scallion, allow to marinate for 15 minutes.

2. Place water in a large saucepan and bring to a boil. Add the fish with its marinade and lemongrass. Reduce heat and simmer for 20 minutes.

3. Meanwhile, combine tamarind pulp and boiling water and allow to soak for 15 minutes. Strain mixture through a fine sieve and discard pulp.

4. Add the tamarind liquid, sugar, bamboo shoots, pineapple and tomatoes to the pan. Simmer for 4–5 minutes until fish is tender.

5. Divide bean sprouts amongst serving bowls and spoon hot soup over. Sprinkle with fresh herbs and deep-fried shallots. Serve with lime wedges and sliced chili on the side.

Serves 4–6

CABBAGE PARCELS IN SOUP

Ingredients

24 cabbage leaves

6 scallions, chopped

4 tablespoons cilantro, finely chopped

1 cup ground pork

½ cup ground shrimp

ground black pepper

6 cups chicken or pork bouillon

2½ tablespoons fish sauce

Method

1. Blanch cabbage leaves in boiling water and cut away any tough sections from their bases.

2. Cut white roots from scallions and finely chop 4 white heads. Slice 2 for garnish. Halve green stalks lengthwise to make strips.

3. Thoroughly mix scallions and 2 tablespoons of cilantro with pork and shrimp. Season with pepper. Bring the bouillon to a boil.

4. Place 1 tablespoon of the mixture onto each cabbage leaf. Fold the leaf base over, then the outer edges and roll up. Carefully tie up each roll with a length of green scallion and place parcels gently into boiling bouillon to cook for 6 minutes.

5. Lift parcels into bowls, pour a cup of bouillon over each and garnish with remaining sliced scallions and cilantro. Dip rolls into fish sauce when eating.

Serves 6

DUCK AND NUT SOUP

Ingredients

14 oz duck or chicken

peanut oil

8 cups bouillon, or water with 2 teaspoons salt

2 cups mixed nuts, crushed

15 oz lychees or loganberries

To garnish

cilantro

Method

1. Cut duck into bite-sized pieces. Fry in a little peanut oil until golden. Boil bouillon or water with salt. Add duck and simmer for 45 minutes. Skim until broth is clear.

2. Add nuts and simmer another 45 minutes. Add lychees or loganberries 5 minutes before serving. Garnish with cilantro.

Serves 6

VERMICELLI AND CHICKEN SOUP

Ingredients

1 cup chicken breast chunks

8 oz Chinese mung bean vermicelli

$\frac{1}{2}$ cup dried wood ear mushrooms, soaked or
   $\frac{1}{2}$ cup canned button mushrooms, sliced

salt to taste

$\frac{1}{2}$ teaspoon black or white pepper

2 tablespoons scallions, chopped

Bouillon

8 cups water

3 teaspoons fish sauce

1 onion, quartered

3 pounds pork bones

1 pound chicken wings, bones
   and/or leftover meat scraps

1 pound of 2 of the following: whole carrot,
   quartered cauliflower, whole green beans
   and/or quarter of a cabbage

Method

1. Make bouillon by boiling all ingredients together then simmering for 1 hour. Strain reduced bouillon and discard the bones and vegetables.

2. Boil chicken chunks in bouillon for 15 minutes, skimming scum from the surface. Add vermicelli and soaked dried mushrooms, stalks removed, or canned mushrooms, and cook until vermicelli is done.

3. Season with salt and pepper and serve sprinkled with chopped scallion.

Note: You can use packaged bouillon if you prefer.

Serves 6

meat

EAST MEETS WEST

It's amazing that *pho* (beef soup) sellers ladle out their addictive national dish 24 hours a day, considering that meat, and certainly beef, is relatively expensive in Vietnam. Family members often work in shifts around the clock to keep their *pho* stalls open.

Home cooks utilize beef in many ways, usually in dishes loaded with other ingredients to save on cost while still enjoying the flavor of beef. The most common meat is pork, which is both cheaper and more available than beef. Ground pork is often combined with seafood to give extra texture and taste to an appetizer or main dish. (See the appetiser and seafood sections of this book.) All meats combine magically with fish sauce –an essential in almost every Vietnamese dish.

Vietnam's climate and terrain are unsuitable for the raising of sheep, so lamb and mutton are not included in authentic menus, but can be prepared instead of beef and sometimes pork in your own kitchen. Goats roam villages and around humble countryside dwellings in Vietnam, but their meat doesn't make frequent appearances in Vietnamese restaurants or at street stalls.

In Vietnam, buffalo, frog, horse, rabbit, veal and venison are also eaten. Choose cheap cuts of beef for slow pot cooking and do try caramelized pork, a Southern specialty. Meat, as well as chicken liver, is often used to make Vietnamese pâté, which can be served as a luncheon dish with salad and baguette. Meat in wrappers or skewered for barbecues is also very popular.

Some recipes in this section call for garnish. All can be served as part of a multi-course meal, but for a simple family meal, serve just one course with rice or noodles and a salad or vegetables.

COCONUT PORK STEW

Ingredients

2 pounds boneless pork, cut into large cubes
4 tablespoons vegetable oil
$2\frac{1}{2}$ cups coconut milk
6 hard-boiled eggs
3 scallions and $\frac{1}{2}$ cup bean sprouts to garnish
nuoc cham dipping sauce (see page 17)

Marinade

3 cloves garlic, crushed
pinch salt
$1\frac{1}{2}$ tablespoons sugar
4 tablespoons fish sauce

Method

1. Combine marinade ingredients and add pork, stirring so that pork is completely covered. Marinate for at least 2 hours.

2. Heat oil in a heavy-based pan and add pork cubes, turning to sear all sides. Drain off any oil, add coconut milk and bring almost to a boil. Reduce heat, skim off surface scum and simmer, covered for about 45 minutes, until tender.

3. Peel hard-boiled eggs, add to pan and cook for about 10 minutes. Serve with dipping sauce, garnished with 3 scallions cut into narrow 2 inch strips and $\frac{1}{2}$ cup of bean sprouts.

BEEF CURRY

Ingredients

2 pounds stewing beef, cubed

1 large onion, sliced

4 cloves garlic, crushed

2 tablespoons fresh ginger, crushed

2 red chilies, seeded and chopped finely

3$\frac{1}{2}$ tablespoons hot curry powder

2 teaspoons turmeric

1 teaspoon black ground pepper

1$\frac{1}{2}$ teaspoons salt

1 cup water

4$\frac{1}{2}$ tablespoons fish sauce

$\frac{1}{3}$ cup vegetable oil

1 tablespoon sugar

3 large carrots, chopped

3 tablespoons cornstarch

2$\frac{1}{4}$ cups coconut milk

To garnish

cilantro

Method

1. Combine beef, onion, garlic, ginger, chilies, curry powder, turmeric, pepper and 1 teaspoon of salt. Cover with plastic wrap and marinate in refrigerator overnight. Turn occasionally.

2. Heat oil in a large, heavy-based saucepan on high heat. Add beef, turning to seal in flavors, before pouring in the water, $\frac{1}{2}$ teaspoon salt and fish sauce. After boiling, cover with lid and turn down heat to simmer for about 1 hour until meat is cooked. Add sugar and carrots and cook until carrots are done (about 15 minutes).

3. Add cornstarch to coconut milk, stirring to dissolve, and pour into curry, stirring for 10–15 minutes until curry thickens. Serve in a casserole dish with rice and salad. Garnish with cilantro.

Serves 4

CARAMELIZED PORK

Ingredients

oil for frying

1 ½ pounds pork, cubed

2 cloves garlic, finely chopped

2 medium onions, sliced

⅓ cup sugar

¾ cup water

1 ½ tablespoon fish sauce

1 ½ tablespoons lime juice

1 seeded red chili, sliced and minced

½ teaspoon five spice powder

2 scallions, chopped, to garnish

Method

1. Heat oil in a heavy-based pan, add pork cubes and turn until brown. Add garlic and onion and cook, stirring to separate onion rings until transparent. Remove from heat.

2. To make caramel, mix sugar with water in a separate saucepan and stir over low heat until sugar dissolves. Bring to a boil then turn down to simmer, still stirring, until liquid is golden. Take pot off heat and carefully add fish sauce and lime juice. Return to heat, stirring quickly to remove any lumps, until the sauce reduces a little.

3. Quickly return pork, garlic and onions to reheat, add chili and five spice and then caramel. Cook for 1 minute, stirring until combined. Transfer to serving dish and sprinkle scallions on top.

Note: For easier washing up, immediately fill pot in which caramel has cooked with boiling water.

Serves 4

SIZZLING SPARE RIBS

Ingredients

8 dried mushrooms

2 scallions

1 green bell pepper

1 red chili

1 pound pork or beef spare ribs

oil for deep-frying

$\frac{1}{2}$ teaspoon salt

$\frac{1}{2}$ teaspoon sugar

1 teaspoon dark soy sauce

$\frac{1}{3}$ cup water

Marinade

$\frac{1}{2}$ teaspoon salt

$\frac{1}{2}$ teaspoon dry sherry

1 tablespoon light soy sauce

2 teaspoons cornstarch

Sauce

$\frac{1}{2}$ teaspoon cornstarch

dash of sesame oil

ground black pepper

1 $\frac{1}{2}$ tablespoons fish sauce

To garnish

mint sprigs

Method

1. Soak mushrooms for 40 minutes in hot water. Remove stalks and discard. Cut scallions into 1 $\frac{1}{2}$ inch pieces. Seed green bell pepper and chili and cut into pieces. Combine marinade ingredients.

2. Chop spare ribs into large bite-sized pieces and marinate 30 minutes. Deep-fry until brown. Remove from oil. Sauté scallions and mushrooms in a little oil, add ribs with $\frac{1}{2}$ teaspoon salt, sugar, dark soy sauce and $\frac{1}{3}$ cup water and stir-fry. Add bell pepper, chili and combined sauce ingredients.

3. Stir-fry, stirring, until bell pepper just starts to lose crispness. Serve on a pre-heated heavy-metal grill pan so meat sizzles. Serve garnished with mint sprigs.

MEAT

VIETNAMESE BEEF (opposite)

Ingredients

1 pound fillet steak

$\frac{1}{2}$ cup vegetable oil

1 cup scallions, sliced

1 pound canned bamboo shoots,
   drained and sliced

pinch salt

$1\frac{1}{2}$ tablespoons fish sauce

2 cloves garlic, minced

$\frac{1}{4}$ cup sesame seeds, toasted

Method

1. Slice steak into thin 2 inch strips. In a pan,
   heat half the oil and stir-fry beef for
   1 minute, then remove from pan.

2. Heat remaining oil and sauté scallions and
   bamboo shoots for 3 minutes. Add
   salt and fish sauce and cook, stirring, for
   5 minutes. Add garlic and cook for a further
   2 minutes.

3. Return steak to pan and cook until just
   tender. Remove from heat, add sesame
   seeds, stir through and serve.

Serves 4

BEEF WITH EGGPLANT

Ingredients

1 pound eggplant, halved lengthwise

3 cloves garlic

vegetable oil

8 oz ground beef

2 tablespoons fish sauce

salt

freshly ground black pepper

Method

1. Char-grill eggplant over a barbecue or under a
   grill until skin blackens. Cool, peel and cut into
   pieces. Peel and mince garlic.

2. In a heavy-based pan, heat oil, then add garlic,
   stirring until soft. Add ground beef and cook,
   stirring it with a spoon until beef loses its
   pinkness. Add eggplant, fish sauce and salt and
   pepper to taste. Turn down heat to simmer
   before covering. Cook and cover about 25
   minutes or until eggplant has lost its firmness.

Serves 4

BARBECUED PORK BALLS

Ingredients

1 tablespoon dry sherry

1 teaspoon salt

1 teaspoon sugar

3 cloves garlic, minced

1 pound pork, finely ground

1 $\frac{1}{2}$ tablespoons ground rice

1 tablespoon fish sauce

1 $\frac{1}{2}$ tablespoons peanut oil

Equipment

bamboo skewers, pre-soaked to prevent
   burning

Method

1. Combine sherry, salt, sugar and garlic. Add
    pork, combine and let stand for 2 hours.

2. Add ground rice, fish sauce and peanut oil,
    mix well then form mixture into small balls,
    about walnut size. Put balls onto bamboo
    skewers, squeezing tightly so balls adhere
    to skewers.

3. Barbecue or grill, turning often, until pork
    is cooked.

Serves 4

BEEF, CAULIFLOWER AND MUSHROOM STIR-FRY (opposite)

Ingredients

8 oz steak, sliced into 2 inch strips

$\frac{1}{4}$ cauliflower, divided into florets

$\frac{1}{2}$ cup water or bouillon

7 oz fresh whole button mushrooms

1 $\frac{1}{2}$ teaspoons cornstarch

2 tablespoons fish sauce

1 teaspoon oyster sauce

ground black pepper

vegetable oil

3 cloves garlic, finely chopped

1 medium onion, cut lengthwise into 8 pieces

To garnish

cilantro sprigs

Method

1. Cut cauliflower florets in half. Mix water or
    bouillon with cornstarch, 1 tablespoon fish
    sauce and oyster sauce.

2. Pour 1 tablespoon of fish sauce over sliced
    meat and sprinkle pepper over. Turn meat and
    let stand 20 minutes.

3. In a pan, heat oil over high heat. Add garlic
    and onion and stir-fry until onion separates
    and softens. Add cauliflower and mushrooms.
    Cover, reduce heat and cook for 4 minutes.
    Add meat and cook until meat is cooked to
    your liking. Stir in cornstarch mixture.
    Continue stirring until sauce thickens. Spoon
    onto a serving plate and garnish with cilantro
    sprigs.

Serves 4

beef, cauliflower and
mushroom stir-fry

BAKED PORK LOAF

Ingredients

12 dried mushrooms

8 scallions, finely chopped

2 pounds ground pork

2 tablespoons fish sauce

5 eggs, beaten

pinch salt

ground black pepper

To garnish

cilantro

Method

1. In hot water, soak mushrooms for 40 minutes then squeeze out liquid, remove stems and chop mushroom tops very finely. Place mushrooms, scallions and pork in a bowl. Add fish sauce, eggs and salt and pepper to taste and combine thoroughly.

2. Preheat oven to 400°F. Grease a loaf tin, then add meat mixture, patting down firmly. Cover with foil, sealing well. Sit loaf tin in a large roasting pan, pour hot water into roasting pan until halfway up the loaf tin and place in oven for about 1 hour or until done. Test with a knife, which should come out clean.

3. Allow the loaf to cool a little, then run knife around the sides of the tin and turn out. Slice and garnish with cilantro.

Serves 6–8

SWEET AND SOUR MEAT BALLS

Ingredients

1 cup onions, finely chopped

oil for frying

8 oz ground beef

8 oz ground pork

1 egg, beaten

½ cup rice, cooked

extra salt and pepper

1 cup seasoned all-purpose flour

Batter

1 egg

⅓ cup all-purpose flour

⅔ cup water

Sweet and sour sauce

¼ cup onions, finely chopped

4 tablespoons dry sherry

2 tablespoons white vinegar

2 tablespoons sugar

1 cup beef bouillon

1 cup pineapple juice

4 teaspoons tomato purée

⅓ cup pineapple, chopped

1 teaspoon fresh ginger, chopped

1 clove garlic, finely chopped

pinch chili powder

1 tablespoon arrowroot

water

Method

1. Fry onion in oil until tender. Drain and add to combination of ground meats, beaten egg and cooked rice. Mix well. Add extra salt and pepper to taste. Form mixture into small balls.

2. Combine batter ingredients. Gently toss balls in seasoned flour. Dip in batter and fry until golden. Drain and set aside.

3. For the sauce, fry onions until tender, add sherry, vinegar, sugar, bouillon and pineapple juice and boil 6 minutes. Add tomato purée and boil for a further 4 minutes.

4. Purée pineapple, ginger and garlic with a little water and add to sauce along with chili powder. (Add more to taste if desired.) Blend arrowroot with more water until smooth and add to sauce. Stir until clear and thick, adding more water if too thick. Add meat balls to sauce to heat through before serving.

Serves 4

NOODLE PANCAKE WITH GARLIC BEEF

Ingredients

10 oz fillet steak

3 teaspoons minced garlic

6 tablespoons vegetable oil

$\frac{1}{2}$ red bell pepper, seeded and cut into slivers

$\frac{1}{2}$ teaspoon ground black pepper

14 oz fresh, soft noodles

1 tablespoon sugar

2 teaspoon fish sauce

$\frac{1}{2}$ cup beef bouillon

2 teaspoon cornstarch

2 scallions, chopped

Method

1. Partially freeze steak to make it easier to cut each piece into very thin slices. Place steak on a plate and spread with garlic, 1 tablespoon oil and bell pepper. Cover and refrigerate for 45 minutes.

2. Pour $2\frac{1}{2}$ tablespoons oil into a heavy-based pan, ensuring the base is coated. Separate the noodles with your hands. Heat oil to medium, add noodles and press them down with a spatula. Heat until base is golden and crisp. Don't lift the noodle pancake for about 15 minutes as it will break up.

3. Loosen edges and base of pancake gently. Place a large plate over the pan and quickly invert the pan to settle the pancake on the plate. Gently slide the pancake back into the pan, uncooked side down, and continue cooking for 5–10 minutes. Return pancake to plate in the same manner and keep warm in very slow oven.

4. In same pan, heat over high heat $2\frac{1}{2}$ tablespoons oil. Add meat and bell pepper mixture and sear quickly on both sides. Don't overcook. Mix sugar, fish sauce, bouillon and cornstarch until smooth and add to steak. Turn meat to absorb flavors, then remove. Stir sauce rapidly until thick, returning steak briefly to coat with sauce.

5. Serve steak and sauce on top of pancake and cut into 4 (or 8 if presenting as an appetizer). Top with sauce and garnish with chopped scallions.

Serves 4 as a main course or 8 as an appetizer.

seafood

Seafood
FOR A SONG

Seafood and fish are abundant in Vietnam with its long, curved coastline and its hinterland river systems. Visitors to Vietnam will feel that they are millionaires in Vietnam. This is not just because the currency, the dong, translates into notes confusingly worth millions, but because visitors can dine so royally on crabs, shrimp, oysters, mussels and more for a fraction of the cost at home.

In Vietnam, fish and shellfish are staples along with rice (and a great source of protein) and are inevitably the first foods to sell out at sea- and river-port markets. Because of a general lack of refrigeration, food freshness is imperative. Therefore, many markets and restaurants offer their customers live fish swimming in tanks or in plastic buckets. It's difficult to buy live fish in Western countries, but you can assess the freshness of your purchases by checking that the scales are not flaky and peeling, that the eyes are clear and prominent and that the gills are pink.

And, provided the fruits of the ocean and rivers are not enclosed in thick batter or drenched with rich sauces, they are delights for dieters—especially when prepared in some of the interesting ways described in the following recipes.

Rarely presented as crumbed calamari, squid is widely appreciated in Vietnam but avoid overcooking so that its texture does not become rubbery and tough. Soak it overnight in milk.

Sometimes crab can be difficult to buy fresh, but crab meat in a can substitutes well.

Vietnam has several fish not found in Western waters so some recipes generalize the type of fish required. Like the Chinese, Vietnamese are partial to carp, which foreigners tend to avoid as it is so bony. However, it is a tasty fish when baked and served with a sweet and sour sauce that you'll find in this book.

SALT AND PEPPER SQUID

Ingredients

1 pound squid, cleaned
3 tablespoons all-purpose flour
1 teaspoon baking soda
1 tablespoon cornstarch
1 egg
4 tablespoons cold water
vegetable oil for deep-frying
small onion, cut into little pieces
1 clove garlic, crushed
2 tablespoons fresh parsley or cilantro, chopped
1 teaspoon sugar
$\frac{1}{2}$ teaspoon salt
1$\frac{1}{2}$ teaspoons ground white pepper
$\frac{1}{2}$ teaspoon five spice powder
drops of dry sherry (optional)
parsley or cilantro sprigs
nuoc cham dipping sauce (page 17)

Method

1. Angle-cut squid into square pieces, open up with knife and score each piece with a criss-cross. Dry squid.

2. Make a smooth batter of flour, baking soda, cornstarch and egg.

3. Cover squid with batter and leave for a few minutes. Heat oil in wok or skillet and deep-fry squid for about 3 minutes, then remove squid and most of the oil. In remaining oil, place onion and garlic and cook until just tender. Add parsley or cilantro and stir for 30 seconds. Return squid to pan and sprinkle with combined sugar, salt, pepper and five spice powder. Gently stir through to combine.

4. Toss vermicelli into hot oil for near-instant crispy noodles for the base of a serving plate. Place squid on top, sprinkle a few drops of sherry on top (optional) and garnish with parsley or cilantro sprigs. Serve with nuoc cham dipping sauce.

Serves 4

CLAYPOT FISH

Ingredients

1 tablespoon vegetable oil

13 oz freshwater fish, cut into bite-sized pieces

4 oz pork loin, sliced

10 cloves garlic, finely chopped

1 cup chicken bouillon

½ cup sugar

2 chilies, seeded and finely chopped

1 medium onion, sliced

1 tablespoon fish sauce

1 medium-sized tomato, sliced

Method

1. Heat oil in a pan. Add fish, and fry lightly until just brown. Transfer fish to a clay pot or stove-top casserole. Brown pork in pan and add to fish along with garlic, bouillon, sugar and chili. Stir to combine. Cover and cook on medium heat until sauce is thickened.

2. In pan, sauté onion slices until tender. Add fish sauce to pot and cook, stirring. When cooked, place onions on top of pork and fish. Place fresh tomato on top just before serving.

Serves 4

SHRIMP CURRY

Ingredients

2 tablespoons vegetable oil

2 cloves garlic, finely chopped

12 jumbo shrimp, cooked

1 onion, sliced

1 medium zucchini, sliced

1/2 green bell pepper, seeded and sliced

1/2 tablespoon green curry paste

1 cup coconut milk

1 teaspoon cornstarch

1 tablespoon water

1 teaspoon sugar

1 tablespoon fish sauce

To serve

cilantro and steamed rice

Method

1. Heat oil in pan. Add garlic and shrimp and stir-fry for 2 minutes. Add onion, zucchini and bell pepper, stirring for 2 more minutes. Remove from stove.

2. In another pan, place curry paste and stir constantly for 1 minute. Add coconut milk and bring to a boil. Mix cornstarch with water. Then add sugar, fish sauce and shrimp with vegetables. Garnish with cilantro and serve with steamed rice.

Serves 4

CHILI CRAB WITH LEMONGRASS

Ingredients

1 large crab (3 pound) or 2 smaller crabs

1 tablespoon oil

2 cloves garlic, finely chopped

1 onion, sliced

1 stalk lemongrass, finely sliced

4 chilies, sliced

2 tablespoons fish sauce

2 tablespoons lime juice

$\frac{1}{2}$ cup water

4 scallions, cut into 1 inch pieces

$\frac{1}{2}$ cup bean sprouts and deep-fried shallots,
   to garnish

extra lime juice and nuoc cham dipping sauce
   (see page 17) to serve

Method

1. Clean the crab well. Heat oil in a large
   saucepan, stir-fry garlic, onion, lemongrass and
   chili over high heat for a few minutes.

2. Pour fish sauce, lime juice and water into the
   pan and bring to a boil. Carefully place crab in
   saucepan. Cover with a tightly fitting lid. Cook
   over medium high heat for 10–15 minutes
   until the crab is cooked.

3. Place crab on a serving platter. Add scallions
   to the pan, heat cooking liquid until reduced
   to about $\frac{1}{4}$ cup and pour over the crab.

4. Arrange bean sprouts over the hot crab,
   sprinkle liberally with deep-fried shallots and
   serve with extra lime juice and dipping sauce.

Serves 2–4

BARBECUED SHRIMP

Ingredients

1 pound large shrimp, raw
6 oz thin rice vermicelli
boiling water
2 teaspoons vegetable oil
6 scallions, chopped
½ cup roasted peanuts
½ bunch cilantro, chopped
nuoc cham dipping sauce (see page 17)

Method

1. Slit shrimp down the back, remove vein, wash and pat dry. Cook shrimp over charcoal or on barbecue for about 5 minutes, turning once.

2. Add vermicelli to boiling water and boil for 2 minutes. Drain and rinse under cold running water.

3. Heat oil in wok or skillet, add scallions and fry until softened. Arrange scallions and vermicelli on warmed serving plates, top with shrimp, then sprinkle with shallots and peanuts. Pour hot nuoc cham over top and sprinkle with cilantro.

Serves 4

NHA TRANG EEL

Ingredients

1 eel, about 2 pounds in weight

10 dried black mushrooms

$\frac{1}{2}$ green bell pepper, seeded

1 cup canned pineapple pieces in juice

oil for stir-frying

2 cloves garlic, crushed

2 onions, sliced

2 teaspoon fish sauce

ground black pepper

2 large tomatoes, cut into small wedges

2 teaspoon cornstarch

To garnish

parsley sprigs

Method

1. Wash eel, skin it, remove backbone and cut into bite-sized pieces. Soak mushrooms in boiling water for 30 minutes then remove and discard stems. Cut bell pepper into 1 inch squares. Drain pineapple, reserving $\frac{1}{2}$ cup of the juice.

2. Heat 1 tablespoon oil in pan over medium heat and fry garlic and onions until soft. Add eel, bell pepper, fish sauce and a sprinkle of pepper to taste. Stir-fry until eel has softened, adding more oil if necessary. Add pineapple pieces, tomatoes and mushrooms, stirring to heat through.

3. Combine cornstarch with pineapple juice and add to pan. Serve once sauce has thickened, garnished with parsley.

Serves 4–6

CRAB MEAT BOATS

Ingredients

3 eggplants

3 scallions, chopped

oil for cooking

$1\frac{1}{2}$ cups crabmeat, cooked or canned

cilantro sprigs to garnish

Sauce

2 small, red chilies, seeded and minced

2 tablespoons peanuts, crushed

$\frac{1}{4}$ cup fish sauce

1 teaspoon sugar

3 tablespoons water

Method

1. Halve eggplants lengthwise and brush with oil. Barbecue or grill, turning frequently until flesh softens completely and skin darkens. Carefully peel off skins and discard, but retain split stem for decorative purpose. Keep eggplant boats warm in oven.

2. Fry two-thirds of scallions in oil until golden. Add sauce ingredients, cook until sugar is dissolved then add crab meat and heat through.

3. Place eggplant boats on one large or individual plates. Spoon over equal amounts of crab meat and sauce and garnish with remaining chopped scallion and cilantro sprigs.

Note: Cooked, chopped or small, whole shrimp can be substituted for crab meat if desired.

Serves 6 as a starter, or 3 as a main course.

HANOI-STYLE FRIED FISH (above)

Ingredients

1 pound boneless fish fillets

salt and pepper

$\frac{1}{4}$ cup peanut oil

4 teaspoons turmeric

1 heaping teaspoon ginger, grated

4 scallions, chopped

$\frac{1}{2}$ cup fresh dill, chopped

2 tablespoons crushed peanuts

Dipping sauce

2 tablespoons shrimp paste with soya bean oil

$\frac{1}{4}$ cup fish sauce

1 tablespoon sugar

To garnish

lettuce and mint leaves

Method

1. Prepare dipping sauce by mixing shrimp paste, a little extra oil, fish sauce and sugar. Boil and add more sugar if desired.

2. Season fish with salt and pepper and cut into 1 inch pieces. In a heavy-based pan, heat oil, then add fish, turmeric and ginger. Turn gently and just before fish is done, add scallions, dill and peanuts. Serve with dipping sauce, lettuce and mint on a bed of rice.

Serves 4

SQUID CAKES

Ingredients

2 tablespoons pork fat, finely chopped

2 teaspoon dry sherry

pinch salt

1 teaspoon sugar

2 teaspoons ground pepper

1 small orange chili, seeded and finely chopped

1 pound squid, finely chopped

2 tablespoons parsley, chopped

3 scallions, chopped

3 teaspoons fish sauce

1 egg

vegetable oil, for frying

Sauce

2 teaspoons fish sauce

2 teaspoons lime or lemon juice or vinegar

2 teaspoons sugar

3 teaspoons water

To garnish

1 lime

$\frac{1}{2}$ red bell pepper, seeded

$\frac{1}{2}$ cucumber

cilantro sprigs

Method

1. Boil pork fat to soften then finely chop again. Add sherry, salt, sugar and pepper. Set aside.

2. Meanwhile, reserve a pinch of chopped chili for sauce. Add the remainder to squid with parsley and scallions. Put fish sauce in wok and heat until wok is nearly dry (to flavor it) and add any crystals to squid.

3. Separate egg and lightly beat white and yolk in individual bowls. Combine pork fat mixture with squid and add enough egg white to bind. Oil your hands and make flat cakes of squid. Lightly shallow-fry in wok or frying pan, turning once, adding more oil as necessary. Cakes will expand. Remove squid cakes and allow to cool. Wipe wok or pan clean with a paper towel. Dip cakes in egg yolk to give yellow color and re-fry in more fresh oil.

4. Combine sauce ingredients with reserved chili. Slowly heat until sugar is dissolved.

5. Thinly slice lime and bell pepper. Halve lime rings and arrange in a circle on a plate with thin slices of cucumber. Add hot squid cakes and serve with a bowl of sauce on the side and garnish with cilantro sprigs.

Serves 4

chicken & poultry

OUT
FOR A DUCK

One has only to stroll through a market in Hanoi, Saigon or one of hundreds of villages and towns in Vietnam to realize how popular poultry is with the Vietnamese.

Strung up in busy meat sections, plump, live and feathered in wicker cages, chicken is favored over red meat for its versatility and economy.

In some of Vietnam's most picturesque regions, where strangely shaped rocky outcrops dominate rice paddies, ducks are farmed, forming noisy, moving foregrounds against stunning scenery. Ducks are revered in the kitchen for their adaptability. While meat is not eaten in households every day, duck and chicken are the most favored meats in Vietnam after pork.

Almost every part of the bird is used, even its feet which, some believe, uplift the spirit. Chicken and duck feet are popular with young women who eat them when they want to pamper themselves.

The Greeks regard bull testicles as a delicacy that encourages virility. Vietnam has a similar philosophy about rooster testicles. The proud, strutting rooster's genitalia are tasty, but not included in our recipes. If they're available and you're intrigued, sauté rooster testes and serve with a sweet and sour sauce with diced ham and peas added.

In salads, roasts, grills, stir-fry, slow cook pots, fricassés, curries and appetizers, poultry makes frequent appearances and can be used to replace seafood if diners are allergic to shellfish.

Indeed, most dishes using seafood in this book are amenable to preparation with chicken instead. Some recipes show the influence of former occupying and neighboring countries.

For cutting up poultry Asian-style, a sharp cleaver is indispensable.

STIR-FRIED LEMONGRASS CHICKEN

Ingredients

4 stalks lemongrass

1 pound skinless boneless chicken breasts, cut into 1 inch cubes

1 teaspoon sesame oil

2 tablespoons vegetable oil

1 red bell pepper, seeded and chopped

2 tablespoons roasted salted peanuts, roughly chopped

1 tablespoon fish sauce

1 tablespoon soy sauce

$\frac{1}{2}$ tablespoon sugar

salt

2 scallions, chopped, to garnish

Method

1. Peel the outer layers from lemongrass stalks and finely chop the lower white bulbous parts, discarding the fibrous tops. Put chicken into a large bowl, add lemongrass and sesame oil and turn to coat. Cover and marinate in the refrigerator for 2 hours, or overnight.

2. Heat a wok or large, heavy-based skillet, and add vegetable oil. Add chicken with its marinade and stir-fry for 5 minutes or until the chicken has turned white.

3. Add bell pepper, peanuts, fish sauce, soy sauce, sugar and salt to taste. Stir-fry for another 5 minutes or until chicken and pepper are cooked. Sprinkle with the scallions just before serving.

Serves 4

SPICY ORANGE DUCK

Ingredients

4 pounds duck pieces

vegetable oil

3 tablespoons sugar

2 cups orange juice

2 oranges

finely sliced orange rind

2 small red chilies, seeded and sliced

Marinade

3 tablespoons fish sauce

1 tablespoon peeled ginger root, finely chopped

1 tablespoon red chili, seeded and finely chopped

salt and pepper

1 tablespoon vegetable oil

Method

1. Combine marinade ingredients, coat both sides of duck pieces and marinate, preferably overnight.

2. Heat oil in pan, add duck pieces along with marinade and fry until golden. Turn pieces. Turn heat down a little. When duck is almost cooked, sprinkle half the sugar over. When time to turn again, sprinkle with rest of sugar. While sugar is becoming caramel, add orange juice, stir and remove duck pieces.

3. Peel oranges, cut into segments and arrange on serving plate. Add duck. Stir orange sauce until it reaches desired thickness. Pour sauce over duck pieces and decorate with pared orange rind and extra chilies.

Serves 6

CHICKEN WITH CAULIFLOWER

Ingredients

2 large chicken fillets

2 cloves garlic, minced

salt and ground black pepper to taste

4 tablespoons vegetable oil

2 large onions, each cut into 8

2 cups small cauliflower florets

1 red chili, seeded and chopped

Sauce

2 tablespoons cornstarch

2 teaspoons soy sauce

1 tablespoon vinegar

1 tablespoon fish sauce

1 cup chicken bouillon (made from powder or cube will do)

Method

1. Between 2 sheets of plastic film, pound chicken until thin. Slice chicken into thin strips to make almost 2 cups. Season with garlic, salt and plenty of pepper. Stir and set aside for 10 minutes.

2. Heat pan, add 2 tablespoons oil and sauté chicken quickly. Remove from pan. Reheat pan, add remaining oil and sauté onion until brown, but not cooked. Add cauliflower florets and chili and sauté for a further 10–15 minutes.

3. Mix cornstarch with vinegar and sauces until smooth. Add to cup of bouillon.

4. Combine chicken with vegetables, add sauce and stir as the mixture thickens. Serve with steamed rice or noodles.

Note: Thin rare beef strips can replace chicken.

Serves 4

HONEY ROASTED DUCK

Ingredients

3 teaspoons ground black pepper

3 teaspoons salt

3 tablespoons sugar

2½ tablespoons peanut oil

1 medium to large whole duck

6 tablespoons honey

6 tablespoons light soy sauce

2 tablespoons lime or lemon juice

pinch saffron or turmeric (optional)

To garnish

tomatoes, thinly sliced

cucumber, thinly sliced

1 red chili, seeded and sliced

cilantro

Method

1. Combine together pepper, salt, sugar and 4 teaspoons of oil. Rub duck inside and out and seal flavors inside by securing the opening with a bamboo skewer. Preheat oven to 375°F.

2. Mix honey, soy sauce, lime or lemon juice, remaining 2 teaspoons of oil and optional saffron or turmeric used for its color rather than flavor. Pour over duck, ensuring it reaches the whole surface (a must). Place duck in oven and baste every 20 minutes until golden and cooked through (about 2 hours).

3. Cut duck into serving pieces, and garnish with tomatoes, cucumber, chili and cilantro sprigs.

Note: Chicken, quails, goat and rabbit or other game may be used to replace duck.

Serves 6–8

honey

roasted duck

SPICY CHICKEN SKEWERS

Ingredients
2 pounds boneless chicken fillets

Marinade

2 scallions, chopped

1 stalk lemongrass, peeled and finely sliced

2½ tablespoons sugar

1 small red chili, seeded and crushed

1 tablespoon fish sauce

1 tablespoon soy sauce

1 tablespoon peanut oil

1 tablespoon coconut milk

1½ teaspoons five spice powder

To serve

nuoc cham dipping sauce (see page 17)

peanut sauce (see page 66)

Equipment

bamboo skewers

Method

1. Soak about 25 bamboo skewers in water overnight or in boiling water for at least 45 minutes so they will not burn when cooking. Combine marinade ingredients.

2. Cut chicken into thin strips, add to marinade, ensuring each strip is covered. Cover and refrigerate several hours or overnight.

3. Drain chicken and discard marinade. Thread chicken strips onto skewers. Barbecue or grill for about 3 minutes until brown.

4. Serve as part of a main course or as a starter with nuoc cham dipping sauce or peanut sauce.

Makes 20–25 skewers

TURKEY WITH MUSHROOMS

Ingredients

1 cup dried mushrooms

3 pound turkey hindquarter

2½ teaspoons vegetable oil

2 tablespoons soy sauce

2 tablespoons dry sherry

3 teaspoons sugar

peel from 1½ oranges

salt and pepper, to taste

To garnish

mint sprigs

Method

1. Soak mushrooms in boiling water for 30 minutes. Drain and discard stems. Slice.

2. Chop turkey hindquarter into chunks, using a cleaver to get through the bone. Pour boiling water over pieces to fatten skin, then drain and dry with paper towels. Brown turkey over medium heat, in just enough oil to cover a heavy-based pan. Cook in batches, wiping pan clean with paper towels after each batch and adding more oil as necessary.

3. To a clean pan add fresh oil and return turkey along with soy sauce, sherry, sugar, mushrooms and peel from 1 orange. Bring to a boil.

4. Turn heat down to simmer, cover and cook, stirring and skimming scum from surface occasionally, until turkey is tender. Season with salt and pepper, remove from heat and let stand covered for 5 minutes. Discard orange peel and serve topped with sauce. Garnish with pared peel from remaining ½ orange, and mint sprigs.

Note: Chicken or duck can be used in this recipe instead of turkey.

Serves 6

CHICKEN EGG CAKES

Ingredients

2 oz cellophane noodles

4 dried mushrooms

2 cloves garlic, minced

1 tablespoon vegetable oil

6 eggs

1 pound ground chicken fillet

1½ teaspoons sugar

2 teaspoons fresh cilantro, finely chopped

pinch salt

ground black pepper

To garnish

1 scallion, sliced

6 sprigs cilantro

nuoc cham dipping sauce (see page 17)

soy sauce

Method

1. Soak noodles in boiling water for 10 minutes. Chop into ¾ inch sections. Soak mushrooms in boiling water for 10 minutes, drain and slice. Soften garlic in oil over medium heat. Preheat oven to 300°F.

2. In a bowl, beat eggs and add garlic, chicken, noodles, mushrooms, sugar, cilantro and salt and pepper to taste. Combine thoroughly and pour into lightly greased heatproof soup bowls or one large bowl.

3. Place bowls in a baking dish and fill dish halfway with water. Cover bowls and steam in oven (for 10–15 minutes) or until cakes are set. Remove lids for just long enough for top to turn golden. Garnish with scallions and a sprig of cilantro. Serve with separate bowls of dipping sauce and soy sauce.

Note: Ground pork, beef, shrimp or crabmeat can be used instead of chicken.

Serves 4–6

vegetables

FRESH, FRIED, COOKED IN A PICKLE

Where rice paddies do not carpet the Vietnamese landscape, and no animals graze, vegetables are grown. Vegetable crops are mixed on farms and also in the countryside, where most small dwellings have little gardens. But, as many city Vietnamese inhabit apartments or sparse rooms without space to garden, and poverty is widespread, vegetables from the market are more popular even than meat. Markets offer a great choice of vegetables, which are selected carefully as the Vietnamese are particular about freshness.

The lack of refrigeration in rural areas often means market shopping is done twice daily by the home cook. Block ice is still sold by some vendors, but it's usually sold by the bucketful to be shaved into cool beer.

Metropolitan Asian markets or stores in Western countries usually have good selections of dried, canned and packaged vegetable ingredients if vegetables are unavailable fresh.

Chilies, pineapples, tomatoes, asparagus and avocados were introduced to Vietnam over the centuries and are still popular. Preserved vegetables are sold in small containers in Asian food stores and markets, but are used sparingly to flavor rice or noodles or to add flavors to soups and stews. The taste is piquant and biting.

Tofu, or bean curd, made from soy beans, is widely used. Vegans visiting Vietnam will never go hungry, but will need to check that fish or oyster sauce or shrimp paste has not been used in the preparation of a vegetable dish.

SPINACH WITH PEANUT SAUCE

Ingredients
$1\frac{1}{2}$ pounds mature spinach
3 scallions, sliced
2 cloves garlic, crushed
$1\frac{1}{2}$ tablespoons vegetable oil
$\frac{1}{4}$ cup peanuts, crushed
salt and pepper

Peanut sauce
$\frac{1}{3}$ cup smooth peanut butter
$\frac{1}{2}$ cup coconut milk
$1\frac{1}{2}$ tablespoons sugar
$\frac{1}{3}$ cup sweet chili sauce
2 teaspoons lime or lemon juice
$\frac{1}{3}$ cup vegetable bouillon

To garnish
cilantro sprigs

Method
1. Trim stalks of spinach. Blanch spinach in boiling water to make it limp then place in cool or iced water. Drain completely.

2. Make peanut sauce in saucepan by combining all ingredients and stirring over low heat until smooth.

3. Fry scallions and garlic in oil until tender. Add peanuts and then spinach and peanut sauce. Season with salt and pepper and garnish with cilantro sprigs.

Serves 4

POTATO PATTIES

Ingredients

2 large old potatoes, peeled

pinch salt

¼ cup cornstarch

1 large egg

3 scallions, chopped

1 small onion, minced

3 cloves garlic, minced

2 teaspoons fish sauce

2 teaspoons curry powder

ground black pepper

⅔ cup vegetable oil

To serve

nuoc cham dipping sauce (see page 17)

Method

1. Grate potato or shred in a food processor. Put in a colander, sprinkle with salt and mix through. Let stand 20 minutes then squeeze out natural liquid. Place in a bowl and combine with cornstarch.

2. Beat egg lightly and add it to potato along with remaining ingredients, except the oil. Combine well. Heat oil in a large heavy-based pan. Ladle in potato mixture by the tablespoon. Patties should be about 2½ inch in diameter.

3. Fry until golden (about 4 minutes) turn, and when each patty is crisp, drain on paper towels. Serve hot with nuoc cham dipping sauce.

Note: Taro roots or sweet potatoes can be substituted for potatoes.

Serves 4 as an accompaniment to a main course

CURRIED VEGETABLES

Ingredients

$\frac{1}{2}$ pound new potatoes, peeled and quartered

2 stalks lemongrass

4 oz green beans

4 oz carrots

1 eggplant

salt

$2\frac{1}{2}$ tablespoons vegetable oil

2 scallions, thinly sliced

3 cloves garlic, crushed

3 tablespoons curry powder

2 teaspoons shrimp paste (optional)

2 dried red chilies, chopped

1 cup vegetable bouillon

1 cup coconut milk

1 tablespoon fish sauce

2 lime leaves or strips of lime or lemon peel

Method

1. Prepare potatoes. Remove outer leaves and trim ends and tough tops of lemongrass. Slice as finely as possible. Trim beans. Peel carrots and cut both diagonally into $1\frac{1}{2}$ inches pieces. Slice eggplant into 1 inch rounds, salt and let stand 10 minutes, then drain liquid and quarter each round.

2. Heat oil in a heavy-based pan, add scallions and garlic and sauté until just golden. Add curry powder, shrimp paste if desired, lemongrass and chili and cook for about 6 minutes. Add bouillon, coconut milk, fish sauce and lime leaves or citrus peel. Cover and bring to a boil.

3. Reduce heat to medium, add carrots, potatoes, beans and eggplant. Partially cover and simmer until vegetables are tender and liquid has reduced. Season with salt.

Serves 4

STEAMED STUFFED CUCUMBERS

Ingredients

4 dried black mushrooms
1 pound cucumber
1½ teaspoons cornstarch
13 oz canned water chestnuts
2½ tablespoons glutinous rice flour
sesame oil
½ teaspoon sugar
½ teaspoon salt
4 tablespoons cooked, diced carrot
vegetable oil
pepper
¾ cup bouillon or water

Method

1. Soak mushrooms for 30 minutes, drain then remove and discard stalks, and chop the remainder.

2. Peel cucumbers and cut into ½ inch pieces. Scrape seeds out and discard. Parboil cucumber shells for 1 minute. Rinse in cold water, drain and dust inside with a little cornstarch.

3. Drain water chestnuts and discard liquid. Mash and add rice flour, a dash of sesame oil and ¼ teaspoon each of sugar and salt. Add carrot and mushrooms and mix well. Stuff cucumber circles and place on a plate. Steam in steamer, covered, for 15 minutes.

4. In a separate saucepan, mix a dash of oil with pepper to taste and remaining sugar and salt. Add remaining cornstarch. Stir in bouillon or water until smooth. Heat until thickened and pour over the cooked cucumber pieces.

Serves 4–6

HERBED RICE NOODLES WITH ASPARAGUS AND PEANUTS

Ingredients

3 tablespoons rice vinegar

1 tablespoon sugar

1 small Spanish onion, finely sliced

8 oz dried rice noodles

2 bunches of asparagus

$\frac{1}{3}$ cup fresh mint, chopped

$\frac{1}{3}$ cup fresh cilantro. chopped

1 seedless cucumber, peeled, seeded and
thinly sliced

6 scallions, finely sliced

3 plum tomatoes, finely diced

$\frac{3}{4}$ cup roasted peanuts, lightly crushed

juice of 2 limes

2 teaspoons fish sauce

2 teaspoons olive oil

$\frac{1}{2}$ teaspoon chili flakes

Method

1. Whisk rice vinegar and sugar together and
   pour over the finely sliced onion rings. Allow
   to marinate for 1 hour, tossing frequently.

2. Cook noodles according to package directions.
   (Usually, rice noodles need only to soak in
   boiling water for 5 minutes, otherwise, boil for
   1–2 minutes then drain immediately and rinse
   under cold water.)

3. Cut off the tough stalks of the asparagus, and
   cut remaining stalks into $\frac{3}{4}$ inch pieces.
   Simmer asparagus in salted water for 2
   minutes until bright green and crisply tender.
   Rinse in cold water to refresh.

4. Toss noodles with reserved onion and
   vinegar mixture while still warm. Then, using
   kitchen scissors, cut noodles into manageable
   lengths (4 inch).

5. Add the cooked asparagus to noodles along
   with chopped mint, cilantro, cucumber,
   scallions, tomatoes and roasted peanuts and
   toss thoroughly.

6. Whisk lime juice, fish sauce, oil and chili flakes
   together and drizzle over the noodle salad.
   Serve at room temperature.

Serves 4

TOFU STUFFED TOMATOES

Ingredients

6 large, firm tomatoes

4 oz firm tofu, drained

1 cup fresh mushrooms, chopped

3 cloves garlic, minced

4 scallions, chopped

1 tablespoon fish sauce

1 teaspoon ground white pepper

1 egg, beaten

1 tablespoon cornstarch

1/4 cup vegetable oil

To garnish

1/4 cup cilantro, chopped

Method

1. Cut tops from tomatoes, remove both core and pulp, and set aside. Mash tofu and mix in a bowl with mushrooms, garlic, scallions, fish sauce, pepper, egg and cornstarch. Fill tomatoes with the mixture.

2. Heat oil in a large skillet over high heat then carefully add tomatoes, stuffed side down. Cook for about 4 minutes, turn to low and cook for another 6 minutes.

3. Serve garnished with cilantro and with sweet and sour sauce (see page 43).

Serves 6.

STICKY RICE WITH BEAN SPROUTS

Ingredients

8 oz glutinous rice

water

8 oz fresh bean sprouts or mung dal

pinch salt

Method

1. Cover rice with water. If not using fresh bean sprouts, soak mung dal in water in a separate bowl. Leave both to soak overnight then wash rice and mung dal until water runs clear. Mix rice and mung dal with salt.

2. Line a bamboo steamer or top of a metal steamer with a tea towel, or greaseproof paper and spread rice and mung dal over it. Cover with folded sides of tea towel and/or lid. Steam for about 40 minutes, replenishing water, until cooked. If using fresh bean sprouts, add to cooked rice and fluff through with a fork.

Note: For plain sticky rice, steam as above (without bean sprouts) or boil 4 cups of water with 2 cups of soaked glutinous rice for 10 minutes. Remove from heat, drain, cover and let stand for 15 minutes.

Serves 6

salads

RIPE FOR
EXPERIMENTS

Vietnamese salads differ from many in the world in that they often include seafoods or meats. This means that the salads can make light, nutritious main courses when served with crusty bread, so refreshing in summer. In Vietnam, salads come as part of a multi-course meal, but visitors to Vietnam should check whether the raw ingredients have been washed in bottled water.

With its range of tropical and cool-climate fruits, herbs and vegetables, Vietnam's colorful salads reflect different flavors and textures and are ripe for experimentation if certain ingredients are unavailable. If a daikon (a large white radish) can't be found, for example, use a red-skinned radish.

Vegetarians can omit meats and certain sauces from the following salads. Some of the dressings described in this section can be used to add exciting new flavors to familiar salad favorites.

SAIGON SALAD

Ingredients
8 cooked potatoes
14 oz canned artichoke hearts
14 oz canned button mushrooms

Dressing
4 tablespoons white vinegar
juice of $\frac{1}{2}$ lemon
$\frac{1}{4}$ cup parsley, chopped
large pinch dried dill
salt to taste
ground black pepper

To garnish
parsley sprigs and walnuts, quartered

Method
1. Peel potatoes, slice and place in salad bowl. Combine dressing ingredients well and pour over potatoes.

2. Drain artichokes and mushrooms and discard liquid. Carefully mix with potatoes and dressing and garnish with parsley and walnuts.

Serves 4

GREEN PAPAYA SALAD

Ingredients

1½ pounds green papaya, finely julienned

4 scallions, very finely julienned

half of a daikon radish, very finely julienned

12 Vietnamese mint leaves

12 Thai basil (or regular basil) leaves

¼ bunch fresh cilantro, leaves only

1 clove garlic, minced

Dressing

¼ teaspoon shrimp paste

2 tablespoons boiling water

3 tablespoons rice vinegar

3 tablespoons lime juice

2 tablespoons fish sauce

2 tablespoons sugar

1 tablespoon sweet chili sauce

To garnish

2 tablespoons dried shrimp or crushed peanuts

extra Thai basil and Vietnamese mint leaves

Method

1. Toss papaya with scallions, radish, chopped fresh herbs and garlic.

2. To make the dressing, dilute shrimp paste in boiling water, then whisk with all other dressing ingredients. If the sauce is a little too acidic, add a little extra water to dilute the flavor to your taste. Continue whisking until the dressing is well mixed.

3. Toss dressing through papaya and vegetable mixture, taking care to disperse the dressing thoroughly.

4. Pile onto a plate and sprinkle with peanuts or dried shrimp. Garnish with extra basil and mint leaves.

Serves 8

CHICKEN SALAD

Ingredients

1 onion, finely sliced

1 carrot, julienned

1 radish, finely sliced

1 stick celery, finely sliced

$1/2$ green or red bell pepper, seeded and finely sliced

2 cups cooked chicken, chopped

1 cup lettuce leaves, torn

$1/4$ quarter cucumber, sliced diagonally

Dressing

5 tablespoons lemon juice

$1/3$ cup water

3 tablespoons sugar

To garnish

1 tablespoon mint, chopped

1 small red chili, seeded and sliced

Method

1. Mix dressing ingredients. Combine salad vegetables except lettuce and cucumber in a bowl. Pour over dressing, cover and refrigerate for 1 hour. Transfer to a salad bowl.

2. Add chicken, lettuce and cucumber, toss together and sprinkle with mint and chili rings.

Serves 4

desserts

SWEET SNACKING

Vietnamese dessert, following a family home meal, is inevitably fruit. Vietnam is blessed with many varieties of fruit, including bananas, watermelon, mangosteen, jackfruit, mango, guava, pineapple, pomelo (like grapefruit), rambutan, custard apple, lychees, tamarind, durian and more. Readers in tropical regions will have little difficulty in obtaining most of these fruits.

The French made a big impact on the creation of desserts in Vietnam. Sweetmeats, including green mung bean cakes, cookies and desserts, are delicious snacks, bought between meals from hawkers, market stalls and French-style patisseries.

The Vietnamese have adapted many French dessert recipes in several ways. One adaption is to replace milk and cream with, respectively, coconut milk and cream. These ingredients add a refreshing flavor and are essentially lower in cholesterol and calories than the dairy equivalents. Some desserts, such as the crème caramel to follow, are called flans although no pastry is evident. Dessert soups are also unusual for Westerners, but very cooling in summer. If, in Vietnam, a host offers you 'cake' (or *banh*), don't necessarily expect a rich gateau–although you may get it. The term *banh* covers all sorts of sweet and savory treats, from vegetable rolls and seafood rice crêpes to fruity tarts.

Although the habit in Vietnam is to serve all lunch and dinner dishes together around the rice pot, without dessert, you can break tradition with a triumphantly sweet finale to your own Vietnamese dinner party.

GINGER COOKIES

Ingredients

$\frac{1}{2}$ cup all-purpose
$\frac{1}{2}$ cup superfine sugar
$\frac{1}{4}$ teaspoon baking soda
pinch salt
2 tablespoons ground ginger
1 teaspoon ground cinnamon
2 oz butter
1 tablespoon honey
1 small egg

Method

1. Preheat oven to 340°F. Sift flour, sugar, baking soda and salt into a bowl. Add ginger and cinnamon. Work butter in with hands until texture of breadcrumbs. Beat honey and egg together and gradually add to flour mix to form dough.

2. Form into small balls and place well apart onto greased baking trays. Bake until crisply golden.

Makes about 20 cookies

COCONUT FLAN WITH CARAMEL (CREME CARAMEL)

Ingredients

Caramel

¼ cup sugar

¼ cup hot water

Custard

4 eggs

1 teaspoon vanilla extract

1 cup canned coconut milk

1 cup milk

¼ cup sugar

mint sprig to decorate

Method

1. To make caramel, melt sugar alone in a small, heavy pot, over low heat. Swirl the pot constantly until the sugar becomes golden. Stir in hot water carefully as the mixture will splatter. Quickly stir to dissolve any lumps and boil for about 2 minutes until liquid is clear.

2. Pour caramel into a 4 cup soufflé dish that has been lightly greased with butter or margarine. Tilt the dish to ensure caramel coats the base.

3. To make custard, beat eggs and vanilla in a large bowl. Combine coconut milk and milk with sugar in a saucepan and cook over low heat until sugar dissolves. Remove from stove and beat quickly into eggs and vanilla so eggs do not curdle. Sieve custard only if it is lumpy. Pour slowly on top of caramel in soufflé dish.

4. Preheat oven to 325°F. In the base of a large roasting pan, place 2 layers of paper towels, then place the soufflé dish on top before pouring hot water into the roasting pan until halfway up the soufflé dish. Bake in the center of the oven for about 50 minutes or until a knife inserted into custard is clean when removed. Do not allow water to boil. Remove soufflé dish. Cool in a pan of cold water. Refrigerate, covered with plastic wrap, preferably overnight.

5. To serve, run a knife around the circumference of the dish and place a dinner plate on top. In a quick movement, invert the dish and the créme caramel will slide onto the plate. Serve alone or with whipped cream. Place a mint sprig in the center to garnish.

Serves 6

MANGO CAKE WITH NUTMEG CREAM

Ingredients

1 cup unsalted roasted macadamia nuts

3 large mangoes, about 1½ pounds

8 oz butter, softened

1 teaspoon vanilla extract

1 cup superfine sugar

4 large eggs

2 cups all-purpose

1½ teaspoons baking powder

½ cup roasted macadamia nuts, chopped

confectioner's sugar

2 cups pure cream

1 teaspoon nutmeg

1 mango, sliced, for serving

Method

1. Preheat the oven to 350°F and grease an 8 inch non-stick cake tin with butter.

2. Crush roasted macadamia nuts in a food processor and set aside.

3. Peel mangoes and dice the flesh, saving as much juice as possible, then reserve some nice pieces of mango (about 3 oz) and purée the remaining mango flesh with all the reserved juice. You should have about 1 cup of mango purée.

4. Beat softened butter and vanilla extract with half the sugar. Beat until thick and pale. While beating, add remaining sugar and beat until all sugar has been added. Add eggs, one at a time, and beat well after each addition.

5. In a separate bowl, combine crushed nuts, flour and baking powder.

6. Remove the bowl from the mixer and add the flour mixture, stirring well to combine. Add the mango purée and mix gently.

7. Spoon the batter into the prepared tin, then sprinkle chopped macadamia nuts and reserved diced mango over the batter and swirl through.

8. Bake for 1 hour, then remove the cake from the oven and cool in the tin. When cool, remove from the tin and dust with confectioner's sugar.

9. To prepare the cream, whip cream and nutmeg together until the cream is thick and fragrant. Serve alongside the cake with some mango slices.

Serves 6

ALMOND RICE JELLY

Ingredients

3 oz ground rice

6 oz ground almonds

2 oz powdered gelatin

6 oz superfine sugar

2 oz dried coconut

$4\frac{1}{2}$ cups boiling water

few drops of almond extract

Method

1. Mix together all dried ingredients in a saucepan. Add boiling water while stirring and bring to a boil. Simmer, still stirring, for 10 minutes until thick. Stir in almond extract. Pour into lightly greased serving bowl or mold, cool, cover and refrigerate.

2. Serve with a bowl of canned lychees, gooseberries or fresh guava and cream if desired.

Serves 4

almond rice jelly

GINGER MELON SOUP

Ingredients

1 canteloupe (about 1$\frac{1}{2}$ pounds)

2 oz fresh ginger, peeled

3$\frac{1}{2}$ cups water

4 oz sugar

11 oz glass noodles

juice of 2 limes or lemons

Method

1. Peel canteloupe, remove seeds, cut into small cubes and machine-blend. Keep cool. Slice ginger finely and boil half of it in water with half the sugar until sugar has dissolved. Turn heat down, and add noodles to simmer for 5 minutes. Remove from heat, allow to cool, pour into a bowl, and remove ginger and chill.

2. In a saucepan, boil together remaining sugar, ginger and lime or lemon juice. Simmer until thick. Remove from heat, cool and remove ginger. Chill.

3. In individual bowls set in larger ice-filled bowls, pour equal quantities of gingered melon purée. Top with noodles then lime or lemon mix. Garnish each with a mint leaf and serve with ginger cookies (see page 78) to dunk and soften.

Serves 4

CHINESE
food

the land
AND ITS
PEOPLE

Russia

Mongolia

Gobi Desert   Beijing •

China

Plateau of Tibet   Shanghai •   *Yellow Sea*

Himalayas

Nepal   Guangzhou •

Burma

Laos

Status	People's Republic
Area	3,705,406 sq mile
Population	1,284,304
Language	Mandarin
Religion	Confucian, Buddhist
Currency	Yuan
National Day	1 October

A BOUNTIFUL BOWL

The Chinese have a joke about the residents of Canton, otherwise known as Guangzhou, the capital of Guangdong Province. They claim that the Cantonese will eat anything that flies, except a plane, and anything on four legs, except a table. But this could be said of any of the Han people, who make up 92 percent of China's population.

The Chinese include about 55 minority groups who inhabit 21 provinces, as well as the residents of the Chinese Special Administrative Regions of Hong Kong and Macau, people from five autonomous regions, including Inner Mongolia and Tibet, and those who live on many of the 5,000 islands controlled by the world's second largest country.

The People's Republic of China (PRC) is dwarfed only by Canada, with the world's largest population of more than 1.2 billion. Because two thirds of China consists of mountains, deserts or is barren land, less than 20 percent of its land is cultivated. So it's small wonder that little birdsong is heard in the countryside and that seemingly every grain, fruit, vegetable, edible root, flower, leaf, and animal food source is collected, farmed or hunted.

This book is not about eating China's many strange delicacies such as monkey brains, ox penises, fish eyes, bird saliva,

rooster feet, cat tails, jellyfish, horsemeat, dog (a great delicacy now farmed humanely in many regions), fox paws, sea cucumbers, snails or snakes, although I thoroughly enjoyed eating the last four items while researching this book on several visits to China.

China has one of the great cuisines of poverty as well as of opulence. Chinese food, as it has evolved through 5,000 years of Chinese history and various dynasties, remains a pleasure to prepare and eat and reflects both Chinese life philosophy and health principles.

The ancient philosophy of yin and yang (also a medical theory) is still very important in Chinese cuisine. Yin food is soothing, beneficial to health and cool, while yang is hot and exciting, but is considered sometimes draining. Another key tradition is the combination of *tsai* with *fan*. *Tsai* is cooked food—meat, fish or vegetables—while *fan* is any grain-derived dish, from rice and noodles to porridge and steamed buns. No meal is complete without a balance of the two. Modern shortages of rice and wheat have seen an increasing reliance on sorghum, soy beans, millet and potatoes.

HEAT UP FOR HEALTH

Regarded as the world's healthiest cuisine, Chinese food is traditionally cooked quickly to conserve fuel and energy. Preparation can be meticulously time-consuming, but also contains the essence of simplicity. Once most ingredients are peeled, chopped, sliced, minced, shaped and shredded with

concentration and rhythmic ease with a Chinese cleaver on a wooden board, the wok, a bamboo steamer and long chopsticks or a wooden spoon will take care of the rest.

The marinating of meat, fish, poultry and meat is common. Where ingredients have different textures, but must be cooked simultaneously in a wok, blanching, steaming and poaching are often carried out before stir-frying.

Dried food, for example shrimps and fungus, are soaked in water, with the soaking liquid then used as stock. The hanging and air-drying of poultry following marinating and, sometimes, steaming, ensures that the skin becomes crispy after roasting or deep-frying, just as with Peking duck.

WHAT IS CHINESE CUISINE?

In a vast country of so many provinces comprised of many counties producing such a variety of produce, there is no one true Chinese cuisine. The first Chinese cuisine to be brought to the West was Cantonese, as the first Chinese cooks and chefs to emigrate to the West were mainly from Canton.

However the cuisine of Shanghai has also been influential from the time that a few Western adventurers arrived in the 1860s to the 1930s when about 60,000 Europeans resided there.

China has 11 cuisines—Cantonese, Shanghaiese, Shandong, Beijing, Hunan, Anhui, Yangzhou, Fukienese, Jiangsu, Szechuan and Mongolian. Each cuisine was developed according to the ingredients available in a particular area and the climatic conditions. The Mongolian hot pot and barbecue, for example, are often featured in speciality restaurants in Western countries. There is a considerable overlapping of cuisines in China dating back to times of war and trade when conquerors and traveling merchants brought with them the food traditions of their regions of origin.

Visitors to China can order Peking duck or a Mongolian hot pot in a Cantonese restaurant far south or a fiery, chili-based dish originating from the landlocked Szechuan Province in a restaurant overlooking the Yellow River in Shandong Province. The same combinations of cuisines have been created in Chinese restaurants in the West where chefs offer a range of dishes which can represent China as a whole. It is estimated that China has about 80,000 different dishes.

china

the land AND
ITS PEOPLE

Abroad or within China, chefs and home cooks share the same concepts: a focus on color, fragrance, a variety of texture and, of course, flavor. Enormous artistry is exhibited in dishes prepared for feasts and special occasions. A dragon pagoda may be meticulously carved out of partly-cooked pumpkin over a number of hours only to be demolished in seconds.

While China offers up to 11 distinctive cuisines, the following four are the most popular. They use an amazing 12,807 different herb varieties. The styles are essentially geographic, but draw on features from neighboring regions.

FOUR OF THE BEST

1. Beijing cuisine, incorporating also the Shandong, Anhui and Mongolian cuisines, is marked by the cold-weather climate of the north, an area often snow-clad in winter. The area is also dry and barren so northern cooking is mainly reliant on fresh vegetables and dried imports from more productive regions. This is a hearty, rich and meaty cuisine which shows the influence of the lavish, imperial courts of the past, as well as the innovations of poor peasants. Chili was one of the first international ingredients to be imported by China, and characterizes this cuisine, as well as that of several other regions.

In the North, rice does not thrive. Wheat is the staple. Steamed and fried breads, dumplings and noodles are wonderful replacements for rice. Noodle-making is a superlative art in China. The soups of Shandong, the region around the Yellow River, are also justly renowned, while the Muslims and Mongolians in the North love lamb and goat. And no visit to Beijing itself is complete without trying Peking duck, which is served in specialty restaurants with entertaining aplomb (see the chicken and poultry section).

2. Szechuan and Hunan are China's most ancient provinces, neighbors in the Southwest of China. Hunan (the birthplace of Mao Tse-

Tung) is bordered by Burma, Laos and Vietnam. While Szechuan and Hunan have similar hot and humid climates, the former is mountainous and produces less than Hunan. Szechuan does, however, produce among the world's most beneficial herbs for food and medicine. Hunan is known for its poultry, meat and fish, wild mushrooms, earthy, aged teas and salted air-dried ham. Szechuan cuisine, produced on the upper reaches of the Yangtze River, is better known in the West than Hunan cuisine. Both rely heavily on chili, which dries out the body's dampness in excessive humidity. Combined, the two cuisines present pungent dishes, hot and sour, perfect pork and freshwater fish. In Szechuan cooking, peppercorns, garlic and ginger are also liberally used in addition to chili. These ingredients are deemed medicinally helpful for sweating off illnesses. Hunan cuisine is simple and less spectacular in presentation than other cuisines, but the flavors can be quite complex. Of Szechuan cuisine, it is said: 'One dish, one style. One hundred dishes, 100 different tastes'.

3. Shanghaiese is the cuisine of the Yangtze River delta, including the Huangpo River on which Shanghai, China's most populous city, is located. Jiangsu cuisine focuses on poultry and river fish cooked in their own juices. The eastern coastal area of China also includes Fukienese-style cooking from which the traditions of Taiwan developed. Not only is the great Changjiang (Yangtze) River a great food source, but the region is blessed with fertile soil, good rainfall and undulating countryside as far south as Guangdong Province. The food from the cities of Hangzhou and Suzhou has been praised by poets down the centuries.

4. Cantonese cuisine is less oily and less spicy than other Chinese cuisines, being either lightly steamed, stir-fried or boiled. It is highly

regarded by people with cholesterol and coronary conditions. Unusual delicacies in Guangdong Province include cats, rats, toads, frogs, owls and monkeys. Snake has been prepared in the province for more than 2,000 years. From Guangzhou (Canton) on the Pearl River comes seafood, roast pork, chicken, steamed fish and fried rice, abalone and 1,000-year-old eggs (which are really only weeks old!). One statistician has estimated that Guangzhou alone has about 6,000 different dishes, not counting about 850 varied snacks. Hong Kong, now part of China again, boasts all styles of mainland food, as well as the cuisines of almost every other country on earth.

PUT WHAT IN THE WOK?

Name an item of produce and China has it, whether it has been grown in a specific region or freighted in from elsewhere in this big country. You can peel a pomegranate or suck on a strawberry in Xian (home of the entombed terracotta warriors). Xian also has the greatest variety of dumplings in China and its dumpling dinners are highlights for visitors. You can pick up a pineapple or bite on a banana in Beijing, even though these fruits are not grown there. Table grapes do survive successfully in the cooler winter climate of Beijing. Pork and poultry are the most consumed meats throughout China, while the most eaten fish is carp. This fish is not popular

with Westerners as it has so many bones. Usually presented whole and carefully de-boned at the table, carp is an oily, but filling fish, given character with different herbs and spices.

daily food
IN CHINA

THREE MEALS FOR ALL

Most people in China work, sometimes at several jobs, since the lifting of the restraints under the Cultural Revolution, the rise of private enterprise and the increase in free markets and Westernization. Breakfast is a fast meal, likely to be milk (inevitably tinned or powdered) and either toast or a traditional baked cake with sweet or salty stuffing. Ginseng is a medicinal tea often used to greet the morning with steamed or fried bread. If there's time, congee or rice porridge will be eaten with pickles and, possibly, steamed bread or twisted fried dough-sticks with wok-cooked tofu. Tofu and milk with steamed dumplings is another breakfast alternative. Poor people in the countryside commonly begin with just rice and tea.

Working women and their partners are likely to opt for street stall snacks en route to work, as they do not have the time to cook as their mothers did. Breakfast might be stuffed wontons or dumplings in soup and, during the day, jasmine or green tea in the North and green tea in the South will be drunk. The appetizer and snacks section includes recipes for some of these snacks.

Traditionally, the oldest, most able woman in a household begins to prepare the evening meal in the afternoon, to be cooked when the working family comes home. A childless couple living on their own will typically cook their own meal, based around the *fan*–rice, noodles, steamed bread or pancakes–with one *tsai* (meat or fish) dish and up to two vegetables, plus soup. Young couples are also likely to eat out on cheap snacks or restaurant food.

FESTIVAL FEAST FARE

The most major festival in China is the Chinese New Year festival, which is celebrated in January or February according to the Chinese lunar calendar. There is a three-day lantern festival 15 days into the

New Year. Other festivals include May Day and the two-day celebration of National Day in September or October. Some families and/or communities celebrate the birthday of Guan Yin, the goddess of mercy, on the 19th day of the second lunar month, when people bring food, often vegetarian, to her shrines. The 23rd day of the third lunar month is the birthday of Mazu, goddess of the sea and mother of heaven. Every fishing village and junk has respective temples and shrines to her. Fish-eating coastal communities eat meat on that day out of respect for her. Qing Ming, meaning 'pure and clean', is a special time devoted to honoring ancestors and dead relatives which takes place 106 days after the winter solstice festival. Graves are visited and tidied, and only cold picnic fare is eaten as no home fires are lit for two days out of respect for the dead. The year also includes the Dragon Boat, Lotus, Double Ninth and Double Seventh festivals. The Festival of the Hungry Ghosts is held on the mainland, and in Hong Kong, as well as in Singapore and Malaysia, on the 15th day of the seventh lunar month. Burning money, clothes and offering vegetarian foods to all, appease the spirits of Buddhist Chinese who have died far from home. Mid-autumn is moon festival time when the man in the moon plays matchmaker and people exchange gifts of fruit, sweets and moon cakes.

Decorated outside with red lanterns, restaurants do brisk trade during most festivals. At birthday parties, a written character meaning longevity is placed on the wall. At a wedding, another character means double happiness. More affluent people are more commonly selecting joint-venture Western hotels for marriage celebrations, but while the bride may first wear a Western white gown rather than the traditional red dress, which is donned later, the menu will inevitably be Chinese.

At most meals, cold dishes, from peanuts to roasted pork, condiments and sauces await guests. To these are added hot, sweet and vegetable dishes, rice or noodles and soup. Often the dessert will arrive in the middle of the meal and, according to the customs of the region, soup may come last. In Guangzhou, even at a family dinner, eight dishes plus a soup are served. Nine courses signify everlasting friendship. In Guangdong Province, soup is served first to aid the digestive system. Sometimes desserts are served both first and last, to signify that life should be sweet from beginning to end.

The Chinese aren't very fond of desserts, but fresh fruit may be served after the meal. Chinese apples are amongst the world's biggest. Chopped and tossed in toffee (see page 156), they taste delicious.

At any meal gathering, guests should leave a little food in the main dishes on the table,. The hosts will then be satisfied they have provided adequately. If the diners eat all the food, provision will be seen to be inadequate and the host will lose face.

YOUR CHINESE DINNER PARTY

Imported dinner sets are inexpensive in Chinese stores and are often sold in department stores too. Each person should have a rice bowl, two smaller bowls for dipping sauces, such as soy or chili, and a bread and butter-sized plate. Main dishes are served on large plates placed in the center of the table, along with a large bowl of rice with a lid to keep it warm throughout the meal. Another big bowl contains soup. Two large porcelain ladles are for serving and a smaller spoon is provided for each diner to eat soup with.

In China, people often move food from the main dishes to individual plates or bowls with their own chopsticks, which is not very hygienic outside a family situation. You may like to place an extra serving spoon by each dish. Many restaurants in China set tables with a paper bag containing 'Sterilized Chopstick', meaning that the chopsticks have not been used before nor will be used again.

When buying chopsticks, opt for plastic, wooden or camel bone pairs with the finest points, which will make picking up a single rice grain or a pea easier. To master the art of using chopsticks, rest the lower one on the fourth finger of one hand, holding it with the thumb. The third and forefinger will operate the one above, securing food between the two.

china

INTRODUCTION

GAN BEI – EMPTY THE CUP

'*Gan bei*' is a traditional saying which means 'Good health' or 'Cheers'. The Chinese are not traditionally big consumers of alcohol. In China, the festive table will be set with tumblers for soft drink or water, beer and a smaller port-size glass for *mao tai*, a near-lethal weapon in the form of a sorghum-based spirit which has a mule's kick. Plum wine, in an extra port-sized glass, is often used for toasting at a banquet.

Jasmine or green tea is the usual accompaniment to food, but light beer is also popular and China produces scores of quaffable regional varieties. For your own dinner party, you could serve some light beer and red or white wines, although the flavor of good wine may be wasted if the food is very hot and spicy. Dynasty and Great Wall are the best-known Chinese brands of red and white wine, produced mainly for visitors, but the Chinese wine industry is growing, producing mainly rather light and sweet wines.

For a serious aperitif, try viper vodka. This, as in Vietnam, Korea and Thailand, is sold with a dead snake still in the bottle and, like Chinese wines which contain herbs, is supposed to be of medicinal value, particularly for treating impotence. If in China, try a shot for the novelty of it. At home, straight vodka is probably the nearest replacement for a traditional toast. Many Chinese recipes call for Shaoxing rice wine. Dry sherry is a reasonable replacement and will be listed as such in the following recipes. Chinese brandy is different from Western, but definitely palatable.

China's tea houses remain popular with older people and are well-worth visiting for a fragrant cup of tea and a traditional ceremony combined with conversation, especially the tea houses in Beijing. In recent years, students have been drawn back to tea houses as places of intellectual discussion.

I hope you enjoy the authentic food of China.

Kerry Kenihan

appetizers
& snacks

Finger on the FOOD

In China, when guests sit in a restaurant or a private home, about six cold appetizers in bowls or small plates are set on the table. Usually only one plate of cooked meat such as red roasted pork (see the meat section), smoked ham, or fish will be served with soured or pickled vegetables, shredded vegetables, marbled eggs, edible dried seeds and peanuts.

Diners pick slowly, reserving their appetites for the main dishes, which are served almost simultaneously. Occasionally, one hot dim sum or stall-snack-food dish will appear with the main dishes.

Dim sum is a brunch adventure in which barbecued, fried or steamed dumplings, buns, egg or wonton-wrapped rolls and other snacks are selected from a trolley and eaten in a continuous procession with dipping sauces and tea. Dim sum is particularly popular in Hong Kong, Singapore, Kuala Lumpur and in Chinese restaurants throughout big cities in the Western world, especially on Sundays. In China, the fun way to experience it is on a food-stall-crawl in a street devoted to snacking. The words yum cha are an invitation to eat dim sum and/or enjoy tea.

The following recipes are snack foods, although they could be part of a main meal or form a starter at your dinner party. You could prepare several of these dishes as finger food at a cocktail party. Supply finger bowls and paper serviettes. Store bought wonton and spring roll wrappers are convenient and easily available.

CHICKEN SPRING ROLLS

Ingredients

1 pound chicken stir-fry pieces
$1/4$ Chinese cabbage, finely chopped
$1/2$ red bell pepper, seeded and thinly sliced
4 mushrooms, thinly sliced
1 tablespoon soy sauce
1 tablespoon oyster sauce
2 teaspoons cornstarch
1 tablespoon water
2 tablespoons oil
2 teaspoons fresh ginger, finely chopped
1 small onion, finely chopped
1 package frozen spring roll wrappers
oil for deep frying

Method

1. Chop chicken stir-fry into smaller pieces. Prepare all vegetables, combine the 2 sauces and mix cornstarch and water together. Heat wok; add 2 tablespoons of oil and heat. Add ginger and onion and stir-fry until onion is pale gold in color. Add chicken and stir-fry until white all over (about 2 minutes), toss in vegetables and stir-fry one minute, mixing chicken through vegetables.

2. Pour in combined sauces, tossing to mix through. Push mixture to one side and add blended cornstarch to juices in the base of wok. As juices thicken, stir and toss through vegetables. Spread mixture out onto a flat tray to cool. Wrap one heaping tablespoon chicken mixture in each wrapper according to package directions.

3. Wipe out wok, heat and add fresh oil to approximately 2 inches deep. Heat oil and fry rolls a few at a time until golden color and crisp. Drain on paper towels. Serve hot.

Makes 32 rolls

SESAME SHRIMP TRIANGLES WITH CHILI SAUCE

Ingredients

4 oz cooked peeled shrimp, defrosted if frozen

1 clove garlic, chopped

2 tablespoons beaten egg

1 teaspoon cornstarch

$\frac{1}{2}$ teaspoon sesame oil

a few drops of light soy sauce

3 slices of white bread

2 tablespoons sesame seeds

peanut oil for deep-frying

Dipping sauce

$\frac{1}{2}$ inch fresh root ginger, finely chopped

2 tablespoons hot chili sauce

juice of $\frac{1}{2}$ lime

Method

1. Blend shrimp, garlic, egg, cornstarch, oil and soy sauce to a paste in a food processor. Alternatively, grind shrimp with a mortar and pestle, then mix with the other ingredients.

2. Spread one side of each slice of bread evenly with shrimp paste, sprinkle with sesame seeds, remove crusts and cut into 4 triangles. To make dipping sauce, mix together ginger, chili sauce and lime juice, then set aside.

3. Heat 1 inch of oil in a large skillet over medium to high heat. Add half the shrimp triangles, shrimp-side down, and fry for 4–5 minutes on each side, until deep golden. Drain on kitchen towels and keep warm while you cook the remaining shrimp triangles. Serve with dipping sauce.

Serves 4

HONEY AND CHILI SHRIMP

Ingredients

1 pound jumbo shrimp, raw

Marinade

¼ cup red wine

½ cup honey

¼ teaspoon ground chili

1 teaspoon mustard powder

Equipment

bamboo skewers, soaked for 10 minutes to
   prevent burning

Method

1. Mix all ingredients, except shrimp, together
   to make marinade.

2. Shell and devein shrimp, leaving tails intact.
   Place in a glass dish and add enough
   marinade to coat well. Cover and marinate
   in refrigerator for 1 hour.

3. Thread shrimp onto skewers, either
   through the side or through the length of
   each shrimp.

4. Heat the barbecue to medium-high. Place a
   sheet of baking paper over the grill bars
   and place shrimp on the paper. Cook for
   4–5 minutes each side. They will turn pink
   when cooked. Brush with marinade while
   cooking. Transfer to a platter. Remove
   skewers and serve immediately.

Serves 3–4

CRAB MEAT FRITTERS

Ingredients

3 eggs

1 cup bean sprouts

3 scallions, chopped

14 oz crab meat

salt and cracked black pepper

oil for deep-frying

Sauce

2 teaspoons cornstarch

1 tablespoon sugar

3 tablespoons soy sauce

1 cup chicken bouillon

2 tablespoons dry sherry

Method

1. Beat eggs in a bowl, stir in bean sprouts, scallions and crab meat, and add salt and pepper to taste.

2. Heat sufficient oil to cover the base of a skillet and drop in the crab mixture, one heaping tablespoon at a time.

3. Fry until golden brown on one side, then turn and brown the other side.

4. Remove from pan, and keep warm.

5. To make the sauce, blend together cornstarch and sugar in a pan, add soy sauce and chicken bouillon.

6. Slowly bring to a boil over low heat, stirring all the time. Cook for 3 minutes, or until sauce is thickened. Stir in sherry. Serve fritters with sauce.

Serves 4

STICKY HOT CHICKEN WINGS

(opposite)

Ingredients

12 chicken wings

1 red chili, seeded and finely chopped

1 teaspoon chili powder

2 teaspoons fresh ginger, crushed

rind of 1 lemon or lime, grated

4 tablespoons vegetable oil

1 tablespoon cilantro, chopped

2½ tablespoons soy sauce

4 tablespoons honey

To garnish

citrus rind and cilantro

Method

1. Cut wings in half at the natural joint. In a bowl, combine fresh and powdered chili, ginger and lemon or lime rind. Rub mixture onto wings and cover for at least 3 hours for flavors to be absorbed.

2. Heat 2 tablespoons of oil in a wok or pan on medium heat and add chicken wings. Stir-fry for about 12 minutes or until crispy golden, adding remaining oil when necessary. Remove and drain on paper towels.

3. Place cilantro in wok and stir-fry for 40 seconds. Add chicken wings, stir-fry for 90 seconds, then add soy sauce and honey. Stir-fry for about 2 minutes or until honey is melted and combined. Place wings on serving dish and spoon sauce from wok on top. Garnish with cilantro and lemon or lime rind.

Serves 4

CRISPY FISH BALLS

Ingredients

8 oz boneless fish

4 oz raw shrimp meat

2 scallions, chopped

2½ teaspoons vegetable oil

½ teaspoon five spice powder

salt and pepper

3 tablespoons cornstarch

extra vegetable oil

Method

1. Combine fish and shrimp meat in a food processor or mincer, or chop very finely.

2. In a bowl, mix scallions, vegetable oil, five spice powder, salt and pepper to taste, and add fish mixture. Work through with your hands until combined and refrigerate for 45 minutes.

3. Make balls about the size of walnuts and carefully toss in a bag with cornstarch and some extra pepper. Transfer to a pan on medium heat with enough vegetable oil for shallow frying. Fry in batches until golden. Drain on paper towels.

4. Serve with a sauce of equal quantities of vegetable oil and chili sauce.

Note: Use canned crab meat as a substitute for shrimp meat, or use an extra 4 ounces of fish instead.

Makes about 22

CHINESE DUMPLINGS

Ingredients

4 oz ground pork

vegetable oil

8 oz shrimp meat, finely chopped

4 water chestnuts, chopped

2 scallions, chopped

½ teaspoon salt

2 teaspoons soy sauce

40 egg wonton wrappers

Method

1. Sauté pork in a little oil in a pan for about 1 minute. Add remaining ingredients with the exception of the wonton wrappers and the rest of the oil. Stir, combining completely. Remove from heat and allow to cool to room temperature.

2. To make dumplings, place a teaspoon of the mixture into the center of each wonton wrapper. Brush edges with a little water, pull corners to the center and pinch edges together to seal mixture inside.

3. Heat enough oil in pan or wok for deep-frying. Drop in wontons 8–10 at a time, and fry until golden (about 2–3 minutes). Drain on paper towels. Dumplings can be kept warm in a slow oven for about 1 hour. Serve with soy, sweet chili, plum or chili plum sauce.

Makes 40

PEKING SCALLION PANCAKES

Ingredients

2 eggs

6 scallions, sliced finely

6 oz all-purpose flour

2 strips bacon, finely chopped

1 cup chicken bouillon

pinch of salt

3 tablespoons vegetable oil

Method

1. Beat eggs well, then add scallions, flour, bacon, bouillon and salt and combine to form a smooth batter.

2. To a 10 inch skillet on medium heat, add 2 teaspoons of oil to spread over base of pan. Pour a quarter of the batter into the pan, also ensuring it covers the base.

3. When pancake edge is golden, turn pancake carefully until cooked. Remove and repeat the procedure 3 more times with extra oil to yield 4 pancakes.

4. Serve hot, cut into slices.

Serves 4 as individual starters or 16 or more as finger food with drinks, depending on slice portions.

SPICED SPARE RIBS

Ingredients

2 pounds meaty pork spare ribs

1 teaspoon Szechuan peppercorns

2 tablespoons cooking salt

$\frac{1}{2}$ teaspoon five spice powder

$1\frac{1}{2}$ tablespoons cornstarch

oil for deep-frying

Marinade

$2\frac{1}{2}$ tablespoons light soy sauce

2 teaspoons superfine sugar

2 tablespoons dry sherry

black pepper, freshly ground

To garnish

parsley or cilantro

Method

1. Ask the butcher to chop spare ribs into 2 inch pieces or use a sharp cleaver. Reserve. In a wok or heavy deep pan, stir-fry peppercorns with salt for about 5 minutes, stirring until salt colors. Remove. Then with mortar and pestle pound down peppercorns with five spice powder added.

2. Combine marinade ingredients and set aside. Rub half of the spice mix into spare ribs with your hands, add marinade and turn each rib to ensure each is fully coated. Marinate for at least 3 hours, preferably overnight.

3. Drain marinade from ribs and coat each rib with cornstarch. Add more oil to wok until half full. Deep-fry ribs in batches over medium heat for about 4 minutes, remove, then re-fry until crisp and deeply golden.

4. Drain ribs. Place on warmed serving dish, sprinkle with remaining spice mix and serve garnished with parsley or cilantro.

Serves 4

NUTTY NOODLE SNACK

Ingredients

1 pound noodles or spaghetti

4 tablespoons soy sauce

2 tablespoons vinegar

2 tablespoons peanut or sesame oil

4 scallions, sliced diagonally

Sauce

2 tablespoons sesame paste or peanut butter

2½ tablespoons sesame or peanut oil

2 tablespoons chicken bouillon

Method

1. Boil water, add noodles or spaghetti and cook according to package directions until al dente. Drain, wash in hot water, return to pot and add soy sauce, vinegar, oil and scallions. Meanwhile, heat sauce ingredients, stirring to combine.

2. Divide noodles into 4–6 bowls, top with sauce and serve.

Note: This is a filling snack or lunch on its own but can make a good appetizer, particularly when eaten with pickled vegetables. Can also be served as one of several main courses.

Serves 4–6

soups

Through thick
AND THIN

Soup in China is not an afterthought or a starter. Its main role is to aid digestion, therefore it is generally clear and made with bouillon from boiled meats, fish and/or vegetables.

Thin, savory soups are sipped while eating dry main courses such as fried chicken or fish or roast duck served without sauces. Some of the nicest soups I've slurped in China have been palate-refreshing postscripts to the meal. Bland soup will temper spicy main courses, while a perky soup will contrast with mild dishes.

Thick soups harken back to ancient times before flour refining, when a combination of meat or fish, vegetables and cereals resulted in a stew with a thick soup consistency. Eggs are used to thicken, add flavor and for decorative effect such as in egg flower soup.

Base soups on bouillon or broth made from 4½ lbs of stewing meat—beef, pork or lamb with fat trimmed off or even just the bones. Boil in 1 gallon of cold water with a heaping teaspoon of peppercorns, 4 cilantro or parsley stalks, a large onion and 3 celery sticks and simmer for about two hours. Regularly skim off froth, fat or scum, strain and reheat for about 40 minutes with 3 slices of fresh ginger and salt to taste. Chop meat and return to pot if desired. Substitute meat with chicken trimmings (bones, giblets and so on,) or fish or shrimp heads and shells when these bouillons are needed. Freeze unused bouillon.

Perfectionists would disagree, but if caught short, cheat with bouillon cubes or powder. If you do, reduce the quantity of soy sauce or the soup (or other dish) will be too salty. Vegetarians can cook bouillon using just the vegetables given in the recipe.

FISH NOODLE SOUP

Ingredients
1 pound white fish fillets
vegetable oil
3 oz scallions
1 teaspoon chopped, fresh ginger
1 teaspoon garlic, chopped or crushed
1 red bell pepper, seeded and chopped
4 cups fish bouillon or water
1 tablespoon oyster sauce
½ teaspoon ground black pepper
1 teaspoon sesame oil
1 tablespoon dry sherry
8 oz egg noodles, boiled
1 teaspoon sesame oil, extra
½ red bell pepper, seeded (extra) and chopped for garnish

Method
1. Chop fish into bite-sized pieces. Heat enough vegetable oil to deep-fry fish for 2½ minutes. Remove and drain. Cut scallions into 1½ inch sections, separating white parts from green.

2. Heat 3 tablespoons of oil and brown ginger and soften garlic. Add fish, bell pepper and white sections of scallions. Stir-fry for 3 minutes then add bouillon or water and boil. Add green scallion sections, oyster sauce, black pepper, oil and sherry and simmer for 1 minute, stirring.

3. Add hot, cooked, drained noodles and extra 1 teaspoon of oil. Stir through until hot. Serve immediately, garnished with chopped bell pepper.

Serves 4

GINGER CHICKEN WONTON SOUP

Ingredients

Soup

1 tablespoon sesame oil

1–2 teaspoons chili paste

1 tablespoon soy sauce

2 cloves garlic, minced

1½ oz fresh ginger, sliced

8 cups chicken bouillon

7 oz can bamboo shoots

6 scallions, sliced diagonally

Wontons

4 fresh shiitake mushrooms

1 teaspoon five spice powder

4 oz water chestnuts, drained

3 scallions, chopped

3 sprigs cilantro

2 tablespoons soy sauce

1 tablespoon fresh ginger, grated

1 fresh bird's-eye chili, minced

1 tablespoon sesame seeds

2 chicken breast fillets, skin off

1 pack wonton wrappers

Method

1. First, make the soup. Heat sesame oil in a saucepan and add chili paste, soy sauce, garlic and ginger and sauté for 1–2 minutes. Add bouillon and simmer for 15 minutes then add bamboo shoots and sliced scallions. Set aside.

2. Now make the wontons. Place all the ingredients, except wonton wrappers, in a food processor and 'pulse' the mixture until it is well chopped. Do not overprocess.

3. To shape wontons, separate wonton wrappers and lay them out. Place 1 tablespoon of filling in the center of each wrapper. Working with one wrapper at a time, pick up wrapper and moisten the edges with water. Fold wrapper into a triangle, pinching the pastry together well to enclose the filling. Then wrap the triangle around your finger, carefully pinching together the opposite corners. Shape each wonton in this way.

4. Add the wontons to the simmering soup and cook them for about 4 minutes. Serve immediately.

Serves 6–8

GREEN JADE SPINACH SOUP

Ingredients

1 pound spinach, fresh or frozen

6 cups chicken bouillon

4 oz ground chicken

1 chicken bouillon cube

1 cinnamon stick

2 tablespoons cornstarch

½ cup water

salt and pepper

Method

1. Wash and dry spinach if fresh. Mince in a blender. If using frozen spinach, defrost and purée in blender.

2. Heat bouillon in large saucepan, add chicken and bring to a boil then add spinach and crumbled bouillon cube, stirring well. Add cinnamon stick and simmer for 5 minutes.

3. In a bowl, mix cornstarch with water until smooth and add to soup, stirring until it thickens. Remove cinnamon stick. Add salt and pepper to taste.

Note: While it is not done in China, you might like to add a swirl of yogurt or cream to each bowl, plus a tiny sprinkle of powdered cinnamon. Vegetarians can omit chicken and bouillon cube and substitute vegetable bouillon.

Serves 6

HOT AND SOUR SOUP

Ingredients

6 cups strong chicken, pork or beef bouillon

8 medium-sized dried Chinese mushrooms

1 cup cooked chicken or pork or both, chopped

2 oz cellophane noodles, soaked

7 oz can bamboo shoots, drained

2 tablespoons frozen green peas

7 oz tofu, cut into small cubes (optional)

1 teaspoon fresh ginger, finely grated

1 tablespoon cornstarch, blended with
    4 tablespoons water

1 egg, lightly beaten

1 tablespoon light soy sauce

1½ tablespoons tomato sauce

2 tablespoons vinegar

2 scallions, finely chopped

Optional

2 teaspoons sesame oil

a good pinch of chili powder

ground black pepper to taste

To garnish

scallions

Method

1. Strain bouillon, chill and skim off fat. Soak mushrooms in 6 tablespoons of boiling water for 30 minutes, then drain, remove stalks and chop. Reserve mushroom water and add it to bouillon along with mushrooms, noodles cut into short lengths, chopped bamboo shoots, peas, tofu, ginger and meat.

2. Make sure that the cornstarch and water are well blended before adding to soup. Stir soup continuously. Drizzle beaten egg into soup and stir when it has set. Combine soy sauce with remaining ingredients. Remove pot from heat, quickly add soy sauce mixture to soup, stir well, garnish with scallions and serve immediately.

Note: For a fiery northern or western Chinese flavor, have on the table a bowl containing a mix of a dash of vinegar, ground black pepper, a finely chopped and seeded chili, and sesame oil to add to soup.

Serves 6

VELVET CHICKEN AND SWEET CORN SOUP

Ingredients

1 pound boned chicken breast

large pinch of salt

2 egg whites, beaten to froth

6 cups chicken bouillon

14 oz can creamed corn

2 tablespoons cornstarch blended
   with 3½ tablespoons water

2 tablespoons dry sherry

2 teaspoons light soy sauce

1 teaspoon sesame oil

Garnish

thin slices of Chinese smoked ham or
   cooked bacon

Method

1. Remove fat from chicken then mince, food-process or finely chop it until it is almost a purée. Mix in salt well and fold in egg whites. Bring bouillon to a boil, add corn and return soup to a boil. Thicken with cornstarch mix, stirring for about 1 minute.

2. Stir in chicken purée, sherry, soy sauce and sesame oil and simmer, stirring, for 3 minutes. Serve this soup (which is popular at formal banquets) garnished with finely chopped ham or cooked bacon bits. If you can't buy Chinese ham, substitute Virginia ham.

Serves 6

meat

Marvellous
MEAT

For 7,000 years, the Chinese have revered the meat they cook in their most important color, red. That meat is pork and it's rare for a meal in China to come without it. Pork in sweet and sour sauce has become somewhat of a culinary cliché, but since it is so well loved by Chinese and Westerners alike, a recipe is included in this section.

Pork is so revered for its versatility that when Chinese say 'meat', they mean pork. They also like to red-cook other meats, bending color concepts a little as the red supposedly comes from soy sauce.

The North is not big on beef, but lamb or mutton (no distinction is made between the two) and goat, particularly Mongolian style, is presented in hearty, warming dishes in cold and/or mountainous regions. The Mongols introduced sheep to China in the 13th century, and lamb and mutton are appreciated by Chinese Muslims who are forbidden to eat pork. Mongolian hot pot is a real party piece.

In preparing beef, the Cantonese utilize their secret weapons: simplicity and harmony. Beef is eaten in every region of China, particularly when oxen and domestic cattle employed as beasts of burden reach their use-by-date. The Chinese are not fond of milk products. Only in the far North and northwestern grasslands are cattle found in herds. Venison is also eaten in China.

Ham is rarely used as a pork substitute, but is popular in quick stir-fry or egg dishes. Whole, steamed or glazed ham from Yunnan province is renowned for its quality.

CHINESE FIVE SPICE PORK FILLET

Ingredients
2 tablespoons sunflower or peanut oil
2 small cloves garlic, crushed
2 tablespoons five spice powder
3 tablespoons soy sauce
6 tablespoons dry or medium sherry
2 scallions, finely chopped
pared orange rind, cut into strips
juice of 2 large oranges
salt and black pepper
$1\frac{1}{2}$ pound pork fillet
$\frac{1}{2}$ oz butter, chilled and cubed

To garnish
fresh snipped chives

Method
1. In a small bowl, mix together oil, garlic, five spice powder, soy sauce, sherry and scallions to make a marinade. Add half the orange rind and juice and season with salt and black pepper.

2. Put pork into a non-metallic bowl, pour the marinade over and cover, or place meat and marinade in a roasting bag, tie bag well and shake. Refrigerate for at least 2 hours, or up to 24 hours, turning the meat or shaking the bag once or twice.

3. Preheat the oven to 375°F. Transfer pork fillet and marinade to a roasting tin, loosely cover with foil and cook for 30 minutes. Take off the foil, turn fillet and cook for a further 15 minutes. Cover and leave to stand for 10 minutes. Alternatively, roast in the bag for 45 minutes, then leave to stand for 10 minutes, still in the bag, with the oven door ajar and the heat turned off.

4. Slice the meat. Pour the cooking juices into a small saucepan, add the rest of the orange juice and heat gently. Whisk in butter and adjust the seasoning. Serve the slices of meat with the sauce poured over. Garnish with chives and the remaining orange rind.

Serves 6

BEEF WITH BLACK BEAN SAUCE

Ingredients

1 pound sirloin or rump steak, cut into
 thin strips
1 clove garlic, crushed
1 small red chili, seeded and finely
 chopped (optional)
1 tablespoon dark soy sauce
black pepper
2 teaspoons cornstarch
1 tablespoon water
1 tablespoon white wine vinegar
2 tablespoons vegetable oil
1 yellow and 1 red bell pepper, seeded
 and cut into strips
1 large zucchini, julienned
5 oz snow peas, sliced
3 tablespoons black bean stir-fry sauce
4 scallions, sliced

Method

1. Combine steak strips, garlic, chili (if using), soy
 sauce and pepper in a bowl. In another bowl,
 mix cornstarch with water until smooth, then
 stir in vinegar.

2. Heat oil in a wok or large skillet until very hot.
 Add meat and its marinade and stir-fry for 4
 minutes, tossing continuously, until meat is
 seared on all sides.

3. Add bell peppers and stir-fry for 2 minutes.
 Stir in the zucchini and snow peas and cook
 for 3 minutes. Reduce the heat and add
 cornstarch mixture and black bean sauce. Stir
 to mix thoroughly, then cook for 2 minutes or
 until meat and vegetables are cooked through.
 Scatter with scallions just before serving. If
 desired, serve over egg noodles cooked
 according to package directions.

Serves 4

PORK AND HOKKIEN NOODLE STIR-FRY

Ingredients

1 pound pork stir-fry strips

4 oz bamboo shoots, sliced

14 oz stir-fry vegetables, sliced
  (for example cabbage, carrots, celery
  and bell pepper)

2 tablespoons peanut oil

2 cloves garlic, crushed

1 onion, sliced

1 pound hokkien or egg noodles (or
  cooked rice)

1 cup chicken bouillon
  or salt-reduced stir-fry sauce

2 teaspoons cornstarch

1 tablespoon Shaoxing rice wine
  or dry sherry (optional)

2 tablespoons reduced-salt soy sauce

Method

1. Gather equipment, sauces and fresh
   ingredients before starting to cook. Slice
   pork and vegetables into even, thin
   strips or cut into even bite-size pieces.

2. Heat wok or non-stick skillet until hot. Drizzle
   in oil and swirl to lightly glaze and
   coat the bottom and sides. Stir-fry garlic and
   onion for about 15 seconds until fragrant.
   Stir-fry pork in 1–2 batches until just cooked.
   Allow pan to reheat between batches. Remove
   pork from pan.

3. Add a little more oil to the wok. Stir-fry harder
   vegetables in hot oil for about 30 seconds to
   1 minute or until bright and hot, but still crisp.
   Noodles (or rice) can be added at this stage if
   desired. Save any softer, leafy and easy-to-wilt
   vegetables such as bean sprouts and herbs
   until the end.

4. Return pork to the hot wok and lightly
   combine with vegetables.

5. Make a well by pushing pork and vegetables to
   the side. Add stir-fry sauce, or chicken bouillon
   combined with cornstarch, and pour into pan.
   Stir until it simmers, toss meat and vegetables
   through the sauce, and heat.

6. Combine any remaining ingredients including
   softer, leafy vegetables and herbs. Taste and
   adjust the flavor as required with rice wine or
   sherry and soy sauce. Garnish and serve
   immediately.

Serves 4

HONG KONG BEEF BRAISE
(below)

Ingredients

1 inch fresh ginger root

8 oz carrots

1 pound beef, preferably fillet

4 tomatoes

2 tablespoons vegetable oil

1 onion, sliced

2 teaspoons brown sugar

$\frac{1}{2}$ teaspoon five spice powder

2 tablespoons soy sauce

1 tablespoon dry sherry

2 tablespoons water

salt

Method

1. Cut ginger and carrots into julienne strips. Cut carrot into 2 inch lengths. Thinly slice and cut beef to same length. Cut tomatoes into thin wedges.

2. Heat oil in a wok and fry beef for 3 minutes. Add onion, ginger, tomatoes and carrot strips and stir-fry 3 minutes. Add sugar, five spice powder, soy sauce, sherry, water and salt to taste. Cook gently for 8 minutes.

Serves 4

RED ROASTED PORK

Ingredients

1 pound pork fillet

1 tablespoon sugar

1 tablespoon light soy sauce

$1\frac{1}{2}$ teaspoons black bean sauce

2 teaspoons salt

$2\frac{1}{2}$ tablespoons dry sherry

2 cloves garlic, crushed

1 teaspoon five spice powder

1 teaspoon red food coloring

1 tablespoon honey

1 tablespoon sesame oil

Method

1. Cut pork into long strips, 1 inch thick. In a bowl, combine sugar, soy sauce, black bean sauce, salt, sherry, garlic, five spice powder and food coloring. Add pork strips to marinate for at least 3 hours, but preferably overnight, turning occasionally.

2. Preheat oven to 400°F. Transfer pork from marinade into a roasting pan and roast in oven for 15 minutes in a little oil. Mix sesame oil with honey and spoon it over pork to roast for a further 15 minutes. After pork is cool, cut into thin slivers. Serve hot or cold.

Serves 4

CARAMELIZED PORK LOIN WITH LETTUCE

Ingredients

2 x 14–16 oz pork loin fillets,
   trimmed of visible fat
2 scallions, cut into 2 inch batons
1 red bell pepper, cut into thin strips
1 butter or cos lettuce, leaves separated

Marinade

1 tablespoon brown sugar
2 teaspoons fresh ginger, grated
1 teaspoon five spice powder
1 tablespoon reduced-salt soy sauce
1 tablespoon rice wine or sherry
1 tablespoon oyster sauce
1 teaspoon sesame oil
1 cinnamon stick

Sesame and herb dressing

1 tablespoon fresh basil, shredded
1 tablespoon fresh cilantro, chopped
2 tablespoons rice or white wine vinegar
1 teaspoon reduced-salt soy sauce
½ teaspoon sesame oil

Method

1. To make marinade, place sugar, ginger, five spice powder, soy sauce, wine, oyster sauce and sesame oil in a bowl. Mix to combine. Add cinnamon stick.

2. Place pork in a shallow glass or ceramic dish. Pour marinade over. Turn pork to coat and cover. Marinate in the refrigerator, turning occasionally, for at least 2 hours or overnight. Preheat oven to 425°F.

3. Drain pork and reserve marinade. Place pork in a baking dish. Bake, uncovered, brushing occasionally with reserved marinade, for 25–30 minutes or until cooked to your liking. Cover loosely with aluminium foil. Rest for 10 minutes. Place scallions and red bell pepper in a separate baking dish. Bake for 5 minutes or until vegetables soften slightly.

4. For the dressing, place basil, cilantro, vinegar, soy sauce and oil in a screwtop jar. Shake well to combine.

5. To serve, line a serving platter with lettuce leaves. Cut pork into thick slices. Arrange green onions, red bell pepper and pork on top of lettuce. Drizzle with dressing. Accompany with steamed rice or udon noodles.

Serves 4

MONGOLIAN HOT POT

Ingredients

2 pounds lamb fillet, frozen

2 cakes tofu, thinly sliced

2 oz cellophane noodles

leaves of 1 large bok choy

1 pound spinach leaves

8 cups beef bouillon

6 large scallions

pinch of salt

3 teaspoons dry sherry

Accompaniments

Hoisin sauce

soy sauce

chili sauce

prepared mustard

2 tablespoons fresh ginger, crushed

2 scallions, finely chopped

6 eggs

Method

1. Select cooking equipment: a fondue pot, saucepan on a heating plate or a fire pot (see step 1 on page 129).

2. Defrost lamb, but while still mostly frozen, slice into paper-thin slices across the grain. Arrange on 6 plates to thaw, then drain off any liquid. Cube tofu. Soak noodles in hot water for 10 minutes then drain well.

3. Wash green vegetables, tear into large pieces and place next to lamb on plates. Thinly slice 6 scallions and place in individual bowls. Place small dishes of sauces within easy reach of diners. Mix ginger and the extra scallions, sliced, and place into small bowls. Place a bowl containing one whole egg, lightly beaten, in front of each diner.

4. Heat pot, add bouillon, salt and sherry, and bring to a boil, then reduce to a simmer. Using chopsticks, each diner dips meat and vegetables into their bouillon, then into their own egg and/or other dips. Meat should be rare and vegetables just cooked. After all meat has been eaten, add noodles, remaining vegetables and tofu to bouillon to simmer for about 5 minutes. It can then be eaten as soup. Add any unused egg to the bouillon, if desired, for a flower drop effect.

Note: This recipe works equally well with beef.

Serves 6

SIZZLING BEEF

Ingredients

1 pound rump steak, trimmed of any
   excess fat and cut into thin strips

2 tablespoons soy sauce

2 tablespoons rice wine or sherry

1 1/2 tablespoons cornstarch

1 teaspoon sugar

3 tablespoons peanut oil

5 oz broccoli, cut into bite-size pieces

1 large red bell pepper, seeded and cut
   into thin strips

2 cloves garlic, crushed

3 tablespoons oyster sauce

7 oz fresh bean sprouts

salt and black pepper

Method

1. Put steak, soy sauce, rice wine or sherry,
   cornstarch and sugar into a non-metallic bowl
   and mix thoroughly.

2. Heat 1 tablespoon of oil in a wok or large
   heavy-based skillet, add one third of the beef
   mixture and stir-fry over high heat for
   2–3 minutes until browned. Remove and cook
   remaining beef in 2 more batches, adding a
   little more oil if necessary.

3. Heat remaining oil in wok, then add broccoli and
   6 tablespoons of water. Stir-fry for 5 minutes,
   then add bell pepper and garlic and stir-fry for a
   further 2–3 minutes, until the broccoli is tender,
   but still firm to the bite.

4. Stir in oyster sauce, return the beef to the wok
   and add bean sprouts. Toss over high heat for
   2 minutes or until beef is piping hot and bean
   sprouts have softened slightly. Add salt and
   pepper to taste.

Serves 4

STIR-FRIED NOODLES WITH PORK AND GINGER

Ingredients

1 pound Chinese egg noodles

8 oz ground pork

1 tablespoon soy sauce

1 tablespoon dry sherry

1 teaspoon cornstarch

2 tablespoons vegetable oil

2 scallions, finely chopped
   plus extra to garnish

1 teaspoon fresh ginger root, finely grated

1 carrot, finely chopped

3 tablespoons black bean sauce

5 oz chicken bouillon

Method

1. Cook noodles according to package instructions, then drain well. In a bowl, mix together pork, soy sauce, sherry and cornstarch. Stir well to combine.

2. Heat oil in a wok or large heavy-based skillet, then add scallions and ginger and stir-fry for 30 seconds. Add pork mixture and carrot and stir-fry for 5–10 minutes, until pork has browned. Stir in black bean sauce.

3. Pour in bouillon and bring to a boil. Add noodles and cook, uncovered, for 3–5 minutes, until most of the liquid is absorbed and noodles are piping hot. Garnish with extra scallions.

Note: You can really smell the fresh ginger in this quick and easy Chinese dish. The sherry adds a little sweetness to the tangy sauce that coats the pork and noodles.

Serves 4

SWEET AND SOUR PORK

Ingredients

14 oz lean pork, cubed

pinch of salt

1/2 teaspoon ground black pepper

2 tablespoons dry sherry

1 egg, lightly beaten

4 tablespoons cornstarch

vegetable oil for frying

Sauce

1/2 carrot, cut in julienne strips

1 small green bell pepper

4 scallions, chopped

1 fresh red chili, seeded and finely chopped

2 cloves garlic, crushed

1 teaspoon fresh ginger, grated

3 tablespoons tomato sauce
   or 1 tablespoon tomato paste

1 tablespoon soy sauce

3 tablespoons honey

1 tablespoon cornstarch

1 small can pineapple pieces, drained
   and juice reserved

vegetable oil for frying

Method

1. Prepare vegetables for sauce. Core, seed and cut bell pepper into thin rings and cut each ring in half. Put pork cubes in a bowl, sprinkle with salt and pepper, add sherry, mix and marinate for 30 minutes.

2. Toss pork cubes in a bag containing cornstarch then dip pork in beaten egg and toss in cornstarch again. Heat some oil in a preheated wok or heavy-based pan and deep-fry pork until brown. Drain on paper towels and reserve.

3. Drain off all oil except for about 2 tablespoons, heat and add scallions, bell pepper, chili, garlic and ginger and stir-fry for 2 minutes. Mix tomato sauce or paste, soy sauce, honey, cornstarch and juice from pineapple. When smooth, add to wok and stir until thickened. Add water if too thick. Stir in pork and drained pineapple pieces, heat through and serve.

Note: Pork chops, pre-cooked meatballs of any sort, chicken, uncooked peeled shrimp, and pieces of white fish also team very well with this sauce.

Serves 6

BEEF POT WITH EGGS

Ingredients

2 pounds beef, cubed

6 level tablespoons cornstarch

1 egg, lightly beaten

oil for frying

2¹/₂ cups beef bouillon

2 tablespoons dry sherry

4 tablespoons soy sauce

6 eggs, hard-boiled

7 scallions

Method

1. Toss beef cubes in a bag containing cornstarch, dip beef in egg, re-toss in cornstarch and brown in a pan with a little oil. Add to a lidded saucepan or stove-top casserole dish with bouillon and sherry. Boil and reduce heat to simmer for 30 minutes. Add soy sauce and simmer for 30 minutes more.

2. Shell hard-boiled eggs. With a knife, make a small slit in the side of each egg. Cut scallions into 3 inch lengths. Add scallions and eggs to pot and gently simmer for 5 minutes before serving hot. Serve one egg with beef to each diner.

Serves 6

BEIJING PORK AND CRAB MEATBALL STEW

Ingredients

14 oz lean ground pork

4 oz can or cooked crab meat

1 scallion

1 tablespoon fresh ginger juice

pinch of salt

1 tablespoon cornstarch

oil for deep-frying

4 bok choy leaves, cut in half, lengthwise

1 tablespoon dry sherry

3 cups chicken bouillon

2 teaspoons sugar

2 tablespoons soy sauce

Method

1. Place the following ingredients in a bowl pork, drained crab meat and scallion that has been cut into quarters lengthwise then chopped. Add ginger juice (gained by crushing peeled ginger in a garlic crusher) plus salt and cornstarch. Mix well by hand. Divide mixture into 4 and make 4 large balls. Deep-fry balls very carefully in oil over medium heat until golden brown.

2. Quickly sauté bok choy in 3 tablespoons of oil. Remove and place in a lightly greased pottery casserole or a deep, heavy lidded saucepan. Place meatballs on top of bok choy, sprinkle sherry over and add bouillon mixed with sugar and soy sauce. Cover and cook on stove top on high for 15 minutes then reduce heat and simmer on low for about 45 minutes. Alternatively, place pottery casserole in a hot oven and reduce it to low for the same period.

Serves 4

seafood

Net great RESULTS

The Chinese have farmed fish for 2,000 years after inland inhabitants found it easier to harvest fish rather than cast random lines or nets. Now ponds are filled with clean fresh water, so fish, mainly carp, mullet, catfish, bream and eels don't taste muddy. Fish is most popular in the South and has replaced chicken on many family menus. The tradition of salting fish came about because of the lack of refrigeration.

Fresh shrimp are loved by eastern Chinese and most provinces have fine freshwater fish. However, in Szechuan, Hunan, Jiangxi, Hubei, Anhui and several other landlocked provinces, seafood is transported frozen from coastal regions. Southerners are also into shrimp. Lobsters, abalone and oysters, which are sundried without salt in the South, are used along with clams (which can be substituted with mussels). The northern region is blessed with coastal and Yellow River seafood and freshwater fish.

Shark fin soup is expensive, and conservation groups deplore its consumption. A recipe is therefore not included here. Chinese cultivate carp in several varieties, black carp being most popular. If you can tolerate the bones, you will find that carp is an oily, but very tasty fish. Other fish eaten in China include bass, trout, mullet, pomfret, perch, white-bait, yellowfish and many types of shellfish.

As seafood is so popular in Chinese cooking, why not start your Chinese taste adventure with this chapter? Try the method introduced by the Mongols, of fire pot cooking, which can also be used to prepare Mongolian hot pot (see page 113).

FRIED RICE WITH SHRIMP

Ingredients
5 oz long-grain rice

salt

3 oz frozen or fresh shelled peas

2 tablespoons vegetable oil

3 cloves garlic, peeled and chopped roughly

2 scallions, thinly sliced

1 egg, beaten

4 oz peeled and cooked shrimp, defrosted if frozen

Method
1. Rinse rice in a sieve. Bring a large saucepan of water to a boil, then add rice and $\frac{1}{2}$ teaspoon of salt. Simmer for 10 minutes or until rice is tender, then drain thoroughly. Meanwhile, bring a small pan of water to a boil, add peas and cook for 3–4 minutes until softened.

2. Heat a wok or a large heavy-based skillet over medium heat. Add oil and rotate wok or pan for 1 minute to coat the base and lower sides. Add garlic and scallions and fry, stirring constantly with a wooden spoon, for 30 seconds. Add beaten egg and stir briskly for 30 seconds or until it scrambles.

3. Add cooked rice, peas and shrimp and stir over heat for 3 minutes or until everything is heated through or cooked and mixed in with egg and scallions. Season with a pinch of salt.

Serves 4

CHINESE-STYLE STEAMED GREY MULLET

Ingredients

1 grey mullet, about 1 $\frac{1}{2}$ pounds, scaled, gutted and cleaned

$\frac{1}{2}$ teaspoon salt

1 tablespoon vegetable oil

1 tablespoon light soy sauce

1 large carrot, cut into fine strips

4 scallions, cut into fine strips

1 tablespoon fresh ginger root, grated

1 tablespoon sesame oil (optional)

To garnish

cilantro

Method

1. Make 4 deep slashes along each side of the fish, then rub the fish inside and out with salt, vegetable oil and soy sauce. Cover and place in the refrigerator for 30 minutes.

2. Spread half the carrot, scallions and ginger on a large piece of foil. Place fish on top, then sprinkle with remaining vegetables and ginger and any remaining marinade. Loosely fold over foil to seal. Transfer fish to a steamer. Alternatively, transfer to a plate, then place on a rack in oven at 400°F set over a roasting tin half filled with water. Cover tightly with a lid or with foil.

3. Cook for 20 minutes or until the fish is firm and cooked through. Put sesame oil, if using, into a small saucepan and heat. Drizzle over fish and garnish with cilantro.

Serves 2

BAKED COD WITH GINGER AND SCALLIONS (opposite)

Ingredients

oil for greasing

1 pound piece cod fillet

1 tablespoon light soy sauce

1 tablespoon rice wine or medium-dry sherry

1 teaspoon sesame oil

salt

1 inch fresh ginger root, finely chopped

3 scallions, shredded and cut into 1 inch pieces, white and green parts separated

Method

1. Preheat the oven to 375°F. Line a shallow baking dish with a piece of lightly greased foil.

2. Place cod in dish, skin-side down. Pour over soy sauce, rice wine or sherry, oil and salt to taste, then sprinkle over ginger and white parts of scallion.

3. Loosely wrap foil over fish, folding the edges together to seal. Bake for 20–25 minutes, until cooked through and tender. Unwrap parcel, transfer fish to a serving plate and sprinkle over the green parts of the scallions to garnish.

Serves 4

WALNUT FISH ROLLS

Ingredients

2 scallions, finely chopped

½ teaspoon salt

1 teaspoon sugar

½ teaspoon cornstarch

1 teaspoon soy sauce

1 teaspoon dry sherry

1 egg, lightly beaten

8 fish fillets, spine removed

½ cup walnuts, crushed

2 x 1 oz slices ham, cooked

peanut oil for frying

cilantro sprigs to garnish

Method

1. Combine scallions with salt, sugar, cornstarch, soy sauce, sherry and egg.

2. Dunk fish fillets into scallion mixture and then into bowl of walnuts. Cut each ham slice into 4 and place a piece on each fillet before rolling each fillet up and securing with toothpicks.

3. Deep-fry fish in peanut oil until golden. Drain on paper towels and serve hot, garnished with cilantro sprigs.

Serves 4

FUKIEN FRIED FISH

Ingredients

4 dried Chinese mushrooms

4 whole white sea fish, such as whiting

4 oz shrimp, peeled

1 teaspoon ginger, crushed

2 scallions

1 egg

1 teaspoon water

2 tablespoons cornstarch

oil for frying

Sauce

1 tablespoon dry sherry

1 tablespoon sugar

2 tablespoons canned black beans

1 tablespoon cornstarch

1 cup fish or chicken bouillon

salt

1 tablespoon soy sauce

Method

1. Soak mushrooms for 25 minutes in hot water, then remove and discard stalks, squeeze dry and chop. Leaving heads and tails on, clean fish, wash and wipe dry inside and out. Chop shrimp. Combine with mushrooms, ginger and scallions.

2. Separate egg. Reserve yolk and lightly beat white. Add to shrimp mixture and stuff fish with it. Carefully sew up fish with string, then make 2 slashes per fish, on either side, to enable steam to escape.

3. Beat egg yolk with teaspoon of water and brush over each fish. Let dry and rub cornstarch onto fish, using extra if necessary to completely coat the fish. In a pan, heat 2 inches of oil and fry fish, turning only once. Drain on paper towels and cover with foil to keep warm.

4. In a small pot, place sauce ingredients, bring to a boil then simmer, stirring, for about 3 minutes until sauce is smooth and thickened. Serve fish whole on a large plate.

Serves 4 or 8

SZECHUAN-STYLE SCALLOPS

Ingredients

1 1/2 tablespoons peanut oil

1 tablespoon ginger root, finely chopped

1 tablespoon garlic, finely chopped

2 tablespoons scallions, finely chopped

1 pound scallops, including corals

Sauce

1 tablespoon rice wine or dry sherry

2 teaspoons light soy sauce

2 teaspoons dark soy sauce

2 tablespoons chili bean sauce

2 teaspoons tomato paste

1 teaspoon sugar

1/2 teaspoon salt

1/2 teaspoon sugar

2 teaspoons sesame oil

Method

1. Heat wok until very hot. Add oil and when it is very hot, add ginger, garlic and scallions. Stir-fry for 10 seconds. Add scallops and stir-fry for 1 minute.

2. Add all sauce ingredients except sesame oil. Stir-fry for 4 minutes until scallops are firm and thoroughly coated with sauce.

3. Add sesame oil and stir-fry for another minute. Serve immediately with plain boiled or steamed rice.

Serves 4

CANTONESE SPICY SQUID

Ingredients

1 pound squid
1 teaspoon ginger juice
1 tablespoon dry sherry
3 cups water
a pinch of five spice powder
½ teaspoon salt
2 teaspoons ground white pepper
vegetable oil
½ small green bell pepper, seeded
   and sliced into rings

Method

1. Remove and discard squid heads, backbones and ink sacs. Wash and dry on paper towels. Slit open squid tubes, flatten and score inside meat in a criss-cross pattern with a sharp-pointed knife.

2. Squeeze ginger juice from whole pieces of peeled ginger root using a garlic press. Cut squid into 1 inch squares. In a bowl, combine ginger juice and sherry and marinate squid squares for 45 minutes.

3. Boil water, place in a bowl and immerse squid for several seconds until criss-cross patterns turn into bumps. Drain off water and dry squid thoroughly on paper towels.

4. Deep-fry squid in vegetable oil on medium heat for no more than 20 seconds. Drain on paper towels and sprinkle with combined salt, pepper and five spice powder, turning to cover each piece. Spoon onto serving plate. Garnish with rings of bell pepper.

Serves 4

SEAFOOD NOODLES (opposite)

Ingredients

8 oz thin egg noodles

½ red bell pepper, seeded

½ green bell pepper, seeded

1 large squid tube, cleaned

2 teaspoons cornstarch

2 tablespoons vegetable oil

salt

black pepper

1 teaspoon garlic, crushed

1 teaspoon ginger, crushed

1 scallion, chopped

4 oz fresh mussels, cooked

8 oysters

1½ tablespoons soy sauce

1½ tablespoons dry sherry

Method

1. In boiling salted water, cook noodles according to package directions until al dente. Rinse in cold water and drain. Cut bell peppers into matchstick-thin lengths. Cut squid into thin rings. Halve rings and toss in cornstarch.

2. Heat oil in wok or skillet, add squid for 1 minute, stir-frying. Remove, drain on paper towel, lightly salt and liberally pepper. Add garlic, ginger, bell peppers and scallion to wok and stir-fry for 1 minute.

3. Add mussels, oysters, squid, soy sauce, dry sherry and noodles to stir-fry until heated through. Pile onto warmed serving dish.

Serves 4

SHELLFISH CUSTARD

Ingredients

1 pound clams or mussels in shells

3 scallions, sliced

2 teaspoons fresh ginger, crushed

oil for frying

6 egg whites, beaten well

3 eggs

1¾ cups seafood bouillon

2 tablespoons cornstarch

½ teaspoon salt

½ teaspoon ground black pepper

1 tablespoon dry sherry

lemon wedges and parsley to garnish

Method

1. Remove beards from the clams or mussels and gently scrub shells before thoroughly rinsing in water. Dry scallions and ginger and cook with oil in a covered wok or pan on medium heat. Remove shells when most have opened, having shaken the pan occasionally to aid this. Discard any shells that have not opened.

2. Remove shellfish meat and place in a serving dish that fits on top of a saucepan for steaming. To make custard, gently mix egg whites with whole eggs and chicken bouillon smoothly blended with cornstarch. Add salt, black pepper and sherry. Add mixture to shellfish in dish.

3. Place dish on top of saucepan and steam over quickly boiling water until custard is set. Serve with lemon wedges and garnish with parsley. Serve in dish or, alternatively, steam and serve in individual mini heatproof soufflé dishes.

Serves 4

SHANGHAI SCALLOPS

Ingredients

1 green bell pepper, seeded

1 pound scallops

2 tablespoons peanut oil

2 teaspoons garlic, crushed

3 scallions, finely chopped

½ teaspoon fresh ginger, crushed

3 tablespoons dry sherry

3 tablespoons soy sauce

4 tablespoons sweet chili sauce

1 tablespoon cornstarch

⅓ cup fish or chicken bouillon

Method

1. Cut bell pepper into matchstick strips. Wash and dry scallops well. Heat oil in wok or pan over medium heat, add garlic, stir to separate and add scallops. Turn heat to high and fry scallops for 1 minute, turning carefully. (Scallops are tough if overcooked.) Remove scallops.

2. Add bell pepper, scallions and ginger to pan and stir-fry for 1 minute. Add sherry, soy sauce, chili sauce and cornstarch mixed smoothly with bouillon. When sauce is smooth and thick, return scallops to heat through and become coated with sauce.

Serves 4

BOK CHOY, FISH AND CRAB ROLLS

Ingredients

8 large bok choy leaves

8 oz white fish fillets

8 oz crab meat, fresh or canned

3 slices fresh ginger, chopped

1 teaspoon salt

1 egg white, lightly beaten

1 teaspoon vegetable oil

Dipping sauce

soy sauce

1/2 red chili, seeded and cut into rings

Method

1. Dunk bok choy leaves individually in boiling water quickly to soften. Drain and pat dry. Chop fish and fresh crab meat or drain liquid from canned crab meat. In a bowl, combine fish, ginger, salt, egg white, oil and crab meat.

2. Lay out bok choy leaves on a flat board and divide mixture amongst them. Fold and roll leaves around to form neat parcels. Place rolls in greased metal or bamboo steamer, 4–8 at a time, and steam quickly for 10 minutes, keeping batches warm.

3. Serve with small bowls of soy sauce mixed with chili rings.

Serves 4

SHANDONG SHRIMP, FISH, CHICKEN AND PORK HOT POT

Ingredients

6 dried black mushrooms

4 oz shrimp, peeled

7 oz white fish fillets

4 oz chicken fillet

4 oz pork tenderloin

6 oz bok choy and spinach leaves, mixed

2 oz cellophane noodles

6–7 cups chicken bouillon

1 extra teaspoon salt

2 oz bean sprouts

Dipping sauce

soy sauce

½ red bell pepper, seeded and cut into slices

Method

1. Select equipment for preparing this table top meal. A large fondue pot or saucepan on top of an electric or gas ring will do or a fairly deep electric frypan. But, if you intend to make frequent healthy hot pot preparations, fun for entertaining and also family meals, invest in a fire pot. A fire pot is otherwise known as a steamboat that is charcoal fueled with a chimney surrounded by a moat, like a ring tin, in which to cook. They are available at Asian stores.

2. Put dried mushroom to soak for 30 minutes. Then devein shrimp. Cut the shrimp into 3–4 pieces, depending on size, and remove heads. Wash and dry and place in a bowl. Thinly slice fish, chicken and pork and put in separate bowls.

3. Tear leaves of washed bok choy and spinach (or use just one if desired) and place in a bowl. In warm water, soak cellophane noodles until soft, then drain, cut into 4 inch lengths and put into a bowl. Then take soaked mushrooms, discard the stems, divide into 4 pieces, then place in a separate bowl.

4. Boil bouillon in fire pot or other pot and add salt, mushrooms and bean sprouts. You can either add the meat and vegetables or leave guests to make their own selection from bowls and dip morsels into the simmering bouillon for a few seconds to eat at their leisure. Vegetables should be cooked al dente and meats and fish until done to taste. Diners take noodles from the soup into their individual bowls and top with their choice of meat and vegetables. Add extra bouillon only if the mixture becomes too thick.

5. Serve with small bowls of soy sauce and/or soy sauce mixed with bell pepper for dipping. Reserve some greens and noodles to eat with the bouillon as soup at the end of the meal.

Serves 4–6

CHINESE LOBSTER STIR-FRY

Ingredients

1 pound lobster meat, fresh or frozen

1 small clove garlic, minced

2 tablespoons oil

$\frac{1}{2}$ cup chicken broth

1 small red bell pepper

8 oz bean sprouts

8 oz water chestnuts

8 oz broccoli

13 oz Chinese cabbage, chopped

$\frac{1}{2}$ teaspoon salt

$\frac{1}{4}$ teaspoon pepper

1 egg, beaten

rice to serve

Method

1. If frozen, thaw and chop lobster meat into bite-size pieces. In a skillet, sauté lobster and garlic in oil for 1 minute. Add broth and vegetables and simmer, uncovered, for 5 minutes. Season with salt and pepper.

2. Add a little of the hot broth to lightly beaten egg. Stir the egg mixture into the rest of the broth. Heat gently, but do not boil. Serve with rice.

Serves 4

chicken
& poultry

Shoot for
CLAY

One reason why chicken and duck dishes are many and varied on Chinese menus is that poultry is prolific in China. It can be raised free-range on little land for subsistence, with the farmer taking any surplus to the markets. Every part of poultry is utilized, from gizzards to duck tongues to rooster feet and, more familiarly, chicken livers.

A second reason for the popularity of poultry is that it is essentially quickly cooked, saving on fuel. This is unless you're slow cooking a tough bird or preparing the famed Peking duck authentically (see page 134). Our recipe is simplified, yet original, but you shouldn't serve it with plum sauce as some restaurants do. Hoisin sauce is the appropriate accompaniment.

Poultry is also preferred by the Chinese because almost anything can be done with it. Shredded, sectioned, ground or whole, it boils, broils, roasts, sautées, steams, simmers and stir-fries with equal facility and its meat, without skin, is suitable for dieters, being low in fat and cholesterol. Chicken is also among the world's most economical meats.

In this section is a special dish, beggar's chicken (see page 136). Dining at the Shang Palace in beautiful Hangzhou's Shangri-La Hotel looking over the ethereal West Lake, I asked for the recipe. This posed a problem because this traditional Hangzhou dish is always enclosed in West Lake clay. Legend has it that an emperor happened upon a poor man who had dug a hole and cooked his buried chicken in charcoal and wood cinders covered with lake clay. He shared his meal with the emperor, who then elevated it to imperial status. And so the Shangri-La chefs had to think up a substitute for lake clay for someone to prepare the recipe at home. This recipe is a guaranteed conversation piece, as it is tasty and surprisingly easy to prepare.

CHICKEN LIVERS WITH SHRIMP AND BROCCOLI

Ingredients
8 oz chicken livers
2¼ tablespoons cornstarch
1½ cups fresh mushrooms
13 oz broccoli
2 tablespoons vegetable oil
2 scallions, chopped finely
4 oz shrimp, peeled
salt
black pepper
1 tablespoon soy sauce
5 tablespoons water

Method
1. Trim chicken livers of membranes. Wash and dry, slice thinly and lightly toss in 2 tablespoons of cornstarch. Wash and dry mushrooms. Meanwhile, boil broccoli, fresh or frozen, in a pot of salted water for 5 minutes or until al dente.

2. In a wok or skillet, heat oil and fry chicken livers for 90 seconds. Add mushrooms to cook for the same time then add scallions, drained broccoli and shrimp with salt and pepper to taste. Combine well.

3. Mix remaining cornstarch with soy sauce and water until smooth. Add to skillet and bring to a boil, stirring until thickened slightly. Cook for a further 2 minutes and serve.

Serves 4

FRAGRANT DUCK WITH PINEAPPLE

Ingredients

2 boneless Barbary duck breasts, about 6 oz
each, skinned and cut into strips

1 teaspoon five spice powder

2 tablespoons soy sauce

2 tablespoons rice wine or dry sherry

1 teaspoon sugar

1 tablespoon peanut oil

1 orange or red bell pepper, seeded and cut
into thin strips

2 inch piece fresh ginger root, cut into
julienne strips

2 scallions, white and green parts separated
and thinly shredded

6 oz fresh pineapple, cut into bite-sized pieces,
plus juice

salt

Method

1. Place duck, five spice powder, soy sauce,
rice wine or sherry and sugar in a shallow
non-metallic bowl. Cover and marinate for
20 minutes.

2. Heat oil in a wok. Remove duck from
marinade and reserve. Stir-fry duck over high
heat for 2 minutes. Add bell pepper, ginger and
white scallions and stir-fry for a further 3–4
minutes, until bell pepper starts to soften.

3. Add pineapple and juice and the marinade.
Stir-fry for 1–2 minutes. Season with salt if
necessary. Serve right away, sprinkled with
green scallions.

Note: Fresh pineapple cuts through the richness
of the tender duck breasts marinated in Chinese
spices. Serve this dish with plain boiled noodles
or some fragrant Thai rice.

Serves 4

PEKING DUCK (opposite)

Ingredients

2 pound duck

2 tablespoons soy sauce

$2\frac{1}{2}$ tablespoons brown sugar

1 teaspoon red vinegar

To serve

Hoisin sauce

1 small cucumber, cut into julienne strips

6 scallions

Mandarin pancakes

4 cups all-purpose flour

pinch of salt

$1\frac{1}{4}$ cups boiling water

peanut or sesame oil

Method

1. Plunge duck into a large pot of boiling water for 3 minutes. Drain it, dry it, truss it and hang it up in an airy room to dry completely overnight. Combine soy sauce, brown sugar and vinegar, rub into duck and re-hang for 4 hours. If you can't hang the duck, place on a rack where ventilation is good. Place drip pan beneath.

2. Place duck on a rack well above a roasting pan half filled with hot water and cook in preheated oven at 375°F for 30 minutes. Lower heat to 300°F for 1 hour, then adjust to original temperature until skin is crisp and brown all over and the duck is tender.

3. Cut scallions to the size of the cucumber strips, about 2 inches, or for authentic flair, make brushes of the scallions by cutting them into 3 inch lengths. With a sharp knife, make 2 parallel cuts at each end, about 1 inch deep. Repeat, intersecting these cuts as if drawing a tick tact toe puzzle. Chill green side down, in iced water until the ends curl.

4. To make pancakes, sift flour and salt into a bowl. Make a well in the center, add boiling water and mix to a stiff dough, kneading until smooth. Cover with a damp cloth and leave to rest 15 minutes. On a floured board, shape dough into a roll about 2 inches in diameter. Cut the roll into $\frac{1}{2}$ inch wide slices to roll into pancakes about $3\frac{1}{2}$ inch in diameter. Sandwich 2 pancakes together with peanut or sesame oil and roll out pancake pairs to 6 inches. Repeat with remaining dough. Makes 8 pancakes.

5. Heat a heavy-based pan on high, but don't let it smoke, before turning it down to a gentle temperature and dry-frying each double pancake for about 1 minute. Pancake should inflate a little and just be slightly marked with brown. When cool enough to touch, separate each pancake and fold in half. To keep pancakes hot while carving duck, cover with foil on a warmed dish.

6. Carve skin then meat, keeping separate. Arrange on a plate with cucumber. Serve pancakes and scallion strips or brushes on individual small plates for each diner. Each diner then spreads a little Hoisin sauce on the pancakes, tops with some meat then skin, a cucumber matchstick and scallion to roll up and enjoy.

Serves 6

CANTONESE CHICKEN WITH CASHEWS

Ingredients

14 oz chicken breast, sliced

1 tablespoon cornstarch

1 teaspoon salt

1 teaspoon peanut oil

1 tablespoon soy sauce

1 teaspoon sugar

peanut oil for frying

1 cup cashew nuts

3 scallions, chopped

1 small onion, chopped

1 inch fresh ginger, sliced finely

2 cloves garlic, sliced finely

3 oz snow peas

2 oz bean sprouts

canned or fresh pineapple pieces (optional)

Method

1. Toss chicken pieces in cornstarch. Combine salt, peanut oil, soy sauce and sugar and coat chicken with it. Let stand 10 minutes. Drain chicken and reserve marinade. Heat some oil in wok or skillet, fry chicken for 4 minutes and remove.

2. Fry cashews until golden. Remove and drain on paper towels. If necessary, add more oil then stir-fry onions, ginger and garlic for 2 minutes, add snow peas and bean sprouts, stir-frying for 3 minutes. Drain off excess oil.

3. Return chicken and other ingredients to pan. Mix retained marinade until smooth and add to pan. Add optional pineapple pieces (syrup drained off if canned). Mix well and serve when sauce is thick and transparent.

Serves 4

SHANGRI-LA BEGGAR'S CHICKEN

Ingredients

4 oz pork fat

4 oz pork leg meat

$\frac{1}{2}$ oz onions, finely chopped

$\frac{1}{2}$ oz fresh ginger, thinly sliced

2 tablespoons soy sauce

$2\frac{1}{2}$ tablespoons dry sherry

2 teaspoons chicken bouillon powder

salt and pepper to taste

1 teaspoon five spice powder

3 pounds young chicken

2 lotus leaves

Clay dough

2 pounds cooking salt

4 cups all-purpose flour

$1\frac{1}{2}$ cups water (approximately)

Method

1. Slice pork fat and leg meat thinly and reserve. Finely chop onions and thinly slice ginger.

2. Mix remaining ingredients together with the exception of the lotus leaves, rub over chicken and marinate for at least 2 hours or overnight.

3. Make clay dough by combining unsifted flour and salt in a bowl. Gradually stir in water and mix to a firm dough with your hands. A little more water may be needed. However if the dough is too soft it will be difficult to handle.

4. On a table, place 2 very large lotus leaves (If unavailable, substitute 2 big sheets of foil). Brush top leaf (or top foil sheet) with some oil and place chicken in the middle. Pull skin at neck end down under chicken and tuck wing tips beneath it.

5. Carefully pour remaining marinade into chicken cavity plus pork fat and onions, holding chicken up slightly so marinade won't run out. Seal end of chicken with a skewer. Wrap other lotus leaf or foil piece around chicken and secure like a parcel.

6. Preheat oven to 425°F. Roll dough out to about $\frac{1}{2}$ inch thick so it will completely encase the chicken. Fold dough over chicken. Press edges and ends together, ensuring there are no holes from which steam could escape.

7. Place chicken in a lightly oiled baking dish to bake in oven for 1 hour. Reduce heat to low and bake for a further 3 hours. Remove chicken from oven and break the clay covering with a mallet or hammer.

8. Lift chicken onto a warmed serving dish. Open up lotus leaves and garnish with cilantro leaves.

Note: Cooking salt in the dough does not affect the taste of the chicken. It just ensures the dough bakes rock hard to protect the chicken during the lengthy cooking.

Serves 6–8

DUCK SALAD

Ingredients

2 tablespoons vinegar

2¹/₂ tablespoons sugar

2 tablespoons peanut oil

2 tablespoons soy sauce

1 teaspoon mustard, home-mixed or prepared

pinch of salt

4 oz carrot

4 oz cucumber

4 oz bok choy or cabbage

1 cooked duck

Method

1. Mix dressing of vinegar, sugar, peanut oil, soy sauce, mustard and salt thoroughly. Shred carrot and cucumber into paper thin strips with a potato peeler. Cut end off bok choy, wash leaves very carefully and shred as thinly as possible.

2. Arrange vegetables on a serving plate and top with shredded duck. Add dressing just before serving.

Note: Salads are rarely prepared in China, except at luxury hotels. However, this recipe will use up leftover whole duck from other dishes. Substitute chicken if desired.

Serves 4

CHILI CHICKEN (opposite)

Ingredients

1 egg white

salt

6 tablespoons oil

1½ tablespoons cornstarch

1 pound chicken meat, cut into bite-sized pieces

2 green or red bell peppers

2 fresh small chilies, seeded and chopped

2 small dried chilies, chopped

1 teaspoons fresh ginger, crushed

2 tablespoons soy sauce

2 tablespoons dry sherry

Method

1. Lightly beat egg white. Mix smoothly with salt, 1 tablespoon of oil and cornstarch. Rub mixture to thinly coat chicken.

2. Cut bell peppers into 2 inch squares. Heat rest of oil in a wok or pan and quickly stir-fry chicken. Remove. To the wok add fresh and dried chilies, bell peppers and ginger, and stir-fry for 2 minutes.

3. Return chicken to wok with vegetable mixture and stir-fry until bell peppers are al dente. Add soy sauce and sherry and stir-fry for a further 2 minutes.

Note: This dish is quite fiery, so vary amounts of chili according to taste.

Serve 4

CRISPY DUCK IN LEMON SAUCE

Ingredients

3 pound duck

2 tablespoons soy sauce

1 tablespoon peanut oil

4 scallions, chopped

2 inch fresh ginger, peeled

peanut oil for frying

To garnish

lemon slices, chopped scallion and cilantro sprigs

Lemon sauce

¼ cup lemon juice

¼ cup water

1 teaspoon cornstarch

2 teaspoons sugar

1 teaspoon dry sherry

pinch of salt

Batter

1 egg

1½ tablespoons cornstarch

1 tablespoon water

1 tablespoon soy sauce

½ teaspoon baking soda

pinch of salt

½ teaspoon pepper

Method

1. Trim neck skin and leg fat from duck and divide into 4. Remove wings and reserve if you prefer not to eat them. Mix soy sauce with oil and brush it over duck, then place it in a metal steamer over a saucepan or in a bamboo steamer. When water boils add scallions, ginger and, if desired, wings to make an aromatic bouillon. Reduce heat to simmer, place duck in steamer, cover and cook until duck is almost tender.

2. To make the sauce, mix the lemon juice with water, cornstarch, sugar, sherry and salt until smooth. Boil in a pot until sugar has dissolved and sauce has thickened. Reserve.

3. If still intact, remove wings and also drumsticks from duck. Chop wings into 2 and drumstick meat into chunks and chop remainder of duck into 3 inch segments. To make batter, lightly beat egg and mix with cornstarch, water, soy sauce, baking soda, salt and pepper in a shallow dish until smooth. Dunk duck pieces in batter.

4. In enough oil to cover duck, fry it in small lots until crispy and golden. Drain on paper towels. Keep batches warm by covering serving dish with foil and placing in low oven. Quickly reheat lemon sauce and pour over. Garnish with lemon slices, chopped scallion and cilantro sprigs. Remove wings from steaming bouillon and reserve bouillon for another use.

Serves 8

DRUNKEN CHICKEN

Ingredients

3 pound chicken

2 medium onions

2 teaspoons salt

3 x 1 inch pieces fresh ginger, peeled
   and sliced

water

1¼ cups dry sherry

2 teaspoons sugar

cilantro sprigs for garnish

Method

1. Wash chicken. Quarter onions and place
   in a pot with salt and ginger. Add
   chicken with enough hot water to cover
   and bring to a boil for 5 minutes. Cover and
   simmer for 15 minutes.

2. Transfer chicken to a large non-metallic bowl.
   Add sherry and sugar to cooking liquid, pour
   over chicken, rotate several times to ensure
   chicken is completely immersed and cover
   tightly with plastic wrap. Refrigerate for
   48 hours, stirring and basting with marinade
   occasionally.

3. Drain chicken, discarding onions and chop
   through bone into serving-sized pieces. Serve
   cold, garnished with cilantro.

Note: In China, this dish is popular as an appetizer
which can also be served with cocktails.

Serves 6

TANGERINE DUCK

Ingredients

1 pound duck breast

pinch salt

2 teaspoons sugar

3 teaspoons soy sauce

1 teaspoon dry sherry

2 teaspoons vinegar

1 teaspoon sesame oil

2 teaspoons cornstarch

oil for deep-frying

1 green chili, seeded and chopped

½ inch fresh ginger, finely chopped

1 tablespoon dried tangerine peel, grated

2 scallions, finely chopped

½ teaspoon cornstarch

1 tablespoon water

Method

1. Remove skin and fat from duck and cut into 1 inch pieces. Mix with salt, sugar, soy sauce, sherry, vinegar, sesame oil and cornstarch. Marinate for 30 minutes. Reserve marinade.

2. Heat wok or pan, add enough oil to deep-fry and when oil starts to smoke, add duck to cook until golden. Drain pieces on kitchen paper and drain off all but 1 tablespoon of oil.

3. In remaining oil, stir-fry chili, ginger, tangerine peel (use orange if this is unavailable) and scallions for 3 minutes.

4. Return duck to pan and stir-fry for 1 minute. Mix reserved marinade with ½ teaspoon of cornstarch and water and add to duck, stirring for 3 minutes. Serve with steamed rice.

Serves 6

GARLIC CHICKEN WITH VEGETABLES

Ingredients

3 plump, boneless chicken fillets

1 teaspoon cornstarch

2 tablespoons water

¼ cup red bell pepper, slivered

¼ cup green bell pepper, slivered

⅓ cup fresh mushrooms, sliced

⅓ cup bamboo shoots, sliced

1 celery stalk, thinly sliced

½ cup snow peas

⅓ cup carrot, sliced

2 scallions, sliced thinly

6 cloves garlic, minced

sesame oil

1 teaspoon fresh ginger, grated

2 tablespoons soy sauce

⅓ cup chicken bouillon

2 tablespoons oyster sauce

1 tablespoon black bean sauce

chili powder to taste

To garnish

black sesame seeds

Method

1. Dice chicken. Mix cornstarch with water until smooth and combine with chicken. Let stand while preparing vegetables.

2. Sauté chicken and garlic in a little oil for about 3 minutes until chicken is cooked. Remove. To the same wok or pan add bell peppers, mushrooms, bamboo shoots, celery, snow peas and carrot. Stir together and add an extra 2 tablespoons of water. Cover and cook for about 3 minutes.

3. Add remaining ingredients, except sesame seeds. Return chicken to wok or pan. Cook for 3–5 minutes to combine flavors and until the required tenderness of vegetables is reached. Serve sprinkled with black sesame seeds.

Note: This is an ideal, healthy, economical family meal, served with rice. It can encourage children to enjoy vegetables. Cut back on garlic and chili powder only if really necessary.

Serves 6

vegetables

Very VEGETABLES

No vegetarian will go hungry in China. Every multi-course table offers several vegetable dishes, which many Chinese prefer to meat dishes. They gain their necessary carbohydrates through the accompanying rice or noodles.

Taoists and Buddhists introduced vegetarianism to China hundreds of years ago. Eggplant has been cultivated since 600 BC and is believed to have been introduced by Malay traders, as it was originally known as Malay purple melon. Garlic is a very old vegetable, cultivated since 3,000 BC, while ginger is a relative newcomer (since 600 BC). Crisp, crunchy, lightly cooked vegetables, which characterise Chinese food, replace salads as water was, and still is, generally not clean in China. For centuries, vegetables were never eaten raw because, even after washing them in cool boiled water, cooks could not be sure that impurities from the soil were eliminated. Hence, raw salads are rarely on a restaurant or home menu. The nearest dish to salad is a quickly cooked vegetable served cold.

Some vegetable dishes include seafood flavors and versatile, protein-rich tofu, which was discovered in the Han Dynasty between 206 BC to 220 AD. It is made from puréed soy beans and is available in cakes to be sliced or cubed. Hoisin sauce is derived from tofu with garlic, sugar, vinegar and spices added. Eggs are frequently combined with vegetables, as eggs are so abundant in China.

Often, simple vegetable cooking is finished with bouillon to add extra flavor, and a little oil to add a high gloss to vegetable colors. Attractive presentation is very important. Strict vegetarians should be aware that some vegetable dishes contain meat or fish-based bouillon and sometimes, pieces of meat or fish. Adjust accordingly.

STIR-FRIED VEGETABLES

Ingredients

2 tablespoons vegetable or peanut oil

2 inch piece fresh ginger root, peeled and finely chopped

3 cloves garlic, peeled and finely chopped

2 tablespoons dry sherry

1 yellow bell pepper, seeded and chopped into 1 inch pieces

1 red bell pepper, seeded and chopped into 1 inch pieces

2 medium carrots, peeled and thinly sliced on the diagonal

12 oz broccoli, cut into 1 inch florets and thinly sliced stalks

12 oz crimini mushrooms, wiped and thickly sliced

2 tablespoons soy sauce

8 scallions, cut into $1/2$ inch diagonal slices

Method

1. Heat a large wok or heavy-based skillet over high heat for 1 minute. Add oil and rotate wok or skillet to coat the base and lower sides.

2. Add ginger and garlic and stir-fry for 30 seconds. Add sherry and cook for a further 15 seconds. Add bell peppers and carrots and continue to stir-fry for 5 minutes or until vegetables start to soften.

3. Add broccoli, mushrooms and soy sauce, and stir-fry for 3 minutes or until all vegetables are just tender. Add scallions and stir-fry for 1 minute. Serve immediately.

Serves 4

CHILLED CELERY (below)

Ingredients

1 bunch celery

pinch of salt

1 tablespoon soy sauce

1 teaspoon brown sugar

1 teaspoon sesame oil

$\frac{1}{2}$ teaspoon ginger, crushed

Method

1. Scrub celery. Cut sticks into 1 inch lengths, place in a pot, cover with cold water and bring to a boil. Drain at once then cool completely under cold running water.

2. Drain celery completely. Add salt, soy sauce, sugar, sesame oil and ginger. Stir well, refrigerate and serve cold.

Serves 6

TOMATO SCRAMBLE

Ingredients

6 eggs

salt and pepper to taste

6 medium-sized tomatoes

6 tablespoons vegetable oil

2 tablespoons soy sauce

3 scallions, cut into quarters

Method

1. Beat eggs with salt and pepper to taste. Pour boiling water over tomatoes and remove skins.

2. Add oil to wok or pan and tilt to cover surface. Add eggs. When almost set, move to side of wok and add drained tomatoes to cook until hot then scramble them gently with set egg. Add scallion lengths and soy sauce in drops. Stir through once then serve.

Note: This easy dish often forms part of a main meal, and not a Western-style breakfast, particularly in China's northern summer when tomatoes are abundant.

Serves 6

GREEN VEGETABLE STIR-FRY WITH SESAME SEEDS (opposite)

Ingredients

2 tablespoons sesame seeds

2 tablespoons peanut oil

1 clove garlic, roughly chopped

1 inch fresh ginger root, finely chopped

5 oz broccoli, cut into very small florets

2 zucchinis, halved lengthwise and finely sliced

6 oz snow peas

1 tablespoon rice wine or medium-dry sherry

1 tablespoon dark soy sauce

1 tablespoon oyster sauce

Method

1. Heat wok. Add sesame seeds and dry-fry for 2 minutes or until golden, shaking the wok frequently. Remove and set aside.

2. Add oil to wok, heat for 1 minute, then add garlic and ginger and stir-fry over medium heat for 1–2 minutes until softened. Add broccoli and stir-fry for a further 2–3 minutes.

3. Add the zucchini and snow peas and stir-fry for 3 minutes. Pour in rice wine or sherry and heat for 1 minute. Add soy and oyster sauces, mix well, then stir-fry for 2 minutes. Sprinkle toasted sesame seeds over just before serving.

Note: Toasted sesame seeds add a nutty taste to this quick and healthy Chinese dish.

Serves 4

BRAISED BOK CHOY WITH MUSHROOMS

Ingredients

1 pound bok choy or cabbage

1 green bell pepper, seeded

$\frac{1}{2}$ red bell pepper, seeded

1 scallion, finely sliced

2 tablespoons sesame oil

1 tablespoon soy sauce

$1\frac{1}{2}$ teaspoons sugar

1 cup button mushrooms

salt

black pepper, freshly ground

2 tablespoons water

Method

1. Wash and dry bok choy or cabbage. Cut out the hard base or core and wash leaves carefully. Slice thinly. Slice bell peppers into julienne strips. Add with bok choy and scallions to a hot pan with oil and stir-fry for 3 minutes. Add soy sauce, sugar and mushrooms. Add salt and pepper to taste.

2. Add water and cook, stirring, until liquid reduces. Mushrooms will be still fairly firm. Cover and steam for 4 minutes if firm mushrooms are not to your taste.

Serves 4–6

SHELLEY'S CABBAGE AND CHINESE NOODLE SALAD

Ingredients

Salad

½ curly green cabbage

4 baby bok choy

8 scallions

½ bunch fresh cilantro

¾ cup flaked almonds

½ cup pinenuts

4 oz cooked Chinese noodles

Dressing

4 tablespoons peanut oil

2 tablespoons balsamic vinegar

2 tablespoons fresh lime or lemon juice

1 tablespoon brown sugar (optional)

1 tablespoon soy sauce

salt and cracked pepper to taste

Method

1. Finely shred cabbage and transfer to a large mixing bowl. Thoroughly wash bok choy then slice widthwise and add to cabbage.

2. Wash scallions then slice finely on the diagonal. Add to cabbage mixture together with the washed and roughly chopped cilantro.

3. Under the broiler or in a dry skillet, toast almonds and pinenuts and set aside to cool. Alternatively, toast nuts in a microwave by spreading nuts over the microwave plate and cooking them on high for 2 minutes. Mix gently to distribute then cook for a few more minutes until the nuts are as golden as you wish. Allow to cool.

4. Mix the nuts and noodles with cabbage salad. To make the dressing, beat all the ingredients together with a whisk until thick. Drizzle over the salad, toss thoroughly then serve immediately.

Serves 4

LONGEVITY MUSHROOMS WITH ASPARAGUS

Ingredients

10 dried Chinese mushrooms

1 bunch fresh asparagus, or drained canned
  equivalent

3/4 cup vegetable bouillon

1 cup fresh button mushrooms

1 teaspoon cornstarch

sesame oil

thin strips of red bell pepper or tomato skin

Method

1. Soak dried mushrooms for 10 minutes in
   boiling water. Remove stalks and discard. Cut
   tough lower stalks from asparagus and steam
   until al dente. Heat bouillon, add dried and
   fresh mushrooms and cook until tender. Add
   asparagus to absorb flavors.

2. Arrange asparagus in the center of a serving
   dish, button mushrooms at one end and
   Chinese mushrooms at the other. Quickly add
   cornstarch to thicken the remains of the
   bouillon, add a few drops of sesame oil and
   pour over vegetables. Place bell pepper strips
   or tomato skin in an attractive pattern over
   the asparagus.

Serves 4

PAK CHOI IN OYSTER SAUCE

(below)

Ingredients

14 oz pak choi

3 tablespoons oyster sauce

1 tablespoon peanut oil

salt

Method

1. Trim the ends of the pak choi stalks then
   separate the leaves and rinse thoroughly. Mix
   together oyster sauce and oil.

2. Put pak choi into a large saucepan of lightly
   salted boiling water and cook, uncovered, for
   3 minutes or until tender. Drain thoroughly,
   return the pak choi to the pan, add oyster
   sauce and oil mixture and toss to coat evenly.

Serves 4

RICH FISH-FLAVORED EGGPLANT
(opposite)

Ingredients

2 medium eggplants

oil for frying

salt

2 tablespoons dried shrimp

1 teaspoon ground cayenne pepper

2 teaspoons thick bean sauce

2 scallions, finely chopped

2 slices fresh ginger, chopped finely

3 cloves garlic, finely chopped

1 teaspoon sugar

$\frac{1}{2}$ cup crème fraîche

$\frac{1}{2}$ cup fish or vegetable bouillon

$3\frac{1}{2}$ tablespoons light soy sauce

1 teaspoon cornstarch

1 tablespoon dry sherry

Method

1. Peel eggplants and cut into potato-chip-sized pieces. Gently rub in salt to draw out bitterness and leave for 15 minutes. Wash and dry with paper towels. Soak dried shrimp in boiling water for 10 minutes then drain and chop.

2. In a wok or skillet, heat oil. Fry eggplant until it is yellow. Remove. Pour off oil, add bean sauce and ground pepper, stirring quickly. Add scallions, ginger, garlic, sugar and crème fraîche. Stir for about 1 minute then pour in bouillon and soy sauce with cornstarch stirred smoothly into it. Salt to taste. Add eggplant and stir to coat with sauce. Lower heat and cook for 5 minutes. Add sherry, stir and cook for 2 minutes more and serve.

Serves 4–6

VEGETARIAN FRIED RICE

Ingredients

1 large onion

3 scallions

1 bunch cilantro

6 eggs, lightly beaten

pinch of salt

4 tablespoons vegetable oil

5 cups cooked rice

1 cup peas, shelled, fresh or frozen

1 cup button mushrooms

$\frac{1}{2}$ cup sweet corn kernels, fresh cooked or canned

3 tablespoons soy sauce

Method

1. Cut onion into 8 pieces. Roughly chop scallions. Wash cilantro and chop into 1 inch pieces. Beat eggs and add salt.

2. In a large heavy-based pot, heat 2 tablespoons of oil on high. Add onion and stir-fry 2 minutes. Add scallions then rice. Stir together and remove after cooking for 2 minutes. Add 2 more tablespoons of oil to pot. Add peas and mushrooms and stir-fry $2\frac{1}{2}$ minutes. Add cilantro, corn and soy sauce. Stir-fry for 1 minute.

3. Add rice, combine thoroughly then pour in eggs. Stir through then allow mixture to sit on pan base for 1 minute before turning again.

Note: Any fresh or par-cooked or drained canned vegetable can be used in fried rice. Non-vegetarians can add thinly sliced ham, bacon bits, seafood, fish bits, shredded chicken or pork. Some cooks prefer to cook half the eggs either as scrambled or an omelette to cut into thin strips. The above method ensures the egg flavor is well distributed.

Serves 6–8

SNOW PEAS WITH GARLIC

Ingredients

12 oz snow peas

2 teaspoons garlic, crushed

2 teaspoons vegetable oil

¾ cup vegetable bouillon

1 teaspoons sugar

salt

1¼ teaspoons cornstarch

Method

1. Bring water to a boil in a wok. Add snow peas and return to boil for 3 minutes. Strain. Reserve snow peas. Put oil in wok and quickly stir-fry garlic. Add snow peas, bouillon, sugar and salt to taste. Bring to a boil, stir, simmer for 2 minutes and remove snow peas to a serving dish. Thicken bouillon with cornstarch and pour over snow peas.

Serves 6

desserts

DESSERTS

Delicious
DESSERTS

Desserts are not high on the Chinese list of food priorities. Carefully selected seasonal fresh fruits are preferred as they once were in ancient Greece and Rome. If you live in the tropics, you can't go wrong with kiwi fruit (originally named Chinese gooseberries) served with fresh coconut and coconut cream, or pineapple or banana fritters in a sweet batter and deep-fried as they are in China's south.

Sweets have never been part of the Chinese diet, although they became more popular during the T'ang dynasty between 618 and 906 AD when honey was used more in both sweet and savory dishes. Sweet meats have always been part of festivals and special occasions. Due to the recent increased sugar intake, diabetes is an increasing risk for those Chinese citizens who indulge more frequently than just at celebration times.

Light Western-style sponge cakes, elaborately decorated and expensive, are bought by many Chinese from specialist shops in big cities like Beijing and Shanghai despite the dry texture and the artificial multi-colored creams. If our selection leaves you still stumped for a Chinese dinner party dessert, you could always whip up a sponge cake and fill and top it with colored whipped cream.

The following recipes are mainly festive. Eight-treasure rice pudding is traditionally made by a new bride for the family into which she has married. During the Double Seventh festival, some unmarried girls offer gifts such as six fruits within a seventh, a frozen watermelon, to a mythical weaver maid in exchange for guiding their hands in craftmaking and sewing.

In some regions, particularly along the Yangtze, it is not unusual for toffeed apples to be served simultaneously with savory dishes to give the palate some variety (see page 156).

RUM AND LIME BANANA FRITTERS

Ingredients
4 bananas
juice of 1 lime
2 teaspoons superfine sugar
1 tablespoon dark rum
oil for deep-frying

Batter
4 oz all-purpose flour
1 teaspoon baking soda
pinch of salt
5 oz water
2 tablespoons sesame seeds

Method
1. Peel each banana and cut in half crosswise, then slice lengthwise to make quarters. Place banana quarters, lime juice, sugar and rum in a deep, non-metallic dish and mix gently. Cover and set aside for 30 minutes to marinate.

2. Meanwhile, make the batter. Sift flour, baking soda and salt into a mixing bowl. Pour in 5 ounces of water and whisk to form a smooth, thick batter. Stir in sesame seeds and set aside.

3. Heat 2 inches of oil in a wok or a large, deep skillet until smoking hot. Coat banana pieces thoroughly in batter. Fry for 5 minutes or until golden brown, then turn over and cook for 2 minutes to brown the other side (you may have to cook them in batches). Drain on towels towels.

Serves 4

ORIENTAL FRUIT SALAD

Ingredients

3 stalks lemongrass

2 oz superfine sugar

4 oz water

1 small canteloupe

1 mango

14 oz can lychees, drained

fresh mint leaves to garnish

Method

1. Peel outer layers from lemongrass stalks, finely chop lower white bulbous parts and discard fibrous tops. Place lemongrass, sugar and water in a saucepan. Simmer, stirring, for 5 minutes or until the sugar dissolves, then bring to a boil. Remove from the heat and leave to cool for 20 minutes. Refrigerate for 30 minutes.

2. Halve melon and scrape out seeds. Cut into wedges, then remove skin and cut flesh into small chunks. Slice off the 2 fat sides of the mango close to the stone. Cut a criss-cross pattern across the flesh (but not through the skin) of each piece, then push the skin inside out to expose the cubes of flesh and cut them off.

3. Place melon, mango and lychees in serving bowls. Strain lemongrass syrup and pour over the fruit. Decorate with mint.

Serves 4

TOFFEED APPLES

Ingredients

4 medium cooking apples

all-purpose flour for dusting

6 cups plus 1 tablespoon of sesame oil

²⁄₃ cup sugar

3 teaspoons sesame seeds

iced water for serving

Batter

2 eggs, beaten

½ cup cornstarch

½ cup all-purpose flour

a little water

Method

1. To make batter, add beaten eggs to flours. Pour in enough water to make a reasonably thick batter.

2. Peel, core and cut apples into 1 inch wedges, dip in dusting flour and dunk into batter before deep-frying at moderate heat in 6 cups of oil. Use extra tablespoon of oil to coat a large serving plate.

3. When carefully turned apple wedges have softened and turned golden (after a minute or so), drain them and place aside. Heat sugar carefully until melted and golden and toffee-colored. Quickly add apple wedges and cook for 1 minute. Add sesame seeds and toss apple pieces until all are coated. Dip apple pieces into iced water.

4. Serve on an oiled plate immediately.

Note: The ice water, if the apples are dipped into it quickly, will solidify the toffee instantly. Use this same method to present potato, yam, water chestnuts, banana, pineapple and even frozen custard or ice-cream balls in a similar manner. Be careful not to splatter the hot toffee.

Serves 4

MANDARINS IN ALMOND LAKE

Ingredients

2½ cups milk

½ cup sugar

1 teaspoon almond extract

⅓ cup ground rice

12 oz mandarin orange segments, canned

¼ cup flaked almonds

Method

1. In a saucepan, combine milk, sugar, almond extract and rice. Stir continuously and bring to a boil. Simmer, still stirring, for 5 minutes. Transfer to a bowl, cover and cool completely.

2. Drain mandarins. Spoon rice into individual dishes. Arrange mandarins on top and sprinkle with almond flakes.

Serves 4

CITRUS FRUIT SALAD WITH GINGER

Ingredients

1 pink grapefruit

1 large orange

1 tangerine, peeled and divided into segments
  rind of 1 lime, pared with a vegetable
  peeler and cut into matchsticks

2 oz kumquats, halved and seeds removed

juice of 1 small lemon

5 oz ginger beer

3 tablespoons superfine sugar

2 pieces stem ginger in syrup, drained and
  finely chopped

fresh mint to garnish

Method

1. Slice tops and bottoms off grapefruit and
   orange, using a sharp, serrated knife. Cut down
   the side of the fruits, following the curves, to
   remove the skin and pith. Hold fruit over a
   bowl to catch the juices and cut out the
   segments, leaving the membranes behind.
   Place in a serving dish with tangerine
   segments. Reserve the fruit juices.

2. Place lime rind and kumquats in a saucepan
   with water. Simmer for 10 minutes or until
   softened. Add kumquats to the other fruit and
   drain lime rind on paper towels. Reserve
   the liquid.

3. Add lemon juice, ginger beer, sugar and any
   juices from the fruit to the reserved cooking
   liquid. Heat gently, stirring, for 5 minutes or
   until sugar dissolves. Pour mixture over fruit
   and stir in chopped ginger. Sprinkle with lime
   rind and fresh mint.

Serves 4

JAPANESE
food

the land
AND ITS PEOPLE

Status	Constitutional monarchy
Area	145,728 sq mile
Population	127,000,000
Language	Japanese
Religion	Buddhist, Shinto, Christian
Currency	Yen
National Day	23 December

A PARADOXICAL ARCHIPELAGO

As the Shinkansen bullet train rockets southwest from Tokyo, it passes within 62 miles of Mt. Fuji, Japan's highest mountain. For three seasons of the year, Mt. Fuji is snowcapped; this holy volcano has been dormant since 1707. The pilgrims who toil up it are aware of the proverb that while he who climbs the much-photographed symbol of ancient Japan is a wise man, he who makes a subsequent ascent is a fool. The reward for climbing is likely to be a bowl of soup noodles, as take-away food has reached even Mt. Fuji's pinnacle.

Fuji-san is often elusive for passengers on the high-speed train. From the top of Mt. Fuji, sunrise is a misty, ethereal, timeless experience. But the haze surrounding it is often a haze of pollution as this archipelago of more than 6,800 islands is in one of the world's most industrialised countries. Here, you can become lost in a wild forest on a trail to Mt. Fuji where high mineral deposits often prevent compasses from working. Yet you can also be lost in the sea of Tokyo's humanity—a city of 12 million people. Japan is a country of contrasts: old and new, natural and artificial, traditional and sophisticated.

Meanwhile on the bullet train, even if the glistening ice cream cone of Mt. Fuji is in view, it may be ignored by the passengers because they're too busy tucking into their *ekiben*, or train lunch

packs, one of Japan's many practical inventions. The name derives from *bento* meaning lunch box, and *eki* meaning railway station.

Between 1600 and 1867, Japan's doors were completely closed to foreign influences with the exception of trade with China, Korea and Holland. Shortly after this strict Edo (or Tokugawa) era ended, the *ekiben* emerged alongside the development of the first train services. The *ekiben* has developed from a box containing humble rice balls and pickles to about 3,000 different types of boxed taste treats for commuters and longer-distance travelers. Within the *ekiben*, rice (Japan's staple food) is separated from meat, fish, vegetables and/or eggs and is always accompanied by Japanese pickles (*tsukemono*), and frequently by seaweed, sesame seeds and fish flake powder (*furikake*).

While Japanese train travel is fast, the cuisine is not. Food is assembled with the same artistic restraint that has set Japan apart from the rest of southeast Asia and the Western world, despite Western influence on Japan's cuisine since World War II.

The map of Japan is arc-shaped and resembles an awkward seal almost balancing Hokkaido on its nose. Japan's mountains run for 1,864 miles and comprise 80 percent of the land. In total, Japan is almost the size of California. The 126 million people mostly live in the major cities on the four main islands of Hokkaido, Honshu, Shikoku and Kyushu. The largest island is Honshu.

A mainstay of Japanese cuisine is fish, a legacy of the long coastline, but the local supply is not enough to satisfy the Japanese appetite. Tuna must be imported for the raw fish used in sashimi. Much of the imported tuna comes from Port Lincoln in South Australia, the

world's tuna capital. Seaweed is also a vital ingredient, as Westerners who have become addicted to sushi-bar-hopping would understand.

BEING ACCUSTOMED

The Japanese are frenetic workers and have little time to entertain in their generally small apartments and homes. A family spends an average of a quarter of its income on food, much of it eaten out. And why not, when restaurants abound in Japan? The restaurants serve far more than the well known sushi, sukiyaki and tempura, offering dishes in many styles; many eating houses specialize in a certain type of food. You can eat out differently for every meal of the week in Japan, with the only restriction being your supply

of yen. Food, like the rest of the cost of living, is very expensive in Japan.

Japanese people are reserved but polite, but Western visitors tend to retain the status of outsiders (*gaijin*), no matter how good their Japanese. Newcomers should observe local customs, particularly the custom of removing shoes when entering a home or any room with tatami matting. Pointing feet towards a person is a social gaffe. It is impolite to blow your nose in public and to react when seeing men urinating in the street. It is not acceptable to eat in the street unless eating ice cream, although eating while standing or sitting by a street stall or food vending machine is fine.

the land AND ITS

One can meet Japanese friends in an *izakaya*, a pub serving food such as yakitori, chicken on skewers. There, if not alone, it is considered bad form to pour one's own drink whether sake or beer. Your Japanese host should pour for you and guests should reciprocate. In a restaurant, you will be greeted with *'Irasshaimase!'* or 'Welcome!'. Visitors will be appreciated if they have made the effort to master chopsticks and learn a few Japanese phrases. Exchanging business cards is quite a ceremony in Japan. Each Japanese card should be inspected with interest or offense will be taken.

Through the Japan National Tourist Organization, it is possible to arrange to visit Japanese families in their homes, usually after dinner for tea and sweets. Visitors to a home should expect to sit on the floor and will need to bring a gift. Flowers, chocolates and duty-free spirits are all good gifts. Another acceptable gift is frozen meat if it can be brought from your home airport.

Staying in a *ryokan* or traditional inn is unforgettable. After removing shoes and being given slippers, guests are ushered to a tatami-matted room to don a *yukata* (cotton kimono) with its *obi* belt. Tea and sweets are served and a relaxing bath, 'possibly communal', is offered. You need to shower before entering the bath. Make sure you cross your *yukata* left side over right. At a time when very few Westerners were welcomed to *ryokans*, I committed the faux pas of crossing my small son's garment in reverse, a custom for dressing the dead. Such offense was caused that I was discouraged from eating a refined dinner on the floor at a low table with my husband and son. Later, after strolling the garden, I was forgiven because I thanked the maid in Japanese for preparing our futon beds with quilts.

FOOD FOR ALL SEASONS
In Japan, each season is celebrated with many festivals and with food reflecting the changing temperatures and conditions.

Spring brings fragrant young bamboo shoots, mint-flavored pepper tree leaves and, from the sea, red snapper, giant clams and other fish.

In hot summer, red and fatty *katsuo* (or bonito) is eaten as sashimi. Thin flour noodles are served over iced water along with chilled tofu squares, grated ginger, spring onions and grated dried bonito fish. Frozen, dried seaweed becomes jelly or jello, a popular summer snack with vinegar and soy sauce. Another summer treat is *kaki-gori*, shaved ice topped with sweet syrups.

In autumn, giant mushrooms appear in the pine forests. These are cooked in endless ways. Mackerel is an autumn fish, served either marinated or eaten raw.

Winter features sukiyaki, a hearty warming dish and probably the Japanese dish best known by modern Westerners. Sukiyaki is a beef and vegetable dish seasoned with *suiji* (kelp stock) and served with raw egg. Similar to sukiyaki is *shabu-shabu*, which is made with meat sliced very thinly. Sweet potatoes also appear on the menu in winter, along with vinegared daikon (a type of big white radish).

Marinated red bream and small dried fish wrapped in kelp and prepared in soy-based stock are special New Year treats. Salted salmon is given as a New Year gift, while squid and other seafoods herald the new January. Festive colors are red and white, so fish and rice with red azuki beans are served at this time.

Mochi (pounded rice cake) is a New Year rice substitute. It may be cooked with chicken, vegetables and/or fish in miso soup (soup made from soybean paste), or fish or chicken stock with soy sauce. *Mochi* is so important that sumo wrestlers and music stars make celebrity poundings in public at this time. *Mochi* can also be baked and wrapped in dried seaweed as a snack.

PEOPLE

On New Year's Eve, people make resolutions after cleaning their houses. They listen to 108 ancient temple bells via radio or TV, and eat wheat noodles as they farewell the old year and welcome the new.

Another food tradition is on the eve of February 4, when residents throw roasted soybeans from their doorways with the shout 'Go away, devils. Come in, good fortune'. Then they eat as many beans as their years of age for good health and longevity.

Parents honor their daughters on Girls' Day (March 3) with rice crackers and sake (fermented rice wine) at the national doll festival. During this festival, traditional dolls in kimonos and miniature furniture are displayed in every home that houses a small girl. Boys' Day is celebrated on May 5 by eating sweet rice dumplings and flying carp-shaped streamers.

So many festivals are celebrated with food that even the Japanese sometimes have trouble remembering and preparing appropriate delicacies.

Japanese FOOD

GOCHISOUSAMA DESHITA!

The phrase *Gochisousama deshita!* ('That was absolutely delicious!') is echoed in millions of homes and restaurants three times daily in Japan.

Apart from minor Chinese, Korean and Indian influences, which pre-date 1868, the Japanese tradition of presenting simple and elegant meals has remained unchanged for centuries. Japanese food is based on rice and bonito stock (dashi), which is made from bonito, soy sauce and soy bean paste (miso). Soup and rice generally accompany each meal.

The Japanese are masters of subtle seasoning. Hot, sweet, sour, bitter and salty flavors are utilized through condiments such as salt, miso, mirin (sweet rice wine) vinegar and soy sauce. Sauces and seasonings highlight, rather than dominate, the flavors of natural ingredients, which is a relief to those cooks and diners who dislike hot, spicy dishes. The exception is the fiery wasabi. This is an indigenous, indispensable horse-radish accompaniment for sashimi and sushi. And it is hot!

Since the end of the isolationist Edo period, Japan has enthusiastically embraced Western food, including meat, which was not eaten previously because of Buddhist vegetarian principles. Dairy products are still regarded with a certain trepidation. While Westerners have enjoyed Japanese food in restaurants, many have been hesitant to prepare it in their own kitchens, perhaps threatened by the artistry of its presentation or the unfamiliarity of some of the ingredients. But fear not. The ingredients are widely available in Asian food stores and are complemented by your own locally produced fresh ingredients. Peruse these pages for wonderfully tasty recipes and decoration ideas as simple as an autumn leaf or a snow pea pod.

THE RED SUN RISES

A traditional breakfast in Japan will consist of rice, miso soup, a vegetable dish, raw egg and pickles. Grilled fish was traditionally served, but many modern children disdain it, now accustomed to fast-food-chain breakfasts. Older students in possibly the world's most competitive education system may not have time for more than coffee and toast for breakfast. Many Japanese mothers remain at home. Discrimination still exists against employed married women although the number of women in the workforce is increasing. It's a rushed breakfast for a working wife, the main cook.

With about two hours travel to work, a typical salaryman, as he is known if he's a business-suited white-collar worker, may buy his strong coffee en route at a vending machine, foreign fast food chain, coffee house or sandwich bar. The expensive coffee is usually served without milk or sugar. A morning coffee-house snack is typically toast, a hard boiled egg, coffee, and a small salad. The atmosphere of the coffee houses is often peacefully conducive to reading, talking and relaxing to music. Red tea is served as well as coffee. Its color is distinct from green Japanese tea and is a blend of Sri Lankan and Indian teas.

Osechi is a stylish celebration breakfast eaten at New Year. Four tiers of lacquered boxes contain appetizers, vegetables, grilled food and salads to be savored through the whole day.

IT'S IN THE BOX

Western trends have influenced Japanese workday lunches which may comprise pizza, hamburgers or Chinese fried rice. A home wife or mother may prepare her husband and children a *bento* lunchbox and eat the leftovers herself. *Bentos* are also available at convenience stores and department stores where low-priced (for Japan) set-menu lunches can be bought on a tray. Cold *bento* boxes from home are diminishing in popularity as more business is conducted over restaurant lunches. But hot take-away *bento* boxes, from stations and stall counters, retain their popularity with workers who don't need a big lunch. They also provide inexpensive meals for students and for wives wanting an easy solution for the family's evening meal. Some restaurants take telephone orders and deliver hot food (*demae*) to homes or businesses. Food such as Indian tiffin or pizza can also be delivered.

Diners can choose selections from plastic or waxed models of dishes displayed in windows of the *shokudo* or eating places that serve set courses of rice and noodle dishes, and sometimes Western food. Great novelties to Westerners are *kaiten sushi* shops. People sit at counter stools and a wide variety of sushi comes by on a revolving conveyor belt. Food stalls are everywhere and food, particularly instant noodles, and drinks, including alcohol, are available from vending machines.

Robatayaki (or *robatayakiya*) are another type of restaurant which externally can resemble rustic old farmhouses. Here food is cooked on a large charcoal grill. At the *okonomiyaki*, which means 'cook what you like', you do just that. A

vegetable and cabbage batter is wrapped around the meat, vegetables or seafood of your choice.

Other restaurants specialize in one dish such as sushi, sukiyaki or tempura. Ramen, soba and udon noodles are featured at noodle shops. Most department stores have restaurants on the top floor.

THE RISING SUN SETS

After work, many men drop into a pub, a German beer hall, bar, club, hostess bar or a *yakitori* restaurant, for skewered chicken and a few beers or sake. Sake, the national drink, comes in several grades, and is served cold in summer and warm in winter. With between 17 and 32 percent alcohol, it's a potent brew. *Shochu*, a distilled spirit, was once used as a disinfectant, but is now a yuppie shot and packs a punch. Local and imported whisky is also favored.

By the time many fathers return home, their children are in bed. A home dinner is likely to comprise foods cooked several ways: simmered in dashi or soy, steamed (particularly seafood, pork, poultry, tofu and egg dishes), or grilled. Ideally grilling is done over a *hibachi* or mini charcoal broiler. Vinegared foods are served cold as accompaniments. Deep-frying is mostly left to chefs in restaurants.

Restaurants for dining out at night are the same as those for lunch although *yakitoriya* and *robatayakiya* are more popular during the evenings. One restaurant may serve mainly eel while another may offer *oden*, a homely peasant-style fare popular in winter. One type of restaurant specializes in *dojo* or loach, an eel-like creature. *Yakiniku* has been adapted from Korea. At a *yakinikuya*, most popular with men, every cut of meat is available, including offal. Some restaurants are furnished with tables and chairs in Western-style, as are many of the modern apartment blocks occupied by younger people.

Traditionally, all meals at home are eaten on the floor. *Ryotei* restaurants resemble old-style Japanese homes and serve Japanese *haute*

cuisine (*kaiseki*) in private tatami-matted rooms, often with garden views. *Kaiseki* consists of numerous small artistic courses without meat, with rice eaten last, all made from high-quality ingredients. The *ryotei* are so exclusive that often personal recommendation from a client is the only way to gain entry.

Japanese wines are produced in some areas. They are usually blended with Eastern European or South American wines. Japanese tea usually finishes a meal. Powdered green tea is used in the tea ceremony, a ritual developed by Zen Buddhists five centuries after tea was introduced from China in the ninth century.

Enjoy the adventure of preparing Japanese cuisine in your home. It will not be as difficult as you may think.

Kerry Kenihan

sashimi & sushi

The freshness of SASHIMI

Sushi dates back to 794 AD when fishermen realized rice could be preserved if cooked in vinegar.

If you're new to sushi, you may be a little intimidated. There's the language, the customs and a bewildering array of ways to put rice and fish together. There are rice cubes topped with all manner of sea delicacies, bite-sized kelp rolls, and little seaweed 'boats', just to name a few!

Your friends are probably no help at all. Half swear they hate sushi, particularly those who haven't tried it, and the ones who love it are too enthused over the *anago* (sea eel) or the *uni* (sea urchin) to help a novice make an appropriate selection.

But the biggest hurdle when you come 'face to fin' with your first sushi experience is not knowing what you're getting into. Don't worry. All you need are a few facts, a positive attitude, and a couple of tips about how to navigate these new waters.

In the following pages, you will not only learn how to make sushi, but you will get some insight into the whole sushi experience.

Sashimi is another specialty of Japanese cuisine. It is fresh fish served raw. The fish, which must be completely fresh, is sliced paper thin or alternately 2–4 inches thick, cubed, or cut in strips, according to the nature of the fish. The sashimi is accompanied by wasabi and soy sauce. Sashimi is always part of a formal Japanese meal, served early while the palate is still clear in order for its nuances to be appreciated.

LOBSTER SASHIMI (ISE-EBI OTSUKURI)

Ingredients
1 whole lobster (about 2 pounds)
wasabi
sushi soy sauce

To garnish
shiso leaves, cucumber, daikon

Method
1. Remove tail from lobster. Cut along underside of shell and remove tail flesh. Remove intestinal tract.

2. Thoroughly wash lobster flesh with water chilled by ice cubes for 5–10 seconds. Dry with paper towel. Cut into small bite-sized pieces.

3. Arrange lobster shell on a large flat platter. Spoon the flesh into the upturned tail shell. Serve with wasabi paste and sushi soy sauce.

4. Garnish platter with shiso leaves, cucumber and sliced daikon.

Serves 4

SASHIMI & SUSHI

ASSORTED SASHIMI (SASHIMI MORIAWASE)

Ingredients

5 thin bite-sized slices each of tuna, salmon, garfish, snapper, King George whiting and kingfish

1 pound abalone, removed from shell, cleaned and sliced

2 oz silver bream, cut into $1/4$ inch strips

1 scallion, finely chopped

$1/2$ teaspoon pickled ginger, chopped

To decorate

sliced lemon and lime, sprigs of dill, sliced cucumber, seaweed shapes

Method

1. Arrange sliced fish decoratively on a large flat platter. Place sliced abalone into cleaned shell.

2. Combine silver bream, scallion and ginger and stir through. Spoon onto platter.

3. Garnish liberally with lemon, lime, dill, cucumber and seaweed. Serve with wasabi paste.

Serves 5

ASSORTED SUSHI (SUSHI MORIAWASE) SHAPED SUSHI (NIGIRI-ZUSHI)

Ingredients

assorted sliced fish (approximately 1 inch
    thickness) such as tuna, salmon, King George
    whiting, garfish, kingfish or silver bream
shrimp, peeled and deveined
prepared sushi rice (see page 234)
wasabi

Method

1. Cut fish into pieces measuring approximately
   1 x 2 inches.

2. Cook shrimp in boiling water for 1 minute.
   Remove and place in iced water immediately.
   Gently cut along underside of shrimp, not all
   the way through, and open out flat.

3. Wet your hand and take a $^2/_3$ –1 oz portion
   of rice. Gently shape the rice into a
   rectangular shape, wetting hands as often as
   necessary. The rice portion should be slightly
   smaller than the topping.

4. Using your finger, spread a little wasabi on the
   underside of each piece of fish. Place the
   seafood on top and gently press together.
   Repeat with rest of ingredients. Serve with
   pickled ginger (*gari*) and shoyu.

Allow 4 pieces per person

ROLLED SUSHI (TEMAKI-ZUSHI)

Ingredients

nori seaweed sheets
prepared sushi rice (see page 234)
salmon
cucumber
wasabi

Method

1. Cut nori sheet in half. Place nori, shiny side
   down, onto a bamboo mat (*makisu*). Spread
   over about $^1/_4$ cup rice, leaving a $^1/_3$ inch space
   at top and bottom of seaweed.

2. Cut salmon and cucumber into $^1/_3$ inch strips.
   Using your finger, spread a little wasabi along
   the center of the rice. Lay the salmon and
   cucumber strips along the center.

3. Carefully roll up the nori, using the bamboo
   mat. Roll tightly to ensure the filling is held in
   place. Gently remove bamboo mat.

4. Using a wet, sharp knife, cut each roll in half.
   Then cut diagonally through center to create
   4 pieces. Repeat with rest of ingredients.
   Serve with pickled ginger (*gari*) and shoyu.

Allow 4 pieces per person

CALIFORNIA ROLLS
(KARIFORUNIA MAKI) (opposite)

Ingredients

4 shrimp, peeled and deveined

bowl of iced water

2 sheets nori seaweed

1 cup prepared sushi rice (see page 234)

$\frac{1}{2}$ cup shredded lettuce

1 small cucumber, cut into strips lengthwise

$\frac{1}{2}$ avocado, sliced

1 tablespoon *tobiko* (flying fish roe)

$1\frac{1}{2}$ tablespoons mayonnaise

Method

1. Cook shrimp in boiling water for
   1 minute, remove and place in iced water
   immediately. Slice shrimp in half lengthwise.

2. Place nori sheet, shiny side down, on a
   bamboo mat (*makisu*). Spread $\frac{1}{2}$ cup of
   rice over sheet, leaving a $\frac{1}{3}$ inch space at
   top and bottom of seaweed. Place half the
   shrimp, lettuce, cucumber, avocado, flying
   fish roe and mayonnaise across the middle
   of the rice.

3. Carefully roll up the nori, using the bamboo
   mat. Roll tightly to ensure the filling is held in
   place. Remove bamboo mat.

4. Using a wet, sharp knife, cut roll into
   8 even pieces.

Makes 16 pieces

TOFU SUSHI

Ingredients

10 oz tofu (substitute for sushi rice)

fresh ginger, grated

1 shallot, chopped

1 teaspoon soy sauce

assortment of various fish, meat and
   vegetables, cut into cubes about $\frac{1}{3}$ inch

15–20 nori belts

Method

1. Cut the tofu into small cubes (about 2
   inches).
2. Mix the ginger, shallot and soy sauce and
   set aside.
3. Place the topping (fish, meat or vegetable)
   onto the tofu and tie with nori belt.
4. Place the ginger mixture on top then serve.

Note: The garnish already contains soy, so a
bowl of soy and wasabi is not necessary.

To make nori belts. slice sheets of nori into
about 1 inch wide strips.

You can use any type of cooked meat or vegetables as a substitute for fish in this recipe.

Makes 15–20 pieces

SALMON BOX SUSHI (SAKE HAKO SUSHI)

Ingredients

1 sheet konbu (kelp seaweed)

rice vinegar

4 oz salmon, cut into 2 inch thick slices

5 shiso leaves, cut into 2 inch strips

3 cups prepared sushi rice (see page 234)

Method

1. Simmer konbu in rice vinegar for 5–10 minutes until soft.

2. Wet a wooden sushi mold or line a rectangular container measuring 10 x 3 x 2 inches high with plastic cling wrap. Allow the cling wrap to overhang by at least 4 inches each side.

3. Arrange one third of the salmon over the base of the mold to cover. Sprinkle over one third of the shiso leaves. Spoon over half the rice and gently press down. Repeat with one third salmon, one third shiso, the remaining rice, then remaining salmon and shiso. Top with strips of cooked konbu.

4. Place the wet wooden lid on the mold, or cover with overhanging cling wrap. Place a weight on top and leave for at least 4 hours or overnight, refrigerated.

5. Carefully remove the compressed sushi from the mold or container and unwrap. Using a wet sharp knife, cut into 8 equal portions and serve.

Makes 8 pieces

MACKEREL BOU SUSHI
(SABA BOU SUSHI)

Ingredients

1 mackerel fillet, all small bones removed

salt

rice vinegar

2 x 4 inches sheet konbu

6 Japanese mountain pepper leaves

2 cups prepared sushi rice (see page 234)

Method

1. Place mackerel fillet skin-side down in a flat dish. Cover liberally with salt. Leave for 1 hour.

2. Remove mackerel and shake off excess salt. Return mackerel to an empty flat dish and cover with rice vinegar. Allow to marinate for 1 hour. Remove and wipe dry with paper towels.

3. Place konbu in saucepan, cover with rice vinegar and simmer for 5 minutes. Remove and drain.

4. Place konbu onto a bamboo mat (*makisu*). Arrange mountain pepper leaves evenly down the center then place mackerel, skin-side down over the konbu. Spoon rice on top, and press down with wet fingers. Ensure that the rice is of even thickness and flat along the surface. Gently roll the sushi with the bamboo mat to create a curved top, with the mackerel side up. Remove and sit the sushi upright on its rice base. Cut into 6 even pieces with a wet sharp knife.

Makes 6 pieces

ASSORTED CALAMARI SASHIMI (IKA MORIAWASE)

Ingredients

1 large calamari tube, cleaned

1 sheet nori seaweed

2 strips cucumber, seeded

wasabi

soy sauce

2 tablespoons *udonji* (see page 233)

chives

1 teaspoon kinome

white sesame seeds

Method

1. Cut calamari into 3 equal pieces for 3 different dishes.

2. For the calamari roll, make shallow cuts $\frac{1}{5}$ inch apart on the outside of one calamari piece. Turn calamari over, with cut side down. Cut seaweed to the shape of the calamari and place on top. Line up cucumber along center and roll up. Slice into $\frac{1}{2}$ inch rolls. Serve with wasabi and soy sauce.

3. Cut next piece of calamari into 2 inch thick strips. Arrange calamari in a martini glass and pour in *udonji*. Garnish with chives.

4. Cut final piece of calamari into $\frac{1}{5}$ inch thick strips and mix with kinome. Serve in a shallow dish sprinkled with white sesame seeds.

Serves 2

ASSORTED TOPPED OYSTERS (NAMAGAKI)

Ingredients

6 oysters, shell removed

crushed ice

2 tablespoons ponzu soy sauce

grated daikon

momiji oroshi

2 tablespoons *udonji* (see page 233)

yuzu peel

salmon roe (*ikura*)

1 tablespoon *tosazu* dressing (see page 234)

½ tomato, finely diced

½ zucchini, finely diced

1 daikon, finely diced

Method

1. Arrange oysters on a bed of crushed ice.

2. Spoon ponzu soy sauce over oysters and top with a little grated daikon and momiji oroshi to taste.

3. Spoon *udonji* over another 2 oysters and put a pinch of yuzu peel and a little salmon roe on each.

4. Spoon *tosazu* dressing over the last 2 oysters and top with a mixture of finely diced tomato, zucchini and daikon.

Serves 2

LIGHTLY SEARED SUSHI
(ABURI SUSHI) (opposite)

Ingredients

2 medium scallops, roe removed

2 x 2 inch slices of salmon (approximately
   1 x 3 inches long)

2 x 2 inch slices of swordfish (approximately
   1 x 3 inches long)

1 cup prepared sushi rice (see page 234)

wasabi

Method

1. Slice scallops almost in half, through the center. Open out to create an oval shape and press lightly to flatten.

2. Heat a grill plate and lightly oil. Sear scallops, salmon and swordfish on one side for 3 seconds. Remove carefully from grill.

3. Wet your hands and take a $^2/_3$–1 ounce portion of rice. Gently shape the rice into a rectangular shape, wetting hands as often as necessary. The rice portion should be slightly smaller than the topping.

4. Using your finger, spread a little wasabi on the underside of the seafood. Place a piece of seafood on top of the rice grilled side up and gently press together. Repeat with remaining ingredients.

Note: For a more decorative pattern, cook fish on a heated cake rack sitting on a heated grill plate.

Makes 6 pieces

MARINATED FISH SUSHI
(ZUKE)

Ingredients

10 oz tuna fillet

boiling water

$^1/_2$ cup mirin

$^1/_2$ cup sake

2 cups sushi rice (see page 234)

1 tablespoon wasabi

Method

1. Place the tuna fillet on a cutting board over the sink. Cover with a cloth then pour boiling water all over.

2. Immediately place in cold water.

3. Mix mirin and sake in a bowl. Wipe tuna thoroughly dry, then place in bowl and allow to marinate for 2–3 hours.

4. Thinly slice tuna for sushi.

5. Wet your hands and take a $^2/_3$–1 ounce portion of rice. Gently shape the rice into a rectangular shape, wetting hands as often as necessary. The rice portion should be slightly smaller than the topping.

6. Using your finger, spread a little wasabi on the underside of the seafood. Place a piece of seafood on top of the rice grilled side up and gently press together. Repeat with remaining ingredients.

Note: Serve with a sprinkling of white sesame seeds on top.

Serves 4

INSIDE-OUT ROLL (URA MAKI)

Ingredients

4 sheets nori seaweed

2 cups prepared sushi rice (see page 234)

Fillings

sliced eel, sliced cucumber, blanched shrimp, topped with minced boiled egg

tuna strips, salmon strips, sliced cucumber, chili, mayonnaise, sliced avocado, topped with white sesame seeds

calamari strips, plum paste, sliced cucumber and sliced daikon, topped with *tobiko*

semi-dried tomato, crumbled feta cheese and sliced cucumber, topped with finely sliced scallion green tops.

pickled ginger

Method

1. Place a sheet of seaweed on a bamboo mat (*makisu*). Spoon $\frac{1}{2}$ cup rice onto seaweed. Using wet fingers, press rice out evenly, right to the edges.

2. Place a sheet of plastic cling wrap on top of rice and carefully turn mat over so that the rice is now on the bottom. Remove bamboo mat.

3. Arrange one of the fillings along the center of the seaweed, then roll up using the bamboo mat.

4. Carefully remove the plastic wrap. Sprinkle topping over and cut into 8 equal portions with a sharp wet knife. Repeat with other toppings. Serve with pickled ginger.

Makes 32 pieces

ASSORTED SUSHI BALLS (TEMARI-ZUSHI)

Ingredients

3 raw shrimp, shelled and deveined
iced water
3 shiitake mushrooms
6 thin salmon slices (2 x 1 inch each)
6 thin tuna slices (2 x 1 inch each)
6 baby snapper slices (2 x 1 inch each)
3 vinegar-cured sardine fillets
½ cucumber, sliced into thin 2 x 1 inch each pieces
1 boiled egg, minced
1 quantity sushi rice (see page 234)

Toppings

caviar, grated daikon and chili, Japanese mountain pepper leaves, salmon roe, grated ginger and chopped spring onion
pickled ginger for serving

Method

1. Cook shrimp in boiling water for 1 minute. Immediately place into iced water to cool. Carefully cut along underside of shrimp, not all the way through, and open out flat.

2. Cut a shallow 'cross' shape into the top of each shiitake mushroom and cook in boiling water for 1 minute. Remove and drain.

3. Lay out 2 pieces of the same fish, slightly overlapped on a 8 x 8 inch piece of plastic cling wrap. Place a ball of sushi rice, about the size of a golf ball, on top. Bring the corners of the plastic together over the rice, twist and squeeze until the rice forms a perfect ball. Remove plastic and place sushi ball onto a flat serving platter, rice side down. Repeat process with remaining fish, shrimp, mushrooms, cucumber and egg.

4. Top the salmon sushi ball with a little caviar, decorate the snapper with Japanese mountain pepper leaves and place some grated daikon and chili on the mushrooms. Spoon some salmon roe onto the boiled egg and top the sardines with grated ginger and chopped spring onion. Serve with some pickled ginger.

Makes 24

FLOWER ROLLS
(HANA MAKI) (above left)

Ingredients
$\frac{1}{2}$ sheet nori seaweed
$\frac{1}{2}$ cup prepared sushi rice (see page 234)
$1\frac{1}{2}$ x 8 inch wedge of cucumber
$1\frac{1}{2}$ cups salmon, cut into thin strips

Method
1. Place nori sheet shiny side down on bamboo mat. Spread rice over seaweed, leaving a $\frac{3}{4}$ inch gap along one long edge.

2. Place cucumber wedge over bare seaweed edge. Arrange salmon strips down the center of the rice.

3. Using the bamboo mat, carefully roll to form a petal shape, ensuring that skin-side of cucumber sits against the rice. Cut into 6 even pieces and arrange on a serving platter to form a flower shape.

Makes 6 pieces

FOUR-SIDED ROLLS
(SHIKAI MAKI) (above right)

Ingredients
3 sheets nori seaweed
$1\frac{1}{2}$ cups prepared sushi rice (see page 234)
1 piece thin omelette, cut into $1\frac{1}{2}$ x 4 inch rectangle
flying fish roe (*tobiko*)

Method
1. Cut the 2 sheets of nori in half. Place each nori sheet, shiny side down, on a bamboo mat. Spread over about $\frac{1}{2}$ cup of rice on each nori sheet, leaving a $\frac{1}{3}$ inch space at top and bottom of seaweed. Carefully roll up the nori using the bamboo mat. Roll tightly to ensure the rice is held in place. Gently remove bamboo mat and set the 4 nori rolls aside.

2. Place final sheet of nori onto bamboo mat and spread over the remaining $\frac{1}{2}$ cup of rice. Place a sheet of plastic cling wrap on top of the rice and carefully turn over so that the rice is now on the bottom.

3. Place the 4 rolls on the nori, alongside each other. Place the omelette in the center and carefully roll all together to form a square. Remove plastic wrap.

4. Cut sushi into 4 equal portions. Press a little roe onto the cut side and serve.

Makes 4 pieces

cold & hot entrées

Delicious party
STARTERS

Appetizers are rarely part of a home-prepared Japanese meal, but many skewered or rolled dishes make excellent appetizers with their flavor contrasts of mirin or sugar, soy and sake. Typical examples are speared sections of omelette, cucumber and shrimp. Another good appetizer is made from thin slices of raw flounder wrapped in omelette with a core stuffing of asparagus and smoked salmon.

The Japanese savor these snacks at lunchtime or with beer or sake after work.

Yakitori is another delicious party starter. These short skewers of barbecued chicken or chicken livers are said to have been introduced to Nagasaki by Dutch East India Company traders early in the 17th century. These are served at restaurants that serve nothing except accompaniments, for example onions, shiitake mushrooms or small green peppers, with beer and sake.

Beef, raw or slightly sautéed, then rolled around a vegetable such as onion or cucumber and served with a simple teriyaki sauce of sake, sugar and soy sauce is another easy entrée to make.

Because complete Japanese meals are made up of many small dishes, appetizers can be drawn from every section of this book (except the desserts section of course).

SLICED SEARED BEEF WITH PONZU SOY SAUCE (GYUU TATAKI)

Ingredients
3 oz porterhouse steak
1/4 red onion, thinly sliced
1 teaspoon grated daikon
momiji oroshi to taste
1 1/2 tablespoons ponzu soy sauce
1 tablespoon spring onion, finely chopped
wedge of lemon

Method
1. Cook steak under a hot grill for 1–2 minutes on each side. Slice into very thin strips.
2. Arrange beef on a platter, folding each strip and overlapping them slightly.
3. Combine red onion, daikon and momiji oroshi. Serve alongside beef, with ponzu soy sauce, chopped scallions and lemon wedge.

Serves 1

gyuu tataki

STEAMED CRAB DUMPLINGS (KANI MUSHIMONO)

Ingredients

7 oz fish fillet (gurnard or similar)

2 tablespoons arrowroot

1 tablespoon cooking sake

1 tablespoon mirin

1 tablespoon light soy sauce

1 teaspoon sugar

1 egg white

salt to taste

7 oz steamed crab meat, shredded

1/2 onion, chopped

4 scallions, chopped

2 teaspoon ginger grated

1 egg yolk

1/2 cup canola oil

15 wonton sheets

12 small crab claws

ponzu soy sauce

Method

1. Place fish, arrowroot, sake, mirin, soy sauce, sugar, egg white and salt into a food processor and process to form a smooth paste.

2. Spoon paste into a bowl and combine with crab, onion, scallions and ginger.

3. Whisk egg yolk with a few drops of canola oil. Continue to add oil, a few drops at a time, while whisking, to form a mayonnaise-style sauce. Add to crab mixture and stir well.

4. Cut each wonton sheet in half and then slice into very thin strips.

5. Take a heaping tablespoon of crab mixture and carefully form into a ball. Press wonton strips over the ball to coat it. Repeat with remaining crab mixture and wonton pastry to create 12 balls. Press a crab claw into the top of each dumpling.

6. Steam dumplings for 10 minutes. Serve with ponzu soy sauce.

Serves 6

ASSORTED DENGAKU (DENGAKU IROIRO)

Ingredients

½ baby eggplant, sliced
½ small zucchini, sliced
2 baby carrots
1 baby turnip
5 *satoimo* (Japanese taro)
1 yellow squash
varieties of miso (see step 2)

Method

1. Deep-fry eggplant and zucchini for 4 minutes then drain on paper towels. Steam or boil remaining vegetables until tender. Arrange decoratively on a large platter.

2. Top each vegetable with a tablespoon of a different flavored miso sauce (see page 234).

For example:

eggplant topped with *torimiso* and grilled until golden brown
zucchini topped with black miso sauce
carrots topped with walnut miso sauce
turnip topped with white miso sauce
japanese taro topped with *yuzumiso*
yellow squash topped with *shungiku miso*
Serves 2

GRILLED QUAIL

Ingredients

4 quails
4 wonton sheets
oil for deep frying
2 teaspoons butter
2 teaspoons chopped garlic
4 oyster mushrooms
4 shiitake mushrooms
$1\frac{1}{2}$ oz enoki mushrooms
2 scallions, chopped
1 tablespoon chives, chopped
$\frac{1}{4}$ cup shredded leek

Marinade

$\frac{2}{3}$ cup red wine
$\frac{2}{3}$ cup mirin
$\frac{1}{2}$ cup soy sauce
1 teaspoon crushed black pepper
4 bay leaves

Method

1. Cut each quail in half and remove the backbones and ribs from the meat.

2. Combine all marinade ingredients. Place quail halves in a flat glass dish. Pour over marinade. Allow to marinate for 12–24 hours.

3. Score each wonton sheet, $\frac{1}{2}$ inch apart and 2 inches in length. Deep-fry each sheet, one at a time, so that each sheet opens out like a fan. Remove when golden.

4. Heat butter in a frypan, add garlic and mushrooms, pan-fry for 2–3 minutes until mushrooms are tender and golden. Remove from heat and stir in scallions and chives.

5. Cook quail on a hot grill for 3 minutes each side, until well browned.

6. Spoon mushrooms onto a heated serving plate and top with the wonton fan. Arrange quail on top. Garnish with shredded leek and serve.

Serves 4

THREE KINDS DEEP-FRIED TOFU (SANSYOKU AGEDASHI DOUFU)

Ingredients

1 block tofu, cut into 12 cubes

arrowroot

3 teaspoons *aonoriko* seaweed powder

3 teaspoons black sesame seeds

14 oz *udonji* (see page 233)

chives

Method

1. Lightly roll tofu cubes in arrowroot.

2. Deep-fry tofu for 3–4 minutes.

3. Roll 4 cubes in seaweed powder to coat and another 4 cubes in black sesame seeds.

4. Place one seaweed tofu cube, one black sesame seed tofu cube and one plain tofu cube into each serving bowl.

5. Pour 4 oz of *udonji* into each bowl. Garnish with chives and serve.

Serves 4

COLD-SERVED GRILLED EEL LASAGNE (UNAGI WONTON SARADA)

Ingredients

1 grilled eel, approximately 7 oz

Japanese mountain pepper (sansho)

6 sheets wonton pastry

1½ oz mixed lettuce leaves

4 dried shiitake mushrooms, soaked in water
  for 2–3 hours

⅓ cup ponzu soy sauce

2 tablespoons extra virgin olive oil

Method

1. Carefully slice eel lengthwise through the center to create 2 very thin fillets. Then cut each piece in half. Sprinkle with sansho.

2. Cook wonton pastry in boiling water for 2–3 minutes, until tender. Drain.

3. Arrange 2 sheets of cooked wonton pastry over the base of a 4 x 8 inch rectangular container.

4. Arrange half the mixed lettuce leaves on top of pastry. Place half the eel over the lettuce. Top with another layer of wonton pastry. Cover with remaining lettuce, eel and wonton pastry. Gently press down.

5. Squeeze out any moisture from the mushrooms and chop finely. Combine mushrooms, ponzu soy sauce and olive oil to make a sauce. To serve, cut lasagne into four pieces and serve with mushroom sauce.

Serves 4

STEAMED JAPANESE CUSTARD WITH UDON NOODLES AND CRAB (KANI ODAMUSHI)

Ingredients

2 oz udon noodles, cooked

3 spinach leaves, steamed

4 oz Japanese custard mix (see page 234)

4 oz *udonji* (see page 233)

5 small snow peas

2 oz steamed crab meat

2 teaspoons arrowroot

1 steamed crab claw

1 tablespoon leek, julienned

Method

1. Place noodles and spinach into a heatproof serving bowl. Pour custard into the bowl, cover and steam for 10 minutes.

2. Meanwhile pour *udonji* into a saucepan, bring to a boil and add snow peas and crab meat. Cook for 2–3 minutes.

3. Mix arrowroot with 1 tablespoon water and add to the *udonji*. Stir until it has thickened. Pour liquid over custard and garnish custard with the crab claw and leek.

Serves 1

BRUNOISE SCALLOP SALAD, AYA-STYLE (HOTATE KABU REISEI)

Ingredients

4 oz turnip, diced into $1/4$ inch cubes

8 scallops, diced into $1/4$ inch cubes

3 oz pawpaw, diced into $1/4$ inch cubes

$1/2$ cup chopped chives

1 large daikon, cooked

$1/3$ cup flying fish roe

$1/3$ cup caviar

chives

Miso dressing

1 tablespoon sake

1 tablespoon mirin

1 tablespoon light soy sauce

1 tablespoon rice vinegar

2 teaspoons ponzu sauce

4 oz saikyou miso

1 tablespoon onion, chopped

1 tablespoon extra virgin olive oil

2 teaspoons wholegrain mustard

1 teaspoon ginger juice

Method

1. Cook turnip in boiling water until tender, then drain. Cook scallops in boiling water for 5 seconds, drain and cool in refrigerator. Combine turnip, scallops, pawpaw and chives.

2. Combine all miso dressing ingredients, add scallop mixture and stir well. Spoon half of the mixture onto the center of each serving plate.

3. Cut daikon into $1/4$ inch thick strips. Cut 3 strips to measure 3 x 8 inches. Wrap a strip around the scallop mixture. Secure by tying a chive around the outside. Lightly press down the scallop mixture to form a flat surface.

4. Spoon roe and caviar decoratively over the top. Garnish with chives and serve.

Serves 4

CHICKEN YAKITORI

Ingredients

1 pound chicken tenderloins

small bamboo skewers, soaked

Marinade

¼ cup teriyaki sauce (see page 233)

¼ cup honey

1 clove garlic, crushed

¼ teaspoon ground ginger

Method

1. Place chicken in a glass bowl, mix marinade ingredients together and pour over chicken. Cover and place in refrigerator to marinate for several hours or overnight.

2. Thread 2 tenderloins onto each skewer, using a weaving motion. Heat barbecue or electric grill to medium-high. Grease grill bars or plate lightly with oil.

3. Place skewers in a row, from left to right and cook for 2 minutes on each side, brushing with marinade as they cook.

4. Remove to a large plate and serve immediately as finger food.

Serves 4

ORANGE MARINATED SALMON WITH SHISO PESTO (SAKE ORANGE TSUKE SHISO FUUMI)

Ingredients

7 oz salmon fillet

Orange marinade

4 cups water

juice of 1 orange

juice of 1 lemon

8 oz salt

2 oz sugar

3 bay leaves

1 teaspoon five spice powder

12 mint leaves

Shiso pesto

5 shiso leaves

2 teaspoons olive oil

1 tablespoon onion, chopped

1/2 teaspoon mustard

2 tablespoons scallion greens, chopped

Method

1. Combine all marinade ingredients in a saucepan. Stir over medium heat until salt and sugar have dissolved. Remove from heat and cool. Place salmon in a bowl, cover with the marinade and allow to marinate in refrigerator for 8 hours.

2. Remove salmon, wipe dry with paper towels. Brush with a little olive oil and cut into very thin slices lengthwise.

3. Arrange salmon on serving plate, overlapping slices slightly. Blend shiso pistou ingredients to form a smooth sauce. Spoon over salmon.

4. Sprinkle with scallions before serving.

Serves 1–2

tempura

Tasty
TEMPURA

Tempura is a delicious style of cooking in which foods such as vegetables and seafoods are dipped in a light frying batter and deep-fried.

One of the most well-known and popular Japanese foods, food in batter was first introduced to Japan by Portuguese traders and missionaries. It caught on quickly with the Japanese, who refined the batter to a delicate crispness and accompanied it with flavor-enhancing dipping sauces. Although tempura is not difficult to make, here are several tips that help ensure a crisp, light, delicious batter:

1. Use a light, cold-pressed vegetable oil (such as sunflower oil).

2. The temperature of the oil should be 400°F.

3. Lightly combine batter ingredients, leaving some lumps and even some dry flour on the surface.

TEMPURA METHOD

Ingredients
7 oz all-purpose flour (for dipping)
seafood or vegetable items (see following pages)

Batter
1 egg yolk
7 oz all-purpose flour
1 cup iced water
4 ice cubes

Method
1. Make tempura batter by following the steps on opposite page.

2. Dip each seafood or vegetable item in flour and then in batter (twirl it around to properly coat it). Then drop into oil heated to 400°F. Only fry 5 pieces of food at a time.

3. Fry until golden brown. Remove and drain.

Note: The batter should be somewhat thin and watery, and should easily run off a spoon. If it is too thick, thin it with drops of cold water. Ideally, the batter should be used immediately after being made, but may be used up to 10 minutes after being made.

Makes about 1½ cups batter mixture

1. Place egg yolk in a large bowl.

tempura batter

2. Add water and ice cubes.

3. Using chopsticks or a fork, beat the egg yolk and iced water until combined.

4. Sift flour and add to egg and water mixture.

5. Lightly combine ingredients.

TEMPURA JUMBO SHRIMP (EBI TENPURA)

Ingredients

3 jumbo shrimp
all-purpose flour
7 oz tempura batter (see pages 196–197)
1 sheet nori seaweed, cut into 4 squares
oil for deep-frying

Method

1. Remove legs and tail shell from the shrimp. Devein the shrimp neatly.

2. Carefully lift up the shell covering the head of the shrimp, leaving it partially attached at the tip of the head.

3. Make 8–10 shallow cuts along the stomach of the shrimp. Only cut halfway into the stomach. Turn over and squeeze the back of the shrimp so it becomes straight.

4. Dust shrimp lightly with flour and dip into the tempura batter. Deep-fry at 400°F until crisp and golden.

5. Dip nori squares into tempura batter and deep-fry until crispy. Serve shrimp on a flat platter, piled on top of each other. Garnish with nori squares. Serve with tempura sauce (see page 233).

Serves 1

TEMPURA VEGETABLES (YASAI TENPURA)

Ingredients

3 slices lotus root

1 slice eggplant

1 small carrot, sliced in half lengthwise

2 asparagus spears

3 ginko nuts, threaded onto a bamboo skewer

5 scallions, white end only

3 slices sweet potato

2 slices zucchini

all-purpose flour

oil for deep-frying

10 oz tempura batter (see pages 196–197)

5 oz tempura sauce (see page 233)

Method

1. Cut vegetables into 2–4 inch thick slices.

2. Dust vegetables lightly with flour.

3. Heat oil in deep-fryer to 400°F.

4. Dip vegetables into tempura batter and deep-fry until batter is golden and crispy.

5. Drain lightly on paper towels and then serve. Serve with tempura sauce.

Serves 2

TEMPURA CRAB
(KANI TENPURA) (opposite)

Ingredients

6 large crab legs

7 oz of tempura batter (see pages 196–197)

all-purpose flour

1 sheet nori seaweed, cut into 2 inches strips

lemon wedges

oil for deep-frying

Method

1. Carefully break the shell away from the thick end of each crab leg. Leave the thin end of the leg still covered with shell.

2. Make the tempura batter. Dust the meat ends of the crab leg lightly with flour. Dip the meat end of the crab leg into the tempura batter. Deep-fry the whole leg at 400°F until the batter is crisp and golden.

3. Gently tie each of the seaweed strips into a knot, dip into the tempura batter and deep-fry until crispy.

4. Arrange the crab on a large serving plate and garnish with lemon wedges and fried seaweed knots. Serve with tempura sauce (see below).

Serves 3

TEMPURA SAUCE

Ingredients

7 oz fish bouillon

1½ oz soy sauce

1½ oz mirin

Method

1. Mix all ingredients together in a saucepan. Bring to a boil and immediately remove from heat. Allow to cool.

Makes 10 oz

(Use within 1 day.)

ASSORTED TEMPURA
(TENPURA MORIAWASE)

Ingredients

4 raw jumbo shrimp, or 8 raw medium-sized shrimp

4 whiting or plaice fillets

all-purpose flour

oil for deep-frying

8 snow peas

7 oz tempura batter (see pages 196–197)

4–8 fresh shiitake mushrooms, stalks trimmed, then cut in half if large

For serving

1 tablespoon daikon, peeled and grated

1 teaspoon ginger, grated

5 oz tempura sauce (see below)

Method

1. Peel the shrimp, retaining the last tail section, and devein. Make a few slits along the belly to prevent the shrimp from curling during cooking (see step 3 on page 198).

2. Cut the fish fillets into pieces about 2 inches long and roll in all-purpose flour. Heat oil for deep-frying to about 400°F. Meanwhile, cook the snow peas in boiling water for 2 minutes, then drain and rinse with cold running water. Set aside.

3. When the oil is almost hot enough, make the batter.

4. Dip the mushrooms in the batter and deep-fry for 1–3 minutes or until batter is golden yellow. Drain on a rack. Next, dip the shrimp into the batter, and deep-fry one at a time, holding the tail. Then do the same with the fish fillets. When all the ingredients have been deep-fried, arrange a half of each, with the snow peas, on decorative paper, on individual plates.

5. Serve with tempura sauce.

Serves 2

tempura crab

CHILI TEMPURA

Ingredients

oil for deep-frying

1 pound raw large shrimp, peeled and deveined, tails left intact

12 snow peas, trimmed

1 eggplant, cut into thin slices

1 small head broccoli, broken into small florets

Chili tempura batter

3 oz self-raising flour

2 oz cornstarch

1 teaspoon chili powder

1 egg, lightly beaten

1 cup iced water

4 ice cubes

Method

1. To make batter, place self-rising flour, cornstarch and chili powder in a bowl, mix to combine and make a well in the center. Whisk in egg and water and beat until smooth. Add ice cubes.

2. Heat oil for deep-frying in a deep saucepan until a spoon of tempura batter floats to surface (should take 50 seconds).

3. Dip shrimp, snow peas, eggplant and broccoli florets in batter and deep-fry, a few at a time, for 3–4 minutes or until golden and crisp. Serve immediately.

Serving suggestion: All you need to make this a complete meal is to serve tempura with a variety of purchased dipping sauces, chutneys, relishes and a tossed green salad.

Serves 2

soups

Subtle SOUPS

In Japan, soup is eaten as part of breakfast, lunch and dinner or just as a snack. It is the essence of both artistry and sustenance, whether it is served at the end of a meal or as the meal itself, as is often the case with noodle soup. Soup is sometimes served in a lacquered bowl with a lid so that its heat can be held while it is slurped with much gusto for the duration of the meal.

Many Westerners have the impression that Japanese soup is always based on clear bouillon, fermented bean paste or seaweed, with, apart from noodles, little added except for a few vegetables for decoration. However, these clear concoctions are exquisite with hearty injections of pork and vegetables, which satisfy not only the aesthetic eye, but also the appetite. Miso soup, the most Japanese of soups, is enhanced with fatty meats and vegetables, which add color and flavorful nourishment. Spices and sauces give a fine flourish to this dish, which is fully textured and balanced.

Consider the delicious subtlety of a bouillon to which has been added balls of shellfish or minced fish mixed with green vegetables and mushrooms and garnished with a vegetable leaf or sprig of watercress.

Japanese soup bouillons are not just derived from soy beans and seaweed. As in the West, bouillon may be made with chicken, fish or beef. Otherwise unuseable bones can be used, along with vegetable water or, at the last resort, bouillon cubes or bouillon powder. There is nothing wrong with instant bouillon, dashi included, if the home chef is harried or hurried, although total perfectionists would disagree.

The following pages contain recipes for delicious Japanese soups. Once you have mastered these recipes, you can use them as the basis for creating your own unique flavors.

BEEF UDON NOODLE SOUP (NIKU UDON)

Ingredients

3 oz udon noodles
1 cup *udonji*, heated (see page 233)
2 oz eye fillet, sliced very thinly
1 tablespoon spring onion green, sliced
1 tablespoon cooked tempura batter pieces (see pages 196–197)
½ teaspoon white sesame seeds, chopped

Method

1. Cook udon noodles in boiling water for 8 minutes until tender.

2. Pour hot *udonji* into a serving bowl. Spoon in hot cooked udon noodles.

3. Overlap slices of beef onto the noodles, covering half the bowl. Add scallions and tempura batter pieces to the soup.

4. Sprinkle sesame seeds over the soup and serve.

Serves 1

niku udon

JAPANESE NOODLE SOUP
WITH FRESH TUNA

Ingredients

2¼ cups fish bouillon

4 tablespoons dark soy sauce

4 tablespoons sake or dry sherry

2 tablespoons rice or wine vinegar

1 tablespoon superfine sugar

2 tablespoons sesame oil

8 oz fresh udon noodles

4 tuna steaks, about 5 oz each, skinned

2 tablespoons sesame seeds

fresh cilantro to garnish

Method

1. Place the bouillon, soy sauce, sake or sherry, vinegar, sugar and 1 tablespoon of the oil into a saucepan. Bring to a boil and cook uncovered for 15 minutes, or until reduced by about a third.

2. Meanwhile, cook the noodles according to the package instructions until tender but still firm to the bite. Brush the tuna steaks with the remaining oil and coat the edges with sesame seeds. Heat a ridged cast-iron grill pan or heavy-based skillet until very hot. Add the tuna steaks and cook for 2 minutes on each side or until seared.

3. Transfer the noodles to serving bowls, pour over the bouillon, top with the tuna steaks and garnish with cilantro, then serve immediately.

Note: These tuna steaks are seared on the outside, but still succulent in the middle. You may cook them a little longer if you like, but take care not to make them too dry.

Serves 4

SPRING ONION, SESAME AND SHIITAKE SOUP

Ingredients

4 cups chicken bouillon

2 cups beef bouillon

2 oz dried shiitake mushrooms

1 oz piece fresh ginger, sliced

1 teaspoon sesame oil

1 teaspoon five spice powder

1 tablespoon teriyaki sauce (see page 233)

2 tablespoons mirin

4 oz button mushrooms, finely sliced

6 scallions, sliced diagonally

1 tablespoon sesame seeds to garnish

Method

1. Heat chicken and beef bouillon in a saucepan, then add shiitake mushrooms and sliced ginger. Bring to a boil then simmer for 5 minutes. Remove from the heat and allow to rest for 40 minutes.

2. Remove mushrooms from the liquid and carefully slice them, discarding stems. Remove ginger from bouillon and set aside. Line a sieve with some paper towels then pour the bouillon into the sieve. Allow bouillon to drain through the sieve, to strain out all the grit and sand from the mushrooms. Discard the paper.

3. Return strained bouillon, ginger and shiitake mushrooms to saucepan and bring to a simmer. Add sesame oil, five spice powder, teriyaki sauce, mirin and finely sliced button mushrooms and simmer for 10 minutes.

4. Remove ginger, then add sliced scallions.

5. Serve the soup in Japanese bowls, garnished with sesame seeds.

Serves 4–6

CRISPY BUCKWHEET NOODLE SOUP WITH DUCK BREAST (AGE SOBA KAMO SUIMONO)
(opposite)

Ingredients

4 oz soba noodles

4 oz duck breast, cut into 16 thin slices
     arrowroot

8 scallions, white stem only, roots removed

4 cups *udonji* (see page 233)

4 sprigs mitsuba

Method

1. Cook soba noodles in boiling water for 5–6 minutes until tender. Drain well.

2. Divide noodles into 4 and shape each group into a small ball. Deep-fry each ball carefully until golden brown. Take care while frying to retain the shape of each ball. Drain on paper towels.

3. Toss each slice of duck breast lightly in arrowroot. Bring a pan of water to a boil and cook the slices for 1–2 minutes.

4. Place scallions on a hot grill and cook for 1 minute on each side.

5. Heat *udonji* until boiling. Pour 1 cup into each serving bowl. Top with sliced duck, scallions, mitsuba sprigs and soba balls.

Serves 4

RICE CAKE SOUP (ZOUNI)

Ingredients

4 chicken thighs

1 small carrot

4 oz scallions

4 shiitake mushrooms

3 oz spinach, shredded

4 cups *udonji* (see page 233)

4 pieces *mochi* rice cakes

4 sprigs mitsuba

Method

1. Cut chicken thighs into small pieces.

2. Cut carrot, spring onion and shiitake mushrooms into thin slices.

3. Heat *udonji* until boiling.

4. Add chicken pieces, carrot, scallions, mushrooms and spinach to pan and simmer until softened.

5. Meanwhile, grill *mochi* pieces in the oven until softened and a little burned.

6. Add grilled *mochi* to the soup and serve.

7. Place mitsuba sprigs on the top.

Serves 4

age soba kamo

suimono

LOBSTER MISO SOUP (ISE-EBI MISO-SHIRU)

Ingredients

3 tablespoons mixed dried seaweed such as
    ogonori, wakame, tosakanori
4 cups fish bouillon
3 oz miso
½ teaspoon ginger, grated
1 lobster, head section and legs only
7 oz miso-shiru
chives to garnish

Method

1. Soak seaweed in water for 5 minutes
   then drain.

2. Place fish bouillon, miso and ginger in a
   large saucepan. Bring to a boil.

3. Clean lobster head, separate all legs. Add to
   fish bouillon. When soup returns to a boil,
   remove lobster.

4. Heat soup and pour into a large serving
   bowl. Place hot lobster into the bowl.
   Arrange seaweed around lobster. Decorate
   with chives and serve.

Serves 2

mains

A mix of MAINS

MEAT

Teppanyaki, meaning 'grilled on a hot plate' or
Japanese barbecue, has been enjoyed by
Westerners since the end of World War II when it
was introduced into the USA.
Strangely, it is not so popular in Japan,
probably because of the cost of the
ingredients. Teppanyaki Japanese
restaurant eating is thoroughly
entertaining. Wielding whirling knives
and steel spatulas over a central
hotplate, the chef quickly slices,
seasons, tosses and serves out the
tender steak to great applause. Often
a combination of fresh seafood and
chicken plus onions and bean sprouts are thrown
in. Dipping sauces accompany the feast.

A teppanyaki banquet can be achieved at home
with soy sauce, radish, chopped scallions, lemons
and masses of pepper-grinding while the meat and
optional chicken and seafood sizzle.

Sukiyaki is an equally well-known Japanese dish,
originating after a prohibition against meat-eating
was lifted between 1868 and 1912. A hearty dish
served in Japanese winter to those who can afford
the meat, sukiyaki is quality steak slices quickly
cooked in a heavy pan and seasoned with dashi
bouillon and soy sauce. Additions may include
spring onion, tofu, spinach, carrots, Chinese
cabbage, clear noodles, shiitake mushrooms and
chrysanthemum leaves, if available. All should be
dipped in raw egg before eating.

Kobe beef, heavily marbled with fat, is highly revered.
Shabu-shabu is similar to sukiyaki except the meat,
more thinly sliced, and vegetables are dipped in
sesame sauce and citrus with soy sauces beforehand.

In Japan, the quality of steak is expected to be so
high that cows are fed beer and massaged to
produce the best-grade meat. Because of Japan's
mountainous terrain and the difficulty of breeding
cattle, beef is expensive. This is partly why meat
consumption in Japan is much less than in
Western nations.

Pork was introduced from the West. *Tonkatsu* is a
deep-fried, well seasoned battered pork cutlet, cut
into segments and eaten with chopsticks along
with shredded cabbage and separate bowls of rice
and miso soup. Another version of this dish is
pork cooked in sweet soy broth with onions and
beaten egg. *Tonkatsu* is so loved by the Japanese
that specialty restaurants of the same name are
devoted to preparing it in thick cuts, minced or
deep-fried with vegetables on skewers.

CHICKEN AND POULTRY

Yakitori (grilled chicken) and *tori teriyaki* (grilled
marinated chicken) are two popular poultry dishes.
They have tantalized Western palates for many
years as visitors to Japan, restaurant diners and
home cooks have been developing their knowledge
of Japanese food. Grilled duck is also popular.

In Japan, the thinnest slivers of raw chicken, served
with a sauce based on lime juice and marinated
onion, make for superb sashimi. The most
succulent tasting and delicately textured chicken is
said to be bred in the Nagasaki region.

Chicken is wonderful ground with fish and formed
into balls and served with a sauce of seaweed or
fish bouillon, sake, mirin and soy sauce. Sake can
be used to steam chicken and can also be the
base of a sauce for marinated duck.

SEAFOOD AND FISH

When cut well (sashimi-style), and served with
various dipping sauces, tuna, bream, snapper,
flounder or sea bass, and even small species such
as garfish, are delicious and are making their way
onto Western tables. For sashimi, the slicing of the
flesh is all important. While tuna can be cubed as
well as sliced, sea bass slivers, for example, must
be paper thin.

The Japanese regard red snapper as the king of fish.
The bones and head of the snapper are used to
make flavorful bouillon, which, with a little salt and
soy sauce, transforms into a simple, delicious soup.

Sake is often used to impart subtle flavor and tenderize steamed seafood such as abalone and clams. Scallops, clams, and shrimp are often served with vinegared food, cucumber and fresh ginger and dressed with rice vinegar, dashi, sugar and soy. Oysters stewed in thick miso in a claypot are a triumph. Crab is delicious in a hot pot cooked at the table with greens, mushrooms and tofu and eaten with savory sauces and dips, including a touch of chili.

Lobster, octopus, squid and shrimp are served in delicate small entrée-sized portions, while eel has been part of the Japanese diet since recorded history.

Fugu, the deadly poisonous globe or blowfish, is harvested at the rate of more than 3300 tons per year. Obviously, some people survive the do-or-die experience of eating its translucent, raw slivers at the hands of chefs who spend about seven years learning to separate the meat from the fish's internal organs, which are more lethal than cyanide.

VEGETABLES

Influenced by Zen Buddhists, the vegetarian style of cooking, known as *kaiseki ryori*, was instituted to complement tea ceremony ethics and has become known as Kyoto-style cuisine.

Various products have been developed from soy beans: tofu (soybean curd), miso (fermented soybean paste) and soy sauce. Japanese tofu comes in two main varieties: cotton tofu, which has a fluffy consistency, and silken tofu, which is more fragile. Tofu may be served simply in seaweed-flavored bouillon, garnished with a sprig of bamboo leaf. A popular tofu dish is *hiya yakko*, which is chilled tofu topped with scallions, grated ginger, dried bonito flakes and soy sauce. Miso soup accompanies almost every Japanese meal. *Oden*, literally stew on skewers in simmering broth, is an acquired taste. Often served at street corner carts, *oden* can comprise tofu, daikon (white radish), *konnyaku* (a gelatin-like substance) and seaweed, plus hardboiled eggs, fish or fish cakes and sometimes meat. *Oden* is eaten smeared with mustard.

After salt and vinegar were recognized as preserving agents, pickled vegetables became, and remain very much a part of, modern Japanese cuisine.

Familiar vegetables can gain new dimensions when prepared Japanese-style. Bamboo shoots, slim eggplants, spinach, cabbage, cucumbers, small sweet green peppers, fresh soy beans and daikon are just a few popular vegetables. Expect to find onions, celery, snow peas, zucchini, asparagus, herbs and even avocado among ingredients used in Japanese cuisine.

RICE AND NOODLES

Cultivated in Japan for centuries, rice, steamed with side dishes of vegetables, fish and/or seafood, was the mainstay of the country's cuisine until it became fare only for the upper classes following the introduction of flour products from China. Grains and cereals became the staples for commoners. Noodles arrived from China at the same time and, today, any Japanese worth their sushi eats a bowl almost daily.

Japanese versions of noodles (ramen) include soba and udon noodles. Soba are thin buckwheat flour noodles and udon are thick and made from white flour. Mostly served in bonito broth, these noodles are also served cold, heaped on a bamboo screen with cold dipping broth. A popular cold dish is *zaru soba*, noodles with nori (seaweed) bits on top served with a side dish of scallions and wasabi (hot green horseradish paste). *Yakisoba* and *yakiudon* are fried noodles. They are served with thick soy sauce, seaweed flakes, bonito flakes, vegetables and meat. Plain noodles are enjoyed served over either ice or a bowl of boiling water and with a citrus and soy sauce dip and wasabi. Tea-flavored green noodles are also popular.

Rice is always the short grain variety, washed first to rid it of starch and steamed using the absorption method of cooking. An easy sushi for a crowd is to scatter cooked rice on a lacquerware tray and spread it with raw or cooked fish bits and lightly simmered vegetables.

At home, most Japanese use a rice cooker for perfect rice. Rice is not cheap, but is now less expensive than wheat for bread. Rice balls, sometimes flavored with sesame seeds, seaweed or often fish, are contrasts to the bread and buns to which Japanese have become accustomed through Western fast food chains.

Kare raisu or 'curry rice' became popular after Japan's isolationist period. The brown-sauced curry containing a few beef pieces is poured onto a rice mound and, along with the accompaniments of red pickle and pickled scallions, is eaten with a spoon. It is an easily prepared home meal. Curry noodles are also served at stalls where one stands up to eat on the run.

SUKIYAKI

Ingredients

4 oz marbled porterhouse steak, sliced

4 oz Chinese cabbage, shredded

½ onion, sliced

2 shiitake mushrooms

4 pieces carrot, sliced

8 cubes tofu (about 1 inch cubes)

4 scallions

1 oz beef fat

2 oz shungiku (optional)

2 eggs, beaten

Sukiyaki sauce

10 oz mirin

10 oz soy sauce

5 oz sake

5 oz sugar

18 oz suiji (see page 233)

Method

1. To make sukiyaki sauce, place all ingredients in a saucepan and heat until sugar has dissolved.

2. Arrange sliced beef decoratively on a plate. Place all vegetables and tofu on another plate.

3. Heat beef fat in a sukiyaki pan (or other heavy-based skillet) on the serving table. Cook some of each ingredient while adding a little sukiyaki sauce to the pan. Cook for only a few minutes before serving. Guests may choose to dip the cooked ingredients into the beaten egg before eating.

4. Continue to cook remaining ingredients while adding more sukiyaki sauce to the pan as required.

Serves 2

ASSORTED SEAFOOD, BEEF AND VEGETABLES COOKED ON A STEEL PLATE (KAWARA YAKI)

Ingredients

1 jumbo shrimp

4 slices calamari

2 oz porterhouse steak

½ cup bean shoots

2 oyster mushrooms

2 slices red bell pepper

2 slices leek

To serve

¼ cup onion sauce (see page 233)

1 tablespoon deep-fried garlic 'chips'

Method

1. Fry all ingredients on a hot flat grill plate, until just cooked.

2. Cut beef into thin slices and serve decoratively on a heated serving plate. Arrange cooked fish and vegetables on plate.

3. Serve with a bowl of onion sauce and garlic chips.

Serves 1

215

TERIYAKI CHICKEN WITH KINPIRA VEGETABLES (WAKADORI TERIYAKI, KINPIRA)

Ingredients

4 chicken Maryland fillets

1 cup teriyaki sauce (see page 233)

4 green asparagus spears, cut into quarters

4 white asparagus spears, cut into quarters

4 baby carrots, cut into quarters lengthwise

4 baby corn cobs, cut into quarters lengthwise

1 tablespoon sugar

1 tablespoon light soy sauce

2 teaspoons sesame oil

2 teaspoons white sesame seeds

Method

1. Place chicken under a hot grill and cook for 2 minutes on each side. Heat teriyaki sauce in a large skillet. Place chicken into pan and cook for a further 2 minutes on each side. Slice each chicken fillet into $\frac{1}{2}$ inch strips. Arrange carefully onto warmed serving plate.

2. Combine vegetables with sugar, light soy sauce and sesame oil. Stir-fry over high heat for 1–2 minutes.

3. Arrange vegetables beside the chicken, sprinkle with sesame seeds and serve.

Serves 4

ABALONE AND MUSHROOM BAKED IN SALT PASTRY (AWABI SHIOGAMAYAKI)

Ingredients

14 oz abalone

4 inches square sheet konbu, soaked in water
    until soft

2 oyster mushrooms

1 shiitake mushroom

½ oz enoki mushrooms

1 large decoratively sliced white radish

1 slice carrot

pinch yuzu peel

ponzu sauce for serving

Salt pastry

½ cup parsley

1 egg white

1 oz water

4 oz all-purpose flour

1 oz rock salt

Method

1. To make pastry, place parsley, egg white and
   water into food processor and process for
   1 minute. Sieve flour into a bowl and add
   parsley mixture. Knead together until
   smooth. Add rock salt and knead lightly for
   1–2 minutes. Cover and allow to rest.

2. Remove abalone from shell and clean. Wash
   out shell. Place konbu sheet into the abalone
   shell and top with the abalone meat.

3. Arrange mushrooms, white radish, carrot
   and yuzu peel over abalone.

4. Roll out pastry to a ⅓ inch thickness and
   place over abalone shell, sealing top and any
   holes in shell.

5. Bake at 450°F for 20 minutes.

6. Serve with ponzu sauce.

Serves 1

DEEP-FRIED GARFISH WRAPPED IN NORI (SAYORI EBI ISOBE-AGE)

(opposite)

Ingredients

1 garfish
1 shrimp, peeled and deveined
$\frac{1}{2}$ sheet nori seaweed
arrowroot
$\frac{1}{2}$ oz mixed seaweed

Ume sauce

1 teaspoon Japanese plum sauce
1 teaspoon *suiji* (see page 233)
wasabi

To garnish

steamed sugar snap peas, cherry tomatoes
   (halved), lemon wedge

Method

1. To make *ume* sauce, combine ingredients and set aside.

2. Carefully open out the underside of the garfish. With skin-side down, press the opening out flat with the palm of your hand. Gently remove the backbone, with tail still attached.

3. Straighten the shrimp by making shallow cuts along the underside and pushing backwards.

4. Place the garfish flesh, skin side down, on a board. Place the shrimp on top and wrap the fish around the shrimp. Place the fish on one edge of the nori and roll up.

5. Dust the nori parcel with arrowroot and deep-fry at 325°F for two minutes. Dust the fish spine with arrowroot and deep fry until golden.

6. Place mixed seaweed on a serving plate. Cut nori parcel in half diagonally and arrange over seaweed. Arrange fried fish spine decoratively on plate. Garnish with steamed sugar snap peas, cherry tomatoes and a lemon wedge. Spoon or pipe *ume* sauce over sugar snap peas and serve.

Serves 1

GRILLED SESAME CHICKEN WITH GINGER

Ingredients

1 pound skinless chicken breast or thigh fillets, or tenderloin, trimmed of visible fat

Soy and honey marinade

1 tablespoon sesame seeds, toasted
1 tablespoon mirin or sherry
2 teaspoons honey or plum sauce
2 teaspoons reduced-salt soy sauce
1 teaspoon oyster sauce
1 teaspoon sesame oil

Ginger rice

1 tablespoon fresh ginger, finely chopped
1 teaspoon sesame oil
8 oz short or medium grain rice, rinsed and drained
$1\frac{1}{2}$ cups ginger beer
1 tablespoon pickled or preserved ginger, diced
1 tablespoon green onion, finely chopped (optional)

Method

1. To make marinade, place sesame seeds, mirin, honey, soy and oyster sauces and sesame oil in a non-metallic bowl. Mix to combine.

2. Cut chicken into large pieces, add to marinade, stir to coat. Cover and marinate in the refrigerator for at least 1 hour.

3. For ginger rice, place fresh ginger and sesame oil in a large saucepan over a low heat. Cook, stirring occasionally, for 5 minutes. Add rice. Cook, stirring, for 2 minutes. Stir in ginger beer and pickled ginger. Bring to a boil. Reduce heat. Cover and steam for 10–15 minutes or until liquid is absorbed and rice is cooked. Stir in green onion.

4. Meanwhile, preheat grill or barbecue to medium heat. Drain chicken. Cook under grill or on barbecue, brushing occasionally with marinade, for 6–7 minutes or until cooked through and slightly crispy on the outside. The chicken is cooked when the juices run clear when pressed with a fork. Serve chicken with ginger rice and steamed Chinese greens.

Serves 4

deep-fried garfish

JAPANESE BEEF WITH WASABI CREAM

Ingredients

4 rump steaks, 6 oz each, trimmed of fat

4 tablespoons teriyaki sauce (see page 233) or
   soy sauce

4 tablespoons olive oil

6 tablespoons crème fraîche

4 teaspoons wasabi

2 teaspoons peanut oil

7 scallions, finely sliced, plus 1 scallion, shredded

2 cloves garlic, chopped

¼ teaspoon dried crushed chilies

Method

1. Place steaks in a non-metallic dish. Pour over teriyaki sauce and olive oil and turn steaks to coat. Cover and marinate for 1–2 hours in the fridge. Mix crème fraîche and wasabi in a small bowl, then cover and refrigerate.

2. Heat a ridged cast-iron grill pan over medium to high heat. Wipe with the peanut oil, using a folded piece of paper towel. Alternatively, heat peanut oil in a heavy-based frying-pan. Place 2 steaks on the grill, reserving the marinade, then cook for 3 minutes on each side or until cooked to your liking. Remove and keep warm. Cook the remaining 2 steaks, then remove and keep warm.

3. Place sliced scallions, garlic, chilies and reserved marinade into a small saucepan and heat through. Spoon sauce over steaks and top with a dollop of wasabi cream and shredded scallion. Serve the rest of the wasabi cream separately.

Serves 4

DUCK BREAST FILLET TERIYAKI WITH JAPANESE MOUNTAIN PEPPER (KAMO TERIYAKI ARIMAZANSYO FUUMI)

Ingredients

3 cups *suiji* (see page 233)

1 medium-sized daikon, peeled and cut into quarters
   lengthwise

4 duck breast fillets

20 slices lotus root, deep-fried until golden

1/3 cup *japone* sauce (see page 233)

To serve

8 snow peas, steamed scallion, white parts only and roots
removed, grilled

Method

1. Place *suiji* into a medium saucepan and bring to a boil. Add daikon, reduce heat and allow to simmer for about 20 minutes or until tender.

2. Place duck fillets, skin-side down, in a medium hot skillet. Cook for 4–5 minutes on each side until medium rare. Cut each fillet into thin slices. Place a piece of cooked daikon on each serving plate and top with duck slices. Spoon *suiji* and *japone* sauce over duck and place fried lotus root slices on top.

3. Serve with snow peas and grilled scallion.

Serves 4

BRAISED OX TONGUE WITH MISO SAUCE AND RED WINE (GYUUTAN AKAWAINNI AMAMISOZOE)

Ingredients

1 whole ox tongue

1 tablespoon canola oil

1$\frac{1}{2}$ cups red wine

$\frac{1}{2}$ cup mirin

1 cup water

$\frac{1}{4}$ cup miso sauce for ox tongue (see below)

1 leek, shredded

white sesame seeds

parsley sprigs

Method

1. Peel skin from tongue. Heat oil in skillet and cook tongue until well browned all over.

2. Place tongue, red wine, mirin and water into pressure cooker. Seal and cook for 2$\frac{1}{2}$ hours.

3. Remove tongue from cooking liquid, cover and keep warm.

4. Bring cooking liquid to a boil until reduced for 10 minutes.

5. Slice tongue and arrange on serving plates.

6. Drizzle miso sauce over the sliced tongue. Garnish with shredded leek, white sesame seeds and parsley sprigs.

Serves 4

MISO SAUCE FOR OX TONGUE

Ingredients

1$\frac{1}{2}$ tablespoons mirin

1 teaspoon sake

2 oz sugar

1 oz dark miso

1 oz white miso

1 teaspoon sesame paste

1$\frac{1}{2}$ tablespoons sesame oil

Method

1. Combine mirin and sake in a saucepan, heat until boiling. Remove from heat, add sugar and stir until it has dissolved. Add dark miso, white miso and sesame paste to pan. Stir until glossy. Add sesame oil and stir thoroughly.

Makes 6 oz

(Use within 1 month)

GRILLED SALMON MARINATED IN SAIKYOU MISO WITH HERBS (SALMON SAIKYOU YAKI KOUSOU FUUMI)

Ingredients

½ cup saikyou miso

1½ teaspoons sliced garlic

2 tablespoons chopped mixed herbs such as rosemary, thyme, oregano

4 × 7 oz salmon cutlets, deboned

3 oz thin potato strips, deep-fried

1 sheet deep-fried salmon skin, cut into 4 strips

8 white asparagus spears, halved lengthwise

8 green asparagus spears, halved lengthwise

Method

1. Combine saikyou miso, garlic and mixed herbs in a large glass bowl. Place salmon in bowl. Spoon marinade over salmon. Refrigerate for 3 days, turning salmon daily.

2. Remove salmon from marinade and wipe dry with paper towel. Cook under a hot grill for 2–3 minutes each side, until deep golden in color.

3. Top salmon with fried potato strips and deep-fried salmon skin. Serve with cooked white and green asparagus.

Serves 4

desserts

Delightful
DELICACIES

Like other Asian countries, Japan does not make a big deal of dessert. A slice of seasonal fresh fruit served at the end of a meal is usually enough. Fruits that may be served include melons, persimmons, oranges, plums, apples, mangoes, strawberries and kiwi fruit.

Sweets are available, however, in specialty shops. Japanese sweets are known collectively as *wagashi*. The major ingredient is *anko*, a red adzuki bean paste which characterizes the pastries and is also combined with glutinous rice to form pounded rice cakes. Sweet red bean jelly, served in slices, is also popular. Sweeteners were, until early in the twentieth century, derived from distilled leaves, honey and millet jelly but sugar is now commonly used.

Sweets may be served during the traditional Japanese tea ceremony. This ceremony is performed in traditional teahouses or in private homes. Green tea is served in tiny cups, unsweetened. *Wagashi* accompany the tea.

Foreigners can enjoy the formal traditional etiquette of the tea ceremony after a day of high-tech touring. These days, the tea is instant-green, frothy, and bitter. The *wagashi* counteract the bitterness.

Our chef has prepared special dessert recipes to balance and complement your own beautifully presented Japanese meals.

PUMPKIN AND YUZU ICE CREAM (KABOCHA ANDO YUZU AISU)

Ingredients

14 oz milk

4 egg yolks, lightly beaten

4 oz sugar

1 tablespoon arrowroot

2 teaspoons Cointreau

14 oz pumpkin, steamed and mashed

1 tablespoon chopped yuzu peel

Method

1. Place milk, egg yolks, sugar and arrowroot into the top of a double boiler. Stir over boiling water until custard thickens and coats the back of a wooden spoon. Remove from heat and allow to cool.

2. Stir in Cointreau, mashed pumpkin and yuzu peel.

3. Place ingredients into an ice cream maker and churn until frozen.

Serves 4

PURPLE CONGO ICE CREAM (MURASAKI IMO AISU)

Ingredients

14 oz milk

4 eggs yolks, lightly beaten

4 oz sugar

1 tablespoon arrowroot

1 tablespoon Malibu

4 oz purple congo potato, steamed and mashed

10 oz sweet potato, steamed and mashed

Method

1. Place milk, egg yolks, sugar and arrowroot into the top of a double boiler. Stir over boiling water until custard thickens and coats the back of a wooden spoon. Remove from heat and allow to cool.

2. Stir in Malibu, purple congo potato and sweet potato.

3. Place ingredients into an ice cream maker and churn until frozen.

Serves 4

BLACK SESAME ICE CREAM (KUROGOMA AISU)

Ingredients

14 oz milk

7 oz cream

4 eggs yolks

3 oz sugar

$\frac{1}{2}$ cup kuronerigoma (black sesame paste)

Method

1. Place milk, cream, egg yolks and sugar into the top of a double boiler. Stir over boiling water until custard thickens and coats the back of a wooden spoon. Remove from heat and allow to cool.

2. Stir in black sesame paste.

3. Place ingredients into an ice cream maker and churn until frozen.

Serves 4

SKEWERED SWEET DUMPLINGS (KUSHI DANGO MITARASHI)

Ingredients

1 cup rice flour

$\frac{3}{4}$ cup warm water

1 cup water

$\frac{1}{2}$ cup sugar

2 tablespoons soy sauce

$1\frac{1}{2}$ tablespoons potato starch or cornstarch

$1\frac{1}{2}$ tablespoons water

bamboo skewers

Method

1. To make the dough, place rice flour in a bowl and add the warm water.

2. Knead the dough well, and then roll pieces to make small round dumplings.

3. Place the dumplings in a steamer and steam them on high heat for 10 minutes.

4. Cool the dumplings and skewer them onto bamboo skewers (3–4 dumplings per stick).

5. Mix water, sugar, and soy sauce in a pan over medium heat. Mix the water and potato starch in a cup and set aside. When the sauce boils, add the starch mixture and stir quickly.

6. Slightly grill the skewered dumplings and brush the sauce over them.

Serves 4

GREEN TEA TIRAMISU FLAVORED WITH SAMBUCA (MACHA SAMBUCA TIRAMISU)

Ingredients

7 oz marscapone
$1\frac{1}{2}$ tablespoons Tia Maria
2 eggs
$1\frac{1}{2}$ tablespoons superfine sugar
$1\frac{1}{2}$ tablespoons green tea powder
2 tablespoons Sambuca
$1\frac{1}{2}$ tablespoons sugar
3 oz water
2 pieces sponge cake $8 \times 8 \times \frac{3}{4}$ inch thick

Method

1. Stir together marscapone and Tia Maria. Separate eggs and beat egg yolks and sugar until light and fluffy.

2. Beat egg whites until soft peaks form. Gently fold in marscapone mixture and beaten egg yolks.

3. Place green tea, Sambuca, sugar and water in a small saucepan and stir over medium heat until sugar has dissolved.

4. Place a layer of sponge cake on the base of a 8×8 inch square dish. Pour over half of the green tea syrup, then spread with half the marscapone mixture. Top with the remaining sponge, the syrup and the marscapone mixture. Refrigerate for 4 hours or overnight.

5. Carefully cut into 8 triangles. Serve with a sprinkle of green tea powder and some fresh berries.

Serves 4

YUZU AND GREEN TEA BRULEE

Ingredients

4 egg yolks

7 oz thickened cream

6 oz milk

$\frac{1}{3}$ cup superfine sugar

1 tablespoon green tea powder

2 teaspoons Sambuca

$\frac{1}{2}$ teaspoon yuzu peel

2 teaspoons Cointreau

Equipment

8 one-cup-sized ramekins, greased

Method

1. Combine egg yolks, cream, milk and sugar. Mix until smooth. Divide mixture into two equal halves.

2. Into one half, add green tea powder and Sambuca and stir through. To the other half, add yuzu peel and Cointreau and mix well.

3. Pour the Sambuca mixture into 4 of the ramekins. Pour the Cointreau mixture into the other 4 ramekins. Place the 8 ramekins into a bain marie filled with warm water to about $1\frac{1}{4}$ inch deep.

4. Bake at 350°F for 20 minutes.

5. Remove ramekins from bain marie and allow to cool. Refrigerate for at least 2 hours. Carefully turn out one of each brulée onto each serving plate.

6. Sprinkle 1 teaspoon of sugar over each brulée. Place under a hot grill for 2–3 minutes until sugar has caramelized.

Serves 4

BLACK SESAME BLANCMANGE (KURO GOMO BLANCMANGE)
(opposite)

Ingredients
7 oz milk

$3/4$ cup heavy cream

$2^1/2$ tablespoons sugar

1 tablespoon gelatin powder

3 teaspoons Amaretto

2 tablespoons black sesame paste
(kuronerigoma)

2 tablespoons white sesame paste
(shironerigoma)

4 tablespoons *kuromitsu* sauce

Caramelized filo

1 sheet filo pastry

sugar

white sesame seeds

Method
1. To make caramelised filo, place filo pastry on a greased oven tray, lightly sprinkle with sugar and place under a hot grill until sugar caramelizes. Remove from heat and immediately sprinkle with white sesame seeds. Allow to cool then break into pieces and set aside.

2. Place milk, cream and sugar in a saucepan. Heat gently until sugar has dissolved. Remove from heat. Carefully sprinkle gelatin over and stir until dissolved. Stir in Amaretto.

3. Divide mixture into three equal parts. Stir black sesame paste into one third. Mix white sesame paste into another third and leave the last third plain.

4. Pour the black sesame blancmange into the base of four cold dessert glasses. Carefully pour the white sesame blancmange over this. Finally top with the plain blancmange. Refrigerate 1–2 hours until set.

5. Top each blancmange with 1 tablespoon *kuromitsu* sauce and some broken caramelized filo. Serve with some mixed berries.

Serves 4

MASHED SWEET POTATO WITH CHESTNUTS (KURI-KINTON)

Ingredients
2 large yam or Japanese sweet potatoes
(*satsuma-imo*)

$1/2$ cup sugar

1 tablespoon mirin

8 oz jar of sweetened chestnuts

Method
1. Peel yams or sweet potatoes and cut into small cubes.

2. Soak yam cubes in water for a couple of hours. Rinse the yam cubes well.

3. Place water in a deep pan and bring to a boil.

4. Add yam cubes to the pan and cook until softened.

5. Drain the water and place the yam cubes back in the pan.

6. Mash the yam cubes and add sugar and mirin.

7. Stir the yams over low heat until heated through.

8. Fold in the chestnuts. Cool before serving.

Note: This is a special dish for *Osechi* (see page 165).

Serves 4

D ESSERTS

DEEP-FRIED BANANA WRAPPED IN FILO (BANANA TSUTSUMI AGE)

Ingredients

4 sheets filo pastry
4 bananas, peeled
$1/2$ cup red bean paste (*ogura*)
2 teaspoons *yuzu* peel
confectioner's sugar
4 tablespoons *kuromitsu* sauce

Method

1. Lay 1 sheet of filo pastry on a board. Place a whole banana near one corner. Spoon 2 tablespoons red bean paste and $1/2$ teaspoon *yuzu* peel beside the banana. Roll up pastry to fully enclose banana like a parcel.

2. Heat oil to 350°F and deep-fry banana parcel for 3–4 minutes until golden.

3. Repeat with remaining ingredients.

4. Cut banana parcels in half diagonally, dust with confectioner's sugar and serve each with 1 tablespoon *kuromitsu* sauce.

Serves 4

TOFFEED SWEET POTATOES (DAIGAKU IMO)

Ingredients

2–3 sweet potatoes (1 pound)
5 oz demerara sugar
2 teaspoons black or white sesame seeds

Method

1. Cut sweet potatoes across, slightly on the diagonal, into $1/2$ inch thick oval slices. If the potatoes are large, cut in half lengthwise and then into half-moon slices. (Do not peel.) Place in a deep saucepan with water to cover and cook over moderate heat for 10 minutes, or until just soft, but still firm. Drain.

2. Heat a large saucepan or wok and add sugar and 4 oz water. Heat gently until sugar dissolves, then bring to a boil and boil over moderate heat for 7–8 minutes, or until a light brown caramel syrup is formed. Remove from heat.

3. Add cooked sweet potato slices to caramel syrup and lightly toss and coat. Sprinkle with the sesame seeds. Remove sweet potato slices, one by one, and lay on a buttered baking sheet or greaseproof paper. Allow the caramel coating to harden before serving.

Serves 4

TERIYAKI SAUCE

Ingredients

14 oz mirin

12 oz soy sauce

4 oz sake

3 oz sugar

Method

1. Combine all ingredients in a saucepan. Heat until sugar has dissolved. Remove from heat and allow to cool.

Makes 4 cups

(Use within 1 month)

JAPONE SAUCE

Ingredients

2 oz mirin

1 oz sake

2 oz soy sauce

2 teaspoons miso

1 tablespoon sugar

$\frac{1}{2}$ teaspoon sansho

Method

1. Combine mirin and sake in a saucepan and heat until boiling. Add all remaining ingredients and stir until sugar has dissolved. Remove from heat.

Makes 1 cup

(Use within 1 month)

ONION SAUCE

Ingredients

4 oz mirin

1 oz sake

2 onions, chopped

4 oz soy sauce

$\frac{1}{2}$ teaspoon chopped garlic

1 oz canola oil

Method

1. Heat mirin and sake in a small saucepan until boiling. Remove from heat. Place all ingredients, including mirin and sake, into a food processor and process until smooth.

Make 2 cups

(Use within 1 month)

MISO SAUCE FOR OX TONGUE

Ingredients

$1\frac{1}{2}$ tablespoons mirin

1 teaspoon sake

2 oz sugar

1 oz dark miso

1 oz white miso

1 teaspoon sesame paste

$1\frac{1}{2}$ tablespoons sesame oil

Method

1. Combine mirin and sake in a saucepan, heat until boiling. Remove from heat, add sugar and stir until it has dissolved. Add dark miso, white miso and sesame paste to pan. Stir until glossy. Add sesame oil and stir thoroughly.

Makes 6 oz

(Use within 1 month)

TEMPURA BATTER

Ingredients

1 egg yolk, lightly beaten

1 cup iced water

7 oz all-purpose flour

4 ice cubes

Method

1. Mix together egg yolk, water and ice cubes. Sieve flour into a bowl and add egg mixture. Mix roughly with chopsticks or a fork. Do not over mix; mixture should be lumpy. Use immediately while batter is still cold.

Makes $1\frac{1}{2}$ cups

TEMPURA SAUCE

Ingredients

7 oz fish bouillon

$1\frac{1}{2}$ oz soy sauce

$1\frac{1}{2}$ oz mirin

Method

1. Mix all ingredients together in a saucepan. Bring to a boil and immediately remove from heat. Allow to cool.

Makes 1 cup

(Use within 1 day)

SALMON MARINADE

Ingredients

4 cups water

1 orange, cut into $\frac{1}{3}$ inch thick slices

1 lemon, cut into $\frac{1}{3}$ inch thick slices

8 oz salt

1 oz sugar

3 bay leaves

1 teaspoon five spice powder

12 fresh mint leaves

Method

1. Combine water, orange slices, lemon slices, salt and sugar in a saucepan. Stir over medium heat until salt and sugar has dissolved. Remove from heat and allow to cool. Add remaining ingredients.

Makes 6 cups

UDONJI

Ingredients

6 cups fish bouillon

$1\frac{1}{2}$ tablespoons light soy sauce

$1\frac{1}{2}$ tablespoons mirin

sugar to taste

salt to taste

Method

1. Combine all ingredients in a saucepan and heat until boiling. Remove from heat.

Makes 6 cups

(Use within 1 day)

SUIJI

Ingredients

2 cups fish bouillon

2 teaspoons sake

1 teaspoon light soy sauce

salt to taste

Method

1. Combine all ingredients in a saucepan and bring to a boil. Remove from heat.

Makes 2 cups

(Use within 1 day)

SAUCES & BASES

WHITE MISO SAUCE, YUZUMISO, SHUNGIKO MISO, TORIMISO

Ingredients

2 teaspoons mirin

1 tablespoon sake

$2\frac{1}{2}$ oz sugar

4 oz saikyou miso

Method

1. Combine mirin and sake in a saucepan and heat until boiling. Reduce heat, add sugar and stir until it has dissolved. Add miso and stir until glossy. Remove from heat.

Variations: Divide the above sauce into 4 equal parts.

Add $\frac{1}{2}$ teaspoon chopped *yuzu* peel to make *yuzumiso*.

Add 1 tablespoon grated *shungiku* to make *shungiko miso*.

Add 2 tablespoons cooked minced chicken and $\frac{1}{2}$ egg yolk to make *torimiso*.

Use remaining mixture unflavored.

BLACK MISO SAUCE, WALNUT MISO SAUCE

Ingredients

1 tablespoon mirin

1 tablespoon sake

3 oz sugar

4 oz dark miso (hacchou)

Method

1. Combine mirin and sake in a saucepan, heat until boiling. Reduce heat, add sugar and stir until it has dissolved. Add miso and stir until glossy. Remove from heat.

Variation: Divide mixture in half.

Add 2 tablespoons chopped walnuts to make walnut miso.

Use remaining mixture unflavored.

SUSHI RICE (SU-MESHI)

Ingredients

$\frac{1}{4}$ cup rice vinegar (Mitsukan 'shiragiku')

3 oz superfine sugar

$\frac{1}{2}$ teaspoon salt

5 x 2 inch kelp sheet (konbu)

2 pounds sushi rice (*koshihikari*)

4 cups water

Method

1. Combine rice vinegar, sugar and salt in a small saucepan. Heat until sugar and salt have dissolved (do not boil). Pour into a bowl and add kelp. Allow to soak for 1–2 days. Remove kelp.

2. Place rice in a sieve. Wash rice under running water, until it becomes clear. Allow to drain well.

3. Place rice and water into a large saucepan, cover and bring to a boil. Reduce the heat and simmer covered for 12 minutes. Remove from heat and leave for 10 minutes for the rice to absorb all of the water.

4. Transfer the hot rice into a large flat dish or tub. Pour the sushi vinegar syrup over the rice.

5. Turn the rice over and over with a spatula. This helps to create glossy rice. Do not squash the rice or overmix it. Cover the bowl with a wet tea-towel and leave to cool.

Makes 8 cups

SUSHI VINEGAR

Ingredients

$\frac{1}{4}$ cup rice vinegar

3 oz superfine sugar

$\frac{1}{2}$ teaspoon salt

5 x 2 inch kelp sheet (konbu)

Method

1. Combine rice vinegar, sugar and salt in a small saucepan. Heat until sugar and salt have dissolved (do not boil). Pour into a bowl and add kelp. Allow to soak for 1–2 days. Remove kelp.

Makes $\frac{1}{2}$ cup

TOSAZU SAUCE

Ingredients

$2\frac{1}{2}$ tablespoons rice vinegar

1 tablespoon light soy sauce

1 tablespoon mirin

Method

1. Combine all ingredients in a saucepan. Bring to a boil, then remove from heat.

Makes $\frac{1}{3}$ cup

(Use within 1 year)

JAPANESE CUSTARD MIX

Ingredients

1 egg, lightly beaten

7 oz fish bouillon

1 tablespoon mirin

2 teaspoons light soy sauce

1 teaspoon salt

Method

1. Place all ingredients into a bowl or large jug. Whisk lightly, then strain.

Makes 9 oz

INDIAN
food

the land
AND ITS
PEOPLE

Status	Federal Republic
Area	1, 269, 345 sq mile
Population	about 1 billion
Language	Hindi, English, Urdu
Religion	Hindu, Buddhist, Muslim, Christian, Sikh, Jain
Currency	Rupee
National Day	26 January

WISH UPON A MOON

The Maharani of Bobbili from southern India, on holiday in her country's north, was resplendent in a superb silk sari. She had once represented India as an opponent of Australian tennis champion, Evonne Goolagong. Garlanded with cheap baubles bought from floating vendors who had also sold us flowers and sweetmeats from their gondola-like *shikaras*, we sat on an outdoor deck of our houseboat. We were moored in darkness, facing Lake Nagin, replete after a splendid, robust Kashmiri lamb dinner. We were not far from Srinigar, Kashmir's state capital, which is set on Lake Dal, and is the gateway to the fabled Vale of Kashmir, the Venice of the East.

A full moon soared above us, illuminating the snow on the high, white peaks of the Himalayas ahead. The peaks were like iridescent ice creams topping dark, tall, menacing, mysterious cones. The moon's beam crept steadily towards us across the calm lake, which was reflecting the snow-capped mountains. The Maharani whispered : 'As the full moon's light across the water strikes you, make a wish to return to India – and you will.'

My wish came unexpectedly true years later. I revisited many parts of India and Kashmir. I ate, north-Indian-style, on the floors of the homes of the people who had welcomed me on my previous visits to Northern India. I spent a day exploring Srinigar's canals where the *shikara* man prepared me a Moghul-style lunch on a brazier in his little boat.

The food of Jammu and Kashmir is similar to that of its neighboring state, Himachal Pradesh. Kulu is the nation's honeymoon capital. Here, the snows of the lower Himalayas entice newly married couples to frolic in their silken wedding finery, oblivious to cold temperatures, until they shelter around fires in makeshift wooden huts, eating hot freshly cooked snacks with chai (tea).

The Indian sub-continent is the world's seventh largest country. Imagine a nation almost as wide as Australia or the USA. India is a federal republic with a population of more than one billion people: the world's second largest population after China. It is surrounded by Pakistan, Afghanistan, China, Tibet, Nepal, Bhutan, Bangladesh and Burma (Myanmar). West lies the Arabian Sea. South lies the Indian Ocean containing the independent island of Sri Lanka (formerly Ceylon), which shares some of southern India's food traditions. East lies the Bay of Bengal.

Including the national capital territory of Delhi and its capital New Delhi, India has six union territories and 25 states, which are more diverse than the countries of Europe. The idyllic Andaman and Nicobar groups of more than 500 islands that are also controlled by

India, feature tropical rainforests, hundreds of bird species and beaches lapped by waters that scuba divers dream about.

India is a kaleidoscope of civilizations, architecture, music, dance, literature, fairs, festivals and religions, not to mention its huge variety of cuisines. The contrasts of India inspire awe in visitors to the sub-continent. India's scenery is dramatic: the dominant Himalayas descend into desert alongside rolling plains, tropical forests and beaches washed by three seas.

The wildlife of India will stir the imagination of any reader who, as a child, was captivated by pictures of tigers, panthers, elephants and monkeys. India reveres its past—reflected in its sculptures, palaces, temples, tombs, mosques, cathedrals and memorials, and that monument to love, the Taj Mahal.

A SOUL TO BE GLIMPSED

Travelers to India can still travel through seven cities on a royal vintage train, built more than 90 years ago for princely rulers and British viceroys, and eat as royally as they did. It's possible to stay at a former British Hill station or a former Maharajah's palace. Travelers can take a stroll on a golden beach at Goa or dine in a resort restaurant that could have been plucked from a Portuguese village. Goan food was strongly influenced by the Portuguese occupation from 1510–1961.

On my own travels, I have stalked tigers in Corbett National Park and ridden elephants in Rajasthan. In a dusty village of Untouchables where the caste system still unofficially exists, I joined the local women in the dust, grinding spices with a mortar and pestle. Although we did not share a common language, these women shared their modest meal of dal and rice with me. The fiery food, our laughter and my gestures of appreciation were our bonds.

India

The land and
ITS PEOPLE

In New Delhi, a party was given for me by travel agents and their wives in an affluent household. Women finished the preparation of the seemingly endless dishes, while the men drank local Indian beer and talked of politics and their nation. The children were fed first, and slept while the adults conversed. I tasted everything, it seemed, that India had to offer. The food was hot, cold, savory, sweet, sour, fresh and exciting. As a foreign guest, I was not permitted to help in the crowded kitchen.

At dawn, pilgrims, residents and gurus bathed in the mighty Ganges (also known as the Ganga or Mother of India), meditated, threw marigold garlands into the water, prepared funeral pyres and lit breakfast fires to heat their dal and rice. The city of New Delhi, as old as Babylon, blinked in the reflections.

Hundreds of tributaries flow from the Himalayas into the Ganga. Other major Indian rivers are the Indus, which sustains India's wheat bowl, and the Punjab. East lies the river Brahmaputra. Water for crops is dependent on the monsoon season, as well as on these rivers.

Since ancient times, India has attracted people in search of something: often peace and religious enlightenment, but sometimes war. Greece's Alexander the Great invaded India in 327 BC and down the centuries, clans, empires, states, religious groups, sultanates and conquerors have all battled on Indian soil. In 1509, Goa was seized and made Portugal's maritime capital, and from 1616, as the English influence rose, Portugal's power was waning, the English through the East India Company. The English took control of other princely states and their spices. Colonizing French traders were also lured to India by its spices.

Persians, Islamic Moghuls, Romans, Jews, Christians (according to legend, St. Thomas the Apostle had been to Kerala in AD 52), Portuguese and British have all had their impact on India; their influences remain to intrigue tourists.

Visitors are often surprised that 21st century India is also modern, with world-standard facilities, more than America's share of millionaires, and with information technology second only to the USA. India's film industry, based in Mumbai (formerly known as Bombay), is the world's largest. But affluence is also sadly offset by appalling poverty.

Indian people practice more religions than any nation on earth and many eating habits are a result of individual beliefs. Over 820 million people practice Hinduism, which is a lifestyle as well as a series of beliefs. Hindus do not eat beef because the cow is sacred to them. Buddhism was born in India, but has spread so widely that every fourth human being on earth adheres to Buddhist principles. These include vegetarianism, avoiding harm to any living thing and abstinence from alcohol. Jainism arose as a reaction to personal excesses by early Hindu priests. It does not embrace a single god, but believes in the symbiosis of all living things. Almost a bridge between Hinduism and Islam, Sikhism emerged in the 15th century. Male devotees do not cut their hair and can be recognized by their turbans. In the 7th century, Zoroastrianism came to India from Persia and is practiced by people known as Parsis, most of whom live in Mumbai. Parsis have their own vibrant food culture, a blend of Persian and Indian cuisine. Judaism came to India after the fall of Jerusalem in 587 BC. Most Indian Jews later emigrated to Israel. Although legend describes the arrival of St. Thomas, it is St. Bartholomew who is credited with being the first Christian missionary. St. Francis Xavier came to Goa in 1542; thousands of Catholic pilgrims visit the Basilica of the Born Jesus on December 3 to view his casket. The pilgrims eat Portuguese-influenced food in celebration of his life. Protestant German, Danish and Dutch missionaries followed the Portuguese. The Christian religion was protected over two centuries under the British Raj. Arab traders brought Islam to India in the 7th century, and religious tolerance was particularly propounded by the great Moghul emperor Akbar.

In many thickly forested areas scattered around India, 70 million people belonging to 500 tribes, collectively known as Adivasis and believed to originate from the pre-Aryan era, still live by subsistence hunting as in ancient times. But they are being gradually pressured to adopt modern methods of cultivation.

About 300 million people live in cities and towns, but agriculture remains India's most important industry, with 60 percent of the land under cultivation. Basmati rice is grown in the Himalayan foothills, where delectable fruits, including apples and apricots, also thrive. Rice is also grown in the Punjab in the Northwest, but there wheat is the staple food. Breads such as naan, and tandoor (clay oven)-cooked food have come to west India from the Punjab. In the north, sheep and goats graze in cool, hilly conditions, while Bengali food in the east focuses on tropical produce, coconut, fish and mustard. Darjeeling tea, India's best-known tea, grows in the green Assam Hills.

On the Southwest coast, Kerala produces 95 percent of the republic's pepper and 60 percent of its cardamon, on hills where there are also forests and rubber, tea and coffee plantations. Rice is so important to the diet of southern Indians that it is celebrated early each year at the Pongal festival.

The state of Uttar Pradesh, in the East, yields more than half of India's sugarcane and grows more cereals than any other state. Sugarcane is also grown in the state of Maharashtra (whose capital is Mumbai), along with cotton, millet, barley and peanuts. Further south, tropical Goa's main products are fish and nuts such as cashews. Rice and fish are staples of lush southern India and are served heavy with spices.

A recent survey conducted by the Indian-based Oberoi Group of Luxury Hotels reveals that Indian food has replaced roast beef in popularity in England: chicken tikka masala is now the United Kingdom's favorite dine-out dinner. Curry houses have been in existence in Britain since the 1940s, and are now an established part of British cuisine. Some people believe that Indian food always means hot curries, but Indian cuisine may be hot, mildly cool, subtle or pungent and tempered by yogurt and/or coconut.

The word 'curry' is derived from *kari*, the word for a mixture of spices including cumin, coriander, turmeric, fennel, fenugreek, cloves, cinnamon and cardamon, and often garlic, with chili the dominant spice.

Commercial curry powder was created by the British; it would never be found in India. My mother thought she was daringly different in the 1960s when she threw a teaspoon of Clive of India curry powder into a stew and served it with rice. For me as a teenager, it was a crude, but exciting, introduction to a wonderful and enticing cuisine.

India

Daily food
IN INDIA

SPICE OF LIFE

'Find a sparrow. Spice it. Stuff it inside a quail and then the quail into a chicken and the chicken into a sand grouse. Stuff the lot inside a peacock. Put this into a goat. Then place the goat into a camel. Dig a hole in hot sand and throw in the stuffed camel after you've lit a fire and the coals are glowing. Cover with sand and after several hours, remove the lot'–this is how the royal families of India's Rajasthan once feasted in the 6th century.

India celebrates so many festivals, special religious celebrations and national days that they are too numerous to list here. Government of India tourism offices in your own countries will gladly inform you of festival dates (which alter annually) so that you can plan your visit to the subcontinent to coincide with them. Indians welcome foreigners to

share in their religious celebrations, which include the worship of cobras and elephants; of gods and goddesses; fireworks; singing; processions; music and dance; plays; fairs; and, always, festive food after fasting days have ended.

Some cookbook writers list four major cuisines of India. After several visits to India, I have identified seven. You will find a cross-section of recipes from the seven cuisines in this book.

North Indian: The hearty food of the north has Muslim and Moghul influences, resulting in a variety of savory, rich lamb and goat dishes based on cooking with ghee and cream. The cuisine is further enhanced by the tandoor method of cooking, which was indigenous to the northwest frontier, now the Punjab and Pakistan. The tandoor (clay oven), which burns

wood or charcoal, imparts an unparalleled smoky flavor to mildly spiced, tender meats, lake and river fish, poultry, meat and breads. Punjabi food is simple and filling, an amalgamation of the cuisines of the Greeks, Persians, Afghans, Moghuls and northern invaders. If you see a restaurant advertising 'frontier food', it is likely to include tandoor and Punjabi food, which is well worth experiencing before you create your own.

Maharashtrian: The people of the state of which Mumbai is the capital prepare healthy food with an emphasis on rice, vegetables (as Maharastrians people are vegetarians), nuts and nut oils. Often vegetables are spiced with a combination of ground and roasted cumin seeds, sesame seeds, cardamon, cinnamon and coconut. Sweet and sour dishes make for delicious eating.

Parsi: Like Christians, the Parsis have no religious dietary restrictions. Their cuisine is not overly hot and is a favourite with many foreigners. With their Persian heritage, the Parsis are into meat, fish and eggs. For a traditional Sunday meal, Parsis, most resident in Mumbai, serve several dals (lentil sauces), with meat, chicken and meat balls (deep-fried) and caramelized brown rice.

Gujurati: From Maharashtra's neighboring state of Gujurati comes an interesting vegetarian cuisine, called *thali*. The food is oil-free and *thali* restaurant waiters will refill your bowls until you are fully satisfied. *Thali* has become an institution in India's major cities (see next page for more detail). It is not all vegetarian, but is served with meat, fish or poultry, and rice. Gujuratis are fond of relishes and pickles.

Sindhi: The Sindhis migrated to India after the 1947 partition, bringing with them a new cuisine characterised by garlic, mint-flavored chutneys, pickles and very sweet meats. Sindhi food is not necessarily vegetarian. An example is *kofta tas-me*. These are meat balls swathed in a sauce of onion, tomato, chili, ginger, coriander and sprinkled with garam masala.

Bengali: Freshwater and saltwater fish, seafood and the flavor of mustard seed dominate the Bengali diet. Fish is grilled, fried or stewed. Yogurt is offered separately and is sometimes also used in preparation. Bengalis like lightly

fried fish in a sauce Westerners would regard as curry-flavored—yet it is relatively mild. Bengalis also love sweet dishes.

Goan: The Christian Portuguese had a great influence on the tropical state of Goa, as did the Muslims. The use by the Portuguese of vinegar and the sour fruit of lokum and tamarind, have combined with a Christian preference for pork and a non-vegetarian-Hindu taste for lamb. Seafood, fish and fruits are bountiful. Goans also perfected the vindaloo. Try the vindaloo recipe on page 294 and the milder cashew-nut butter chicken on page 289.

South Indian: In the south, one finds Brahmin cuisine, distinctive because strict South Indian Brahmins will not eat tomatoes and beetroot as they are blood-colored. Nor will they eat garlic or onion. Recipes are based on tamarind, chili, coconut, yellow lentils and rice. These, combined with a vegetable, make *sambar*, a staple dish eaten with *rasama*, a peppery, lentil-based consommé. These two dishes are the basis of English-inspired mulligatawny (see page 262). This staple dish is usually eaten twice daily. Steamed dumplings and pancakes made from fermented ground rice and dal have spread from Southern India throughout India. Meat and seafood are enjoyed by non-vegetarians. Some south Indian dishes can be exceedingly hot to Western palates.

DAY BEGINS IN DARKNESS
Before dawn, millions of Indians rise to prepare breakfast. Many rush to feed the family before sunrise because they have employment and may have to travel long distances to reach it. So from 3 am, braziers are alight in the streets. The smoke haze and the aromas of spicy dal sauces permeate the air. As the food cooks, the stallholders weave marigold garlands for festivals or sew by the light of the fire. Women are usually the cooks in India. While some women become doctors, company directors and politicians, as did one of the world's first woman prime ministers, Indira Gandhi, women usually still do the majority of household work in India. Marriages are still arranged and in some cases a wife will never have met her husband before the wedding.

INTRODUCTION

Among the poorer classes, girls often do not go to school, but clean the house and cook while their parents go to work in industry or to the fields. Children who do go to school usually eat curried dal for breakfast in the north, or snacks. In the South, children breakfast on *dosa* (curried lentils and rice), possibly with coconut, which is thinned and crisped on a flat griddle. The *dosa* may be stuffed with onions and potatoes and served on a banana leaf.

The best breakfast I ever enjoyed in India was of sautéed chicken livers with green masala curry paste (recipe page 247) and naan. This also makes a super brunch dish when combined with other dishes.

THALI TIME–LUNCH

Thali is a tremendous innovation. People in business or busy homes call from the street or telephone their local *thali*-man to bring them lunch. He comes on a bicycle with a cart or in a van and delivers a multi-course meal far superior to home-delivered pizza. Invented in Gujurat state and essentially vegetarian, the *thali* arrives in a metal can, like a small bucket, layered with plates of appetizers, and vegetable and rice dishes. In recent times, poultry, meat and fish have been added in response to clients' requests. *Thali* may also include a dessert or sweetmeats. The *thali*-man picks up his shiny pots and payment on the next visit.

You can create your own *thalis* for lunch or dinner from this book. *Thali* is also eaten as a multi-course meal in homes and restaurants in India. All the diner has to specify is vegetarian or non-vegetarian *thali*. Different dishes come every day with some bread, an Indian *paneer* (a light home-made cheese), pickles, chutney and yogurt. In a *thali* restaurant, china bowls are filled with food and placed on a metal tray. *Thali* is also served on banana leaves. No cutlery is presented as Indians traditionally eat every meal with their right hand. The left hand is unhygienic. After practice with your fingers, you will soon become adept. And, if you dine with a Muslim or a Jew, be careful about ordering pork. Pork dishes at the table may be upsetting for strict Jews and Muslims, so choose an alternative meat or vegetable dish.

EVENING DINING

A vegetarian dinner may include about five courses, including bread and/or rice. A meat-eater's meal might be made up of four courses, including a rice pudding. On a very special occasion, up to nine dishes could be served, including rice and bread, plus dessert, pudding, cake or fruit.

Alcohol is not generally drunk in India, especially in strict Buddhist and Muslim homes. Some Sikhs may request a bottle of spirits from a visitor if they have no license to buy or drink it. Indian wine does not have much of a reputation, but an imported rosé from Portugal or a similar region will certainly accompany a Goan meal well. Otherwise light beer, a fresh, dry white wine, lassi or mineral water is generally served at an Indian dinner party. Take flowers as gifts when visiting an Indian family.

Kerry Kenihan

basic recipes

Ingredients, spices and HERBS

INGREDIENTS

The magic of Indian cooking lies in the myriad of herbs and spices used. Every dish derives its unique taste from the different blending of herbs and spices.

There is a myth that Indian food is 'curry'—meat in a sloppy gravy—and is only good when it's hot and your mouth is crying for iced water! This concept of curry originated with the British, who ruled India for more than 200 years. The British invented a standard mixture of 'curry powder'—hot ground cayenne pepper, ground cinnamon, nutmeg, cloves, turmeric, ground cumin and ground coriander. However in India some of these spices are not used together. Indian cooks make their own mixtures of various spices for different dishes. The secret of any dish is the mixture (*masala*) of spices used and the length of the cooking time. Spices and herbs should never be overcooked or they will lose their flavor.

THE SPICES

Asafoetida: This is a hard block of resin which is used as an aid to digestion and to prevent flatulence. It is used mostly when cooking lentils and pulses. In India the block would be heated in a hot oven for 5 minutes and then ground to a fine powder in a mortar and pestle. In Western countries it can be purchased already ground. It is used in minute quantities.

Bay leaves (tej patha): This aromatic, but mellow-tasting leaf, is used in sauces and rice dishes (*pullaos*).

Black onion seeds (kalaunji): These have no connection with onions, but are so called because they resemble onion seeds. They are mainly used in rice dishes and with green, leafy vegetables in stir-fried dishes. Black onion seeds have a strong bitter-sweet flavor.

Black peppercorns (kali mirch): A pungent condiment that is used whole in chutneys. Ground black peppercorns are used mainly in yogurt and salad dishes.

Black salt (Kali namak): This is a hard block of sulphurous rock which is spicy and extremely pungent. It should not be tasted or used by itself! Use black salt only when mixed with other ground, dry spices in chutneys, sauces and toppings. It can be purchased as a piece of rock which you can grind, then keep in an airtight container.

Cardamon (elaichi): Cardamon provides a strong flavor that many Indian dishes require. It also helps digestion and is one of the spices used in *garam masala*.

Cayenne pepper (degi mirch): This is the ground powder of a red pepper originating from Kashmir. It is very hot and should be used in minute quantities in meat dishes and sweet chutneys. It can be used in place of peppers.

Chilies (mirch): These come in several varieties, but the following are four of the most commonly used:

Fresh red chilies: These come in a variety of shapes and sizes. As a general rule, the smaller, narrower and darker the chili, the greater its pungency.

Fresh green chilies: These are 2–4 inches long and are rich in vitamins. They give a distinctive hot taste to food and will keep in an airtight container for 7–10 days.

Ground chilies: Mainly used with fried vegetables as a topping.

Dried chilies: Used in spice bags for *pullaos* and pickles.

Cinnamon (dalchini): This has a sweet spicy flavor. It is used whole in *pullaos*, desserts and chutneys. Ground, it is one of the spices used in garam masala, and is used in meat and chicken dishes and some desserts.

Cloves (laung): These have a pungent taste and aroma. Ground cloves make up one of the main spices in *garam masala* and are also used in tiny amounts in some desserts. Whole cloves are used in rich Indian dishes and chutneys.

Coriander (dhania): The seeds are used whole to flavor lentils and in some vegetable dishes. Ground coriander has a distinctive taste. Don't get carried away and add too much to food or it will be overpowering.

Cumin (jeera): This spice is used both as whole seeds and ground. The whole black seeds have a sweet herbal taste and are used in northern and Moglai dishes and in *biriyanis*. The white or green seeds are used whole or ground. Cumin has a gentle flavor and is used in appetizers, snacks, batters and yogurts.

Fennel (saunf): Fennel seeds are similar to white cumin seeds and are used mainly in pickles, drinks and rice dishes. Fennel seeds are also used to aid digestion after eating. Ground fennel is used in meat, chicken and fish dishes and gives a tangy, almost minty bite.

Fenugreek (methi): The seeds, mainly used in lentil and some vegetable dishes, have a bitter taste. Ground fenugreek is used mainly in meat, chicken and fish dishes. Fenugreek leaves can be bought fresh or dried and are used as a flavoring for vegetables or as a herb. They have a bitter-sweet taste.

Garlic (lahsun): This is the root of a plant and is a very important ingredient in non-vegetarian dishes, some lentil dishes and chutneys.

Garam masala: The name means 'mixed spice' and it consists of cinnamon, cloves, cardamon, cumin, nutmeg, black peppercorns and coriander ground together. It can be bought ready-mixed in the spice section of most supermarkets or you can make your own (see next page). If you buy this spice pre-blended, keep in mind that there are both savory and sweet varieties (the sweet one being used in teas).

Ginger (adrak): Used both fresh and ground, ginger is the aromatic root of a tropical plant. Fresh ginger is a must in all Indian cooking. It has to be peeled before use. Ground ginger is used mainly as a topping with other dry spices for salads, fried vegetable and sweet dishes.

Mango powder (amchur): This is a brownish powder made from sun-dried green mangoes. It has a sour taste and imparts a unique flavor which is loved all over India.

Mustard seeds (rai): These come in three colors: black, brown and yellow. Black mustard seeds are used mainly in vegetarian sauces, to flavor yogurt and in vegetable dishes. Brown mustard seeds are more difficult to find but are used in chutneys and toppings. Yellow mustard seeds are used in lentil and vegetable dishes with a tomato base.

Nutmeg (jaiphal): This spice is used in small quantities to give a subtle flavor to meat and rice dishes. It is also used in sweets and puddings.

Paprika: This spice is used mainly as a topping for salads.

Poppy seeds (khus-khus): These are used as a thickening agent in desserts and give a special texture to food.

Saffron (kesar): This is the world's most expensive spice which comes from Kashmir or Spain. It has an aromatic flavor and is used to color desserts and rice dishes.

Sesame seeds (til): These are mainly used in chutneys, pickles and in some sweets.

Turmeric (haldi): Turmeric is an aromatic, pungent root. It is used ground in order to color and flavor meat and vegetable dishes. Take care when using turmeric as it can stain.

THE HERBS

Basil (tulsi): Indians revere the basil plant. Use the leaves for yogurt and rice dishes and in sauces. Basil has a sweet, sharp taste.

See below for ingredients, spices and herbs.

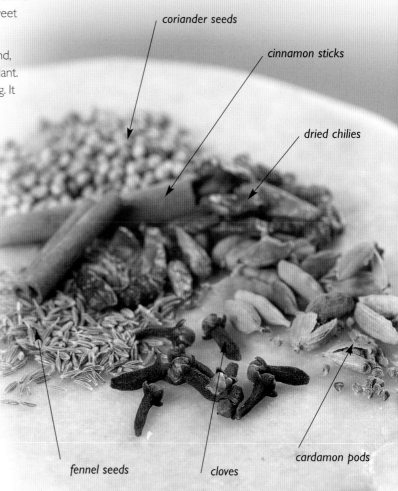

coriander seeds

cinnamon sticks

dried chilies

fennel seeds

cloves

cardamon pods

Chives: Used in salads and herbs in vegetable dishes with other herbs, chives have a mild onion flavor.

Cilantro (hara dhania): Indian cooks use only the leaves of fresh cilantro. When chopped, the leaves have an aromatic flavor and are used as a garnish, in chutneys and for sauces.

Dill (sowa): Used in vegetable dishes, salads and some rice dishes, dill has a clean, delicate flavor.

Mint (phudina): This herb is used in salads and chutneys, and is mixed with other herbs in vegetable dishes.

OTHER INGREDIENTS

Superfine sugar (cheeni): This is used in salads, as well as in some meat and vegetable dishes.

Coconut (nariyal): Used as flakes in lentil (dal) dishes or grated in salads and some vegetable dishes.

Ghee: Clarified butter. Sold in cans, packets or tubs.

Lemon juice (nimbu ras): Used in many recipes to give a tangy taste.

Mustard oil (rai-ka-tel): This is used in small quantities in pickles.

Palm sugar (gur): Used in chutneys and lentil (dal) dishes.

Sesame seed oil (til-ka-tel): Used in salads to give a nutty flavor.

Tamarind (imli): Available as pieces or as a concentrate, tamarind is used in lentil (dal) dishes and chutneys.

Spices, mixes
AND BLENDS

AADOO MIRCH SPICE MIX

Ingredients
2 oz fresh ginger root, grated
1 clove garlic, chopped
1 oz fresh chilies
$\frac{1}{2}$ teaspoon salt

Method
1. Grind ginger and garlic in a blender or food processor, or use a mortar and pestle. Remove stalks from chilies and add with salt. Purée to a smooth paste, scrape into a bowl and cover tightly. Will keep for 1 week in the refrigerator.

Makes about $2\frac{1}{2}$ oz

PANCH FORAN

Ingredients
2 tablespoons black onion seeds
2 tablespoons anise seeds
1 tablespoon black or white mustard seeds
2 tablespoons ground fenugreek

Method
1. Using a mortar and pestle, or a coffee grinder kept especially for the purpose, grind onion seeds, anise seeds and mustard seeds finely. Stir in fenugreek. Use as indicated in recipes.

Makes 6 tablespoons

TANDOORI SPICE MIX

Ingredients
1 small onion, chopped
3 cloves garlic, crushed
1 inch piece of fresh ginger root, peeled and finely chopped
1–2 green chilies, seeded and chopped
1 teaspoon coriander seeds
$\frac{1}{2}$ teaspoon cumin seeds
$\frac{1}{2}$ teaspoon red chili powder
1 teaspoon paprika
$\frac{1}{2}$ teaspoon salt

Method
1. Grind onion, garlic, ginger, chilies and seeds together, using a mortar and pestle, or a coffee grinder kept especially for the purpose. Add chili powder, paprika and salt and mix well.

Makes about 6 tablespoons

GARAM MASALA

Ingredients
2 teaspoons cardamon seeds
2 teaspoons cumin seeds
2 teaspoons coriander seeds
1 teaspoon black peppercorns
1 teaspoon whole cloves
1 cinnamon stick, broken
$\frac{1}{2}$ nutmeg, grated

Method

1. Heat a heavy-based frying pan over moderate heat. Add cardamon seeds, cumin seeds, coriander seeds, peppercorns, cloves and cinnamon stick. Cook, stirring, until evenly browned. Allow to cool.

2. Using a mortar and pestle, or a coffee grinder kept especially for the purpose, grind roasted spices to a fine powder. Add nutmeg and mix well.

Makes about 4 tablespoons

MASALA CURRY PASTE

Ingredients

3 tablespoons fresh ginger root, grated

1 teaspoon ground turmeric

1 teaspoon ground cloves

1 teaspoon ground cardamon

2 cloves garlic, crushed

6 tablespoons fresh cilantro, chopped

6 tablespoons fresh mint, chopped

$\frac{1}{2}$ cup cider vinegar

2 oz peanut oil

2 teaspoons sesame oil

Method

1. Place ginger, turmeric, cloves, cardamon, garlic, cilantro, mint and vinegar in a blender or food processor; process until well combined.

2. Heat oils in a frying pan. Add spice mixture. Cook, stirring, until mixture boils, then remove from heat and allow to cool.

Makes about 1 cup

MADRAS CURRY PASTE

Ingredients

6 tablespoons ground coriander

4 tablespoons ground cumin

1 tablespoon freshly ground black pepper

1 tablespoon ground turmeric

1 tablespoon black mustard seeds

1 tablespoon chili powder

4 cloves garlic, crushed

1 tablespoon fresh ginger, finely grated

$\frac{1}{2}$ cup vinegar

Method

1. Place coriander, cumin, black pepper, turmeric, mustard seeds, chili powder, garlic, ginger and vinegar in a food processor or blender and process to make a smooth paste. Heat oil in a frying pan over medium heat, add paste and cook, stirring constantly, for 5 minutes or until oil begins to separate from paste.

Makes about $\frac{3}{4}$ cup

GREEN MASALA CURRY PASTE

Ingredients

1 teaspoon fenugreek seeds, soaked in cold water overnight

3 cloves garlic, crushed

2 tablespoons fresh ginger root, grated

12 tablespoons fresh cilantro, chopped

12 tablespoons fresh mint, chopped

$\frac{1}{2}$ cup vinegar

1 teaspoon Thai fish sauce

2 teaspoons ground turmeric

1 teaspoon ground cardamon

$\frac{1}{4}$ cup sesame oil

$\frac{1}{2}$ cup vegetable oil

Method

1. Place soaked fenugreek seeds, garlic, ginger, cilantro, mint and vinegar in a food processor or blender and process to make a smooth paste. Add fish sauce, turmeric and cardamon and process to combine.

2. Heat sesame and vegetable oils together in a saucepan over medium heat for 5 minutes or until hot. Stir in paste and cook, stirring constantly, for 5 minutes, or until mixture boils and thickens.

Makes about $\frac{1}{2}$ cup

VINDALOO PASTE

Ingredients

1 tablespoon coriander seeds

1 teaspoon cumin seeds

1 teaspoon mustard seeds

1 teaspoon ground turmeric

1 teaspoon hot chili powder

$1\frac{1}{2}$ teaspoons ground ginger

pinch ground fenugreek

$1\frac{1}{2}$ teaspoons finely ground black pepper

1 tablespoon white wine vinegar, plus extra to serve

Method

1. Using a mortar and pestle, or a coffee grinder kept especially for the purpose, grind whole seeds finely. Add remaining ground spices.

2. Gradually stir in vinegar to make a thick smooth paste. Store in an airtight container and moisten with an additional teaspoon of vinegar just before use.

Makes about 4 tablespoons

Note: Leftover pastes may be stored in sterile airtight containers in the refrigerator for 8–10 days.

Sauces, chutneys and SAMBALS

SPICY TOMATO SAUCE

Ingredients

1 tablespoon oil

1 onion, chopped

1 clove garlic, crushed

2 tablespoons fresh ginger root, grated

1–2 red chilies, seeded and chopped

1 teaspoon ground turmeric

1 tablespoon ground coriander

$\frac{1}{2}$ teaspoon cayenne pepper

2 teaspoons paprika

2 x 14 oz cans chopped tomatoes

1 teaspoon each of sugar and salt

$1\frac{1}{2}$ inch slice creamed coconut

Method

1. Heat oil in a saucepan. Fry onion, garlic, ginger and chilies until onion is golden brown. Stir in remaining spices. Cook for 2 minutes, then add tomatoes, sugar and salt. Bring to a boil, lower the heat and simmer for 20 minutes. Stir in creamed coconut until dissolved; simmer for 20 minutes more. Serve hot, with rice, dal or naan.

Serves 4–6

RAITA

Ingredients

7 oz natural low-fat yogurt

salt and freshly ground black pepper, to taste

1 small onion, very finely chopped (optional)

2 tablespoons chopped fresh mint or cilantro

paprika for dusting

Method

1. In a bowl, beat yogurt with salt and pepper. Stir in onion (if using) and add mint or cilantro. Cover and chill for at least 30 minutes before serving, dusted with paprika.

Serves 4

SPINACH RAITA

Ingredients

1 bunch spinach

1 cup natural yogurt

pinch of salt

pinch of freshly ground black pepper

pinch of paprika

pinch of mango powder

2 small fresh red or green chilies, chopped

Method

1. Steam or microwave spinach until soft. Drain, squeezing to remove excess liquid. Place spinach in a food processor or blender and purée.

2. Place yogurt in a bowl and beat until smooth. Stir in salt, black pepper, paprika, mango powder, chilies and spinach and mix to combine.

Makes 1 cup

SPICED YOGURT

Ingredients

2 cups natural yogurt

$\frac{1}{2}$ teaspoon freshly ground fennel seeds

salt to taste

$\frac{1}{2}$ teaspoon sugar

4 tablespoons vegetable oil

1 dried red chili

$\frac{1}{4}$ teaspoon mustard seeds

$\frac{1}{4}$ teaspoon cumin seeds

4–6 curry leaves

pinch each of asafoetida and turmeric

Method

1. In a heatproof serving dish, mix together yogurt, fennel, salt and sugar and chill until nearly ready to serve.

2. Heat oil in a frying pan and fry chili, mustard and cumin seeds, curry leaves, asafoetida and turmeric. When chili turns dark, pour oil and spices over the yogurt. Fold yogurt mixture at the table before serving.

Serves 4

ROASTED RED BELL PEPPER RAITA

Ingredients

2 red bell peppers

2 teaspoons cumin seeds

7 oz tub Greek yogurt

2 tablespoons finely chopped fresh mint

salt and black pepper to taste

1 teaspoon paprika to garnish

Method

1. Preheat grill to high. Cut bell peppers lengthwise into quarters, then remove seeds, and grill them, skin-side-up, for 10 minutes or until blackened and blistered. Place in a plastic bag and leave to cool for 10 minutes.

2. Meanwhile, heat a wok and dry-fry cumin seeds over high heat for 30 seconds, stirring constantly, or until they start to pop. Remove skins from grilled bell peppers and discard, then roughly chop their flesh.

3. Mix bell peppers with yogurt, cumin seeds and mint and season with salt and pepper. Transfer to a serving dish and garnish with paprika.

Serves 4

BASIC RECIPES

CILANTRO AND MINT CHUTNEY

Ingredients
3 bunches fresh cilantro, leaves only

1 bunch fresh mint, leaves only

6–8 fresh green chilies

3 teaspoons fresh ginger, finely chopped

6 cloves garlic, finely chopped

2 tablespoons lemon juice

1 tablespoon superfine sugar

$\frac{1}{4}$ cup water

salt to taste

Method
1. Place cilantro leaves, mint leaves, chilies, ginger, garlic, lemon juice, sugar, water and salt in a food processor or blender and process to a paste.

2. Spoon chutney into a sterilized jar, cover and refrigerate until ready to use.

Makes 2 cups

FRUIT CHUTNEY

(opposite middle)

Ingredients
4 oz dried peaches, chopped

4 oz dried apricots, chopped

1 pound Granny Smith apples, cored, peeled and chopped

2 teaspoons fresh ginger, finely chopped

4 oz golden raisins

2 cups white vinegar

2 teaspoons salt

14 oz superfine sugar

5 cloves garlic, finely chopped

$\frac{3}{4}$ teaspoon cayenne pepper (optional)

Method
1. Place peaches, apricots, apples, ginger, golden raisins, vinegar, salt, sugar, garlic and cayenne pepper (if using) in a large heavy-based saucepan. Cover and cook over a low heat, stirring occasionally, for 1 $\frac{1}{2}$ hours or until mixture is soft and pulpy.

2. Spoon chutney into hot sterilized jars. When cold, cover and label. Store in the refrigerator.

Makes 6 cups

LIME PICKLE

Ingredients
20 small yellow limes

2 tablespoons salt

1 tablespoon hot chili powder

2 tablespoons sugar

1 tablespoon black peppercorns

Method
1. Wash limes and dry thoroughly on paper towels. Keeping each lime attached at the stalk end, cut into quarters so that can be opened up like a flower. Mix salt and chili powder together and stuff mixture into slits in limes.

2. Pack limes into a large clean jar, sprinkling sugar and peppercorns over each layer. Cover jar with muslin; mature in a sunny place for 10–15 days.

3. To serve, separate limes into wedges and arrange in a small dish.

Note: This is a very hot pickle, so treat it with caution.

Makes 8 cups

MINT AND TOMATO CHUTNEY

(opposite, bottom)

Ingredients
4 large tomatoes, diced

1 bunch fresh mint, leaves removed and coarsely chopped

$\frac{1}{2}$ cup brown sugar

1 cinnamon stick

2 bay leaves

1 teaspoon mixed spice

2 teaspoons fresh ginger root, finely chopped

2 fresh red or green chilies, chopped

$\frac{1}{4}$ cup white wine vinegar

Method
1. Place tomatoes, mint, sugar, cinnamon stick, bay leaves, mixed spice, ginger, chilies and vinegar in a heavy-based saucepan and cook over low heat, stirring every 5 minutes, for 45 minutes or until mixture reduces and thickens. Alternatively, place all ingredients in a large microwave-safe container, cover and cook on high (100%) for 15 minutes. Stir and cook on medium (70%) for 15 minutes longer.

2. Spoon chutney into a warm sterilized jar, cover and label when cold.

Makes 4 cups

MANGO CHUTNEY

(below, top)

Ingredients

8 oz raisins

28 oz canned mangoes, drained and cut into cubes, or 4 ripe mangoes, peeled and cut into cubes

1½ tablespoons fresh ginger, finely chopped

2 cloves garlic, finely chopped

3 teaspoons paprika

1 cinnamon stick

4 cloves

2 bay leaves

½ teaspoon mixed spice

3 tablespoons golden raisins

¼ cup cider vinegar

1–1½ cups brown sugar

Method

1. Place raisins in a small bowl, cover with warm water and set aside to soak for 30 minutes. Drain.

2. Place mangoes, ginger, garlic, paprika, cinnamon stick, cloves, bay leaves, mixed spice, golden raisins, vinegar, sugar and raisins in a large heavy-based saucepan. Cover and cook over low heat, stirring occasionally, for 1 hour or until chutney is thick.

3. Spoon chutney into a warm sterilized jar. Cover and label when cold. Store in refrigerator.

Makes 6 cups

RED CHILI CHUTNEY

Ingredients

10–12 fresh red chilies

10–12 cloves garlic

pinch of superfine sugar (optional)

salt to taste

water

Method

1. Place chilies, garlic, sugar (if using) and salt in a food processor or blender and process until chopped. With machine running, add enough water to form a paste. Store in refrigerator in an airtight container.

Makes 2 cups

SESAME SEED CHUTNEY

Ingredients

½ cup sesame seeds

1 bunch fresh cilantro, leaves only

1 bunch fresh mint, leaves only

5 fresh green chilies

¼ cup tamarind concentrate

6–7 tablespoons water

½ teaspoon salt

Method

1. Place sesame seeds in a cast-iron frying pan and dry-fry over low heat until dark brown in color. Place sesame seeds in a food processor or blender and process until ground. Add cilantro leaves, mint leaves, chilies, tamarind concentrate, water and salt, and process to make a smooth paste. Spoon chutney into a sterilized jar, cover and label. Store in the refrigerator.

Makes 2 cups

TOMATO AND ONION SAMBAL

Ingredients

3 large tomatoes

1 onion

3–4 scallions

2 sprigs fresh cilantro

3 tablespoons lemon or lime juice

salt and freshly ground black pepper to taste

Method

1. Chop tomatoes, onion, scallions and fresh cilantro finely. Place in a small bowl, pour over the citrus juice and add plenty of salt and pepper to taste. Toss well, cover and set aside for 1 hour at room temperature to allow the flavors to blend before serving.

Serves 6

BANANA SAMBAL

Ingredients

2 bananas

1 tablespoon lime juice

Method

1. Slice bananas into a small bowl. Add lemon juice and toss lightly. Serve immediately.

Serves 4

COCONUT SAMBAL

Ingredients

2 oz dried coconut

1 tablespoon onion, finely chopped

1 small red chili, seeded and chopped

1 tablespoon lime juice

Method

1. Mix coconut, onion and chili in a small bowl. Add lime juice, toss lightly and serve.

Serves 4

snacks & appetizers

Tasty tidbits, stunning STARTERS

Everywhere in India, you can smell and hear food sizzling, simmering and baking. Indians may be the world's greatest snackers. In restaurants and homes, snacks are eaten before lunch or dinner. Many people enjoy common starters like these for breakfast but, inevitably, most tidbits are eaten on the run or while relaxing by the sea or in a cinema.

Samosas, with or without meat, are India's most famous snack. These, along with bhajis, pakoras, fritters and more, are usually served with sambals, bland or spicy yogurt raita, chutneys and/or dal. See pages 248–252.

Dal is a national staple. It literally translates as 'split pea' but refers to all pulses. Dal can be eaten as an appetizer or, as our recipes show, served over rice or with bread to make a complete meal. It is the total daily sustenance for millions of Indians. Dried peas should be soaked overnight before cooking, but lentils and other pulses need less softening time. Our recipes make delicious entrées and ideal finger food for parties. Easy to prepare, these dishes are best served immediately after cooking.

VEGETABLE BHAJIS

Ingredients
10 shallots, finely chopped
2 zucchini, coarsely grated
1 eggplant, finely diced
vegetable oil for frying

Batter
4 oz chickpea flour
2 oz ground rice
¼ teaspoon baking soda
1 teaspoon chili powder
1 teaspoon turmeric
1–2 tablespoons curry powder (mild or hot according to taste)
1 teaspoon salt
1 cup water

Method
1. To make batter, put all ingredients into a bowl, then gradually add water, stirring constantly until combined. Add shallots, zucchini and eggplant to batter, mixing well.

2. Pour oil into a wok to a depth of 2 inches and heat over medium to high heat. Check oil is hot enough by dropping in a small piece of vegetable; it should sizzle. Gently place 4 balls of mixture (about 2 tablespoons each) into hot oil and fry for 2–3 minutes, until golden. Turn over and cook for a further 2–3 minutes until crisp.

3. Remove bhajis with a slotted spoon and drain on paper towels. Fry remaining bhajis in the same way.

Serves 4

INDIAN LENTIL SOUP
(DHAL SHORVA)

Ingredients

2 tablespoons ghee or vegetable oil

12 oz red lentils

1 teaspoon mustard seeds

1 teaspoon ground coriander

1 teaspoon ground cumin

1½ teaspoons turmeric

1 cinnamon stick

6 cloves garlic, minced

1 tablespoon fresh ginger root, minced

10 fresh curry leaves, bruised and tied together

1 large onion, finely chopped

1 large green chili, whole but split

8 cups rich vegetable bouillon

2 tomatoes, finely diced

1 small eggplant, finely diced

1 small carrot, finely diced

1 large potato, peeled and diced

juice of 4 lemons

salt to taste

1 bunch fresh cilantro

4 tablespoons yogurt

Method

1. In a large saucepan, heat ghee and add lentils, mustard seeds, coriander, cumin, turmeric, cinnamon stick, garlic, ginger, curry leaves, onion and green chili. Cook over low heat for 5 minutes until spices are aromatic and deep brown in color, and the onion has softened.

2. Add vegetable bouillon and simmer until lentils are soft; about 30–45 minutes.

3. Remove cinnamon stick, whole green chili and curry leaves.

4. Blend with a hand-held mixer or food processor until smooth, then return it to the saucepan.

5. Add diced vegetables and simmer for a further 20 minutes or until vegetables are soft.

6. Add lemon juice, salt and chopped cilantro. Stir well and serve with a dollop of yogurt garnished with a few extra cilantro leaves.

Serves 8

SPLIT LENTIL DAL WITH GINGER AND CILANTRO

Ingredients

7 oz dried split red lentils

3½ cups water

½ teaspoon turmeric

1 tablespoon vegetable oil

½ inch piece fresh ginger root, finely chopped

1 teaspoon cumin seeds

1 teaspoon ground coriander

salt and ground black pepper

4 tablespoons chopped fresh cilantro, plus extra leaves to garnish

½ teaspoon paprika to garnish

Method

1. Rinse lentils and drain well, then place in a large saucepan with water. Bring to a boil, skimming off any scum, then stir in turmeric. Reduce heat and partly cover pan. Simmer for 30–35 minutes, until thickened, stirring occasionally.

2. Heat oil in a small frying pan, then add ginger and cumin seeds and fry for 30 seconds or until cumin seeds start to pop. Stir in ground coriander and fry for 1 minute.

3. Season lentils with plenty of salt and pepper, then add toasted spices. Stir in chopped cilantro, mixing well. Transfer to a serving dish and garnish with paprika and cilantro.

Serves 4

CRUNCHY SPLIT PEAS

Ingredients

3 oz yellow split peas

3 oz green split peas

2 teaspoons baking soda

oil for deep-frying

$\frac{1}{2}$ teaspoon chili powder

$\frac{1}{2}$ teaspoon ground coriander

pinch of ground cinnamon

pinch of ground cloves

1 teaspoon salt

Method

1. Place split peas in a large bowl, cover with water, stir in baking soda and set aside to soak overnight.

2. Rinse split peas under cold running water and drain thoroughly. Set aside for at least 30 minutes, then spread out on paper towels to dry. Heat about 2 inches oil in a skillet and cook split peas in batches until golden. Using a slotted spoon, remove peas and drain on paper towels.

3. Transfer cooked peas to a dish, sprinkle with chili powder, coriander, cinnamon, cloves and salt and toss to coat. Allow peas to cool and store in an airtight container.

Serves 4

SAMOSAS

(opposite)

Ingredients

8 oz all-purpose flour

$\frac{1}{2}$ teaspoon salt

1 oz butter

4–6 tablespoons water

Filling

1 oz butter

1 onion, finely chopped

2 cloves garlic, crushed

2 green chilies, seeded and chopped

1 inch piece of fresh ginger root, grated

$\frac{1}{2}$ teaspoon ground turmeric

$\frac{1}{2}$ teaspoon hot chili powder

13 oz lean ground beef or lamb

1 teaspoon salt

2 teaspoon garam masala (pages 246–247)

juice of $\frac{1}{2}$ lemon

oil for deep-frying

Method

1. Sift flour and salt into a bowl. Rub in butter, then mix in enough water to form a pliable dough. Knead for 10 minutes, then set aside.

2. Make filling. Melt butter in a frying pan. Add onion, garlic, chilies and ginger and fry for 5–7 minutes until onion is golden.

3. Stir in turmeric and chili powder, then add meat and salt. Fry, stirring, until meat is cooked and mixture is fairly dry. Stir in garam masala and lemon juice; cook for 5 minutes more. Remove pan from heat and allow to cool.

4. Divide dough into 15 balls. Flatten each ball and roll out to a paper-thin circle about 4 inches in diameter. Dampen edges of each circle with water and shape into cones. Fill each cone with filling, then pinch opening to seal securely.

5. Deep-fry samosas in batches in hot oil for 2–3 minutes or until golden brown. Drain on paper towels and serve.

Makes 30

Filling variation

1. For a vegetarian samosa filling, fry 1 small chopped onion and 1 teaspoon grated fresh ginger root in 1 tablespoon ghee or vegetable oil until soft.

2. Stir in 13 oz cold mashed potato, 2 teaspoons garam masala and 1 tablespoon mango chutney (with any large chunks finely chopped). Cook over moderate heat until mixture is fairly dry, then cool.

TANDOORI SHRIMP

Ingredients

18 uncooked large shrimp, peeled and deveined, tails intact

12 scallions, trimmed and cut into $1\frac{1}{2}$ inches lengths

2 tablespoons cilantro, finely chopped

2 tablespoons Tandoori spice mix (page 246)

1 cup natural low fat yogurt

2 green bell peppers, seeded and cut into $1\frac{1}{2}$ inch squares

1 tablespoon oil

Method

1. Rinse shrimp and pat dry with paper towels. Place in a glass or china dish along with scallions.

2. Stir fresh cilantro and spice mix into yogurt then add to dish. Toss scallions and shrimp in spiced yogurt until coated. Cover dish and marinate in refrigerator for 2 hours.

3. Thread shrimp, scallions and bell peppers onto kebab skewers. Stir oil into remaining marinade.

4. Cook shrimp kebabs under moderately hot grill or over medium-hot coals 6–8 minutes, turning frequently and basting with marinade. Serve immediately.

Note: If preferred, the shrimp may be left in their shells, in which case the marinating time should be increased to 8 hours or overnight.

Serves 6

samosas

INDIAN DAL

Ingredients

8 oz brown or red lentils

4 cups water

1 teaspoon ground turmeric

1 clove garlic, crushed

1 oz ghee or clarified butter

1 large onion, chopped

1 teaspoon garam masala

$\frac{1}{2}$ teaspoon ground ginger

1 teaspoon ground coriander

$\frac{1}{2}$ teaspoon cayenne pepper

Method

1. Wash lentils in cold water.

2. Place lentils, water, turmeric and garlic in a large saucepan and bring to simmering point. Cover and simmer, stirring occasionally, for 30 minutes or until lentils are cooked. Remove cover from pan, bring to a boil and boil to reduce excess liquid.

3. Melt ghee or butter in a large frying pan, add onion and cook for 5 minutes or until onion is soft. Stir in garam masala, ginger, coriander and cayenne pepper and cook for 1 minute. Stir spice mixture into lentils and serve immediately.

Serves 6

soups

Warm up or
COOL DOWN

Until recently in India, soup was not regarded as a course, except in the northern snow-clad mountains or in the cold, wind-whipped, wintry deserts and plains. There, spicy and hearty soup can constitute a whole meal. A cup of hot northern soup can also be a replacement for tea, to accompany other body and soul-warming dishes.

The winds of change in India and intense interest in its food from abroad has meant that the trend to serve soup in other regions is increasing. In areas of intense heat, soups are served cold, while remaining spicy. They can feature yogurt, appealing green and tropical vegetables and/or fruit including coconut, or herbs such as palate-cooling mint. Cold soup makes a refreshing summer meal starter, particularly if served with an ice cube in each bowl.

The state of Tamil Nadu, along with its warm southern state neighbors, has always favored pepper water, *milagutannir*, to accompany hot dishes. During the British Raj, this was adapted to become mulligatawny (recipe below). This soup, reduced in an uncovered pot until it is very thick, can be poured over rice for a very nourishing casual meal.

MULLIGATAWNY SOUP

Ingredients
1 tablespoon vegetable oil
2 onions, chopped
1 green apple, cored, peeled and chopped
1 clove garlic, crushed
2 tablespoons lemon juice
1 tablespoon curry powder
1 teaspoon brown sugar
1/2 teaspoon ground cumin
1/4 teaspoon ground coriander
2 tablespoons all-purpose flour
8 cups chicken bouillon
1 pound boneless chicken breast or thigh fillets, cut into 1/2 inch cubes
1/3 cup rice
freshly ground black pepper

Method
1. Heat oil in a large saucepan over medium heat, add onions, apple and garlic and cook, stirring, for 5 minutes or until onions are tender. Add lemon juice, curry powder, sugar, cumin and coriander and cook over low heat, stirring, for 10 minutes or until fragrant.

2. Blend flour with a little bouillon and stir into curry mixture. Add chicken, rice and remaining bouillon to pan, bring to a boil, stirring constantly. Reduce heat, cover and simmer for 20 minutes or until chicken and rice are cooked. Season to taste with black pepper.

Note: A dash of chili sauce and a chopped tomato are delicious additions to this soup. Serve with crusty bread rolls, naan or pita bread.

Serves 4

INDIAN SPICED POTATO AND ONION SOUP

Ingredients

1 tablespoon vegetable oil

1 onion, finely chopped

1/3 inch piece fresh ginger root, finely chopped

2 large potatoes, cut into 1/3 inch cubes

2 teaspoons ground cumin

2 teaspoons ground coriander

1/2 teaspoon turmeric

1 teaspoon ground cinnamon

4 cups chicken bouillon

salt and black pepper

1 tablespoon natural yogurt to garnish

Method

1. Heat oil in a large saucepan. Fry onion and ginger for 5 minutes or until softened. Add potatoes and fry for another minute, stirring often.

2. Mix cumin, coriander, turmeric and cinnamon with 2 tablespoons of cold water to make a paste. Add to onion and potato, stirring well, and fry for 1 minute to release the flavors.

3. Add bouillon and season to taste. Bring to a boil, then reduce heat, cover and simmer for 30 minutes or until potato is tender. Blend until smooth in a food processor or press through a metal sieve. Return to pan and gently heat through. Garnish with yogurt and more black pepper.

Serves 4

COOL CUMIN-SCENTED YOGURT SOUP

Ingredients

1 teaspoon cumin seeds

1 teaspoon black onion seeds

1 tablespoon ghee or butter

4 scallions, finely sliced

10 fresh mint leaves

2 teaspoons ground cumin

1 teaspoon turmeric

2 oz cashew nuts

11 oz canned chickpeas, drained and rinsed

1 pound plain low-fat yogurt

7 oz sour cream

7 oz water

salt and pepper to taste

$1\frac{1}{2}$ pounds cucumbers

1 tablespoon sugar

2 tablespoons shredded coconut, toasted

mint leaves and black onion seeds for garnish

Method

1. Heat a frypan (no oil) then add cumin seeds and black onion seeds. Toss them around hot pan until the seeds smell roasted and seem to pop around the pan, about 3 minutes. Remove seeds and set aside.

2. Add the ghee to pan and add the scallions and mint leaves and sauté for a few minutes until scallions have wilted. Add cumin, turmeric and cashew nuts and toss until spices are fragrant and the nuts are golden. Add drained chickpeas and cook for a further 2 minutes. Set aside.

3. In a mixing bowl, whisk together yogurt, sour cream and water until smooth. Season with salt and pepper. Peel cucumbers and scrape out seeds. Cut cucumber flesh into thin slices and add to yogurt mixture.

4. Add scallion and spice mixture, along with sugar, to yogurt mixture and stir thoroughly to combine. Allow flavors to blend for 1 hour before serving.

5. Garnish with toasted coconut, sliced mint leaves and a few black onion seeds.

Serves 6

bread & rice

From Pilau
TO POORI

Rice and bread are the mainstays of almost all Indian meals. Rice has been cultivated in India for more than 3,000 years and for the majority of India's 1 billion people, rice is vital for life. Plain boiled rice provides the balance that the palate and digestive system need to thoroughly appreciate (and tolerate) the tantalizing tastes of fiery toppings.

In most Western homes, rice is served as an accompaniment to meat, poultry, fish and vegetables. In India, it is the reverse. Sometimes Western visitors to India think they are being short-changed when large amounts of rice are piled onto their plates with only a small amount of savory dish to crown it. This is the practice even in the wealthiest of Indian households.

Basmati, a fragrant long-grain rice grown in the Himalayan foothills, is most used in pilaus and biryanis. It is more absorbent than short-grain rice, which is more suitable for desserts. Red rice is eaten in the rural South, which has geographical conditions and a climate more conducive to rice rearing than the wheat-cultivating north; Northerners never miss their daily bread.

Indians enjoy crunchy chapatis or pappadams with each meal. Among the poor or those with religious dietary restrictions, the only companion to chapatis may be dal, which may be eaten with rice. Wholemeal rice (or Indian atta) and all-purpose flour or semolina, are used to produce leavened and unleavened breads by shallow- or deep-frying, or baking. Perhaps no bread is more tempting than warm, soft naan. Traditionally baked in a tandoor (clay oven), naan is especially more-ish when served with tandoori chicken (see page 292). As few Indians have tandoors, naan is not made in the home.

Garlic naan is a favorite with Western diners. Simply add finely chopped and sautéed garlic to your taste to the following plain naan recipe. Pooris are proudly served on festive occasions, especially weddings.

SPICED RICE

Ingredients

1 1/2 cups basmati rice
4 cups water
1/2 teaspoon salt
2 tablespoons lemon juice
2 tablespoons ghee
1 medium red onion, chopped
3 tablespoons cashew nuts
3 tablespoons golden raisins
1/4 teaspoon fennel seeds
1/4 teaspoon cumin seeds
1/4 teaspoon white mustard seeds
1/4 teaspoon ground turmeric
1 teaspoon extra ghee

Method

1. Rinse rice well in a sieve under running water. Bring 4 cups of water to a boil, add salt and lemon juice. Stir in rice and, when water returns to a boil, turn down heat and simmer for 18 minutes, until rice is just tender. Drain in colander and rinse with hot water. Set aside.

2. Heat ghee in a large frying pan. Add onion and cook until transparent. Add cashews and golden raisins and sauté briefly. Add spices and extra teaspoon of ghee and cook, stirring constantly, for 2 minutes.

3. Add drained rice, gently toss to combine ingredients and reheat rice. Serve hot with curries or serve as a side dish with grilled meats and chicken.

Serves 4

FRAGRANT PILAU RICE

Ingredients

large pinch of saffron strands

8 oz basmati rice

1 oz butter

1 shallot, finely chopped

3 cardamon pods

1 cinnamon stick

10 oz water

salt to taste

Method

1. Briefly grind saffron using a mortar and pestle, then mix powder with 1 tablespoon of boiling water and set aside. Rinse rice and drain.

2. Melt butter in a large, heavy-based saucepan. Fry shallot gently for 2 minutes or until softened. Add cardamon pods, cinnamon and rice, and mix well.

3. Add water, saffron mixture and salt. Bring to a boil, then reduce heat and cover pan tightly. Simmer rice for 15 minutes or until liquid has been absorbed and the rice is tender. Remove cardamon pods and cinnamon stick before serving.

Serves 4

COCONUT POORI

Ingredients

7 oz whole wheat flour (or Indian atta flour)

4 oz all-purpose flour

$\frac{1}{2}$–1 teaspoon salt

4 oz dried coconut

1 teaspoon chili powder

$\frac{1}{2}$ tablespoon sugar

2 tablespoons ghee or vegetable oil

approximately 5 oz water,

oil for frying

Method

1. Mix whole wheat flour, all-purpose flour, salt and coconut in a bowl with chili powder and sugar. Add melted ghee or oil and rub through until flour appears crumbly. Stir in the water, only add water as much as necessary to form a soft dough. Knead dough well. Allow the dough to rest for 10 minutes.

2. Divide the dough into 14 pieces, flattening each and rolling each out to a thin circle of 3 inch diameter.

3. Heat oil in a wok and, when hot, add one circle of dough. With a heat-proof implement, push dough under oil until dough is puffed and golden. Allow it to float, turning to cook the other side.

4. Drain on absorbent paper and cook remaining poori the same way.

Note: Although it is important not to overcrowd the wok, 3–4 poori can usually be cooked together.

Makes 14 poori

NAAN BREAD

Ingredients

1 cup plain full-fat yogurt

1½ cups boiling water

2 cups all-purpose flour

3 cups stoneground whole wheat flour

1 tablespoon yeast

2 teaspoons salt

1 teaspoon sugar

2 tablespoons nut oil (peanut or walnut work well)

3 tablespoons black sesame seeds

6 tablespoons sesame seeds

Method

1. First, mix yogurt with boiling water and stir well. Set aside for 5 minutes.

2. Mix all-purpose flour with 1 cup of whole wheat flour and add yeast. Add yogurt mixture and stir with a wooden spoon for 3 minutes, then cover with plastic wrap. Allow this mixture to rest for 1 hour.

3. Add salt, sugar, oil and black sesame seeds and enough of the remaining flour to form a firm, but moist dough. Begin to knead on a floured surface and continue until dough is very silky and elastic. Allow dough to rise in an oiled bowl for 1 hour at room temperature or until doubled in size.

4. Punch down dough and divide into 8 pieces. Shape each into a ball then flatten each piece of dough into a circle about ⅓ inch thick. Transfer to oiled oven trays.

5. Brush surface of dough with water and sprinkle surface generously with sesame seeds. With a blade or sharp knife, score dough from center to edge to look like sunrays.

6. Cover dough and allow to rise for 10 minutes. Bake on oiled oven trays at 435°F for 5–8 minutes.

Serves 4

INDIAN FRESH CORN BREAD

Ingredients

8 oz fresh corn kernels

$\frac{1}{2}$ teaspoon salt

2 tablespoons minced cilantro

5 oz all-purpose flour, plus extra for dusting

1–2 tablespoons ghee, melted

Method

1. In a blender or food processor, grind corn and salt together until it is finely puréed.

2. Transfer mixture to a mixing bowl and add cilantro. Add flour, a little at a time, continuing until mixture is kneadable (it should be a little tacky.)

3. Divide dough into 12 pieces then roll each piece out into a circle about 6 inches in diameter. If dough circles are tacky, use extra flour to absorb dough moisture. Once rolled, brush each with a little ghee.

4. Heat a griddle or frying pan and add a little ghee. Add one piece of dough and cook until piece of dough underside is spotted with brown. Turn over and cook other side. Remove cooked bread and keep warm in foil while cooking other breads the same way.

Note: If you would like to duplicate the smoky roasted flavor that these breads would have when cooked over an open fire, simply hold each bread over a gas cooktop flame for a few seconds. Do not allow to burn. Brush with more ghee and serve.

Serves 4

POTATO NAAN

Ingredients

Dough

1 cup plain full-fat yogurt

1 1/2 cups boiling water

2 cups all-purpose flour

3 cups stoneground whole wheat flour

1 tablespoon yeast

2 teaspoons salt

1 teaspoon sugar

2 tablespoons peanut oil

3 tablespoons black sesame seeds

1 egg, beaten

Filling

1 pound potatoes, peeled and diced

1 onion, finely diced

4 mint leaves, finely sliced

1/4 cup parsley, chopped

1/2 cup cilantro leaves, chopped

1/4 teaspoon cumin

1/4 teaspoon turmeric

salt and pepper to taste

Method

1. First, mix yogurt with boiling water and stir well. Set aside for 5 minutes.

2. Mix all-purpose flour with 1 cup of whole wheat flour and add yeast. Add yogurt mixture and stir with a wooden spoon for 3 minutes, then allow to rest for 30 minutes.

3. Add salt, sugar, oil and black sesame seeds and enough of the remaining flour to form a firm, but moist dough.

4. Begin to knead on a floured surface and continue until dough is very silky and elastic. Allow dough to rest in an oiled bowl for 1 hour or until doubled in size.

5. Meanwhile make potato filling. Cover potatoes, and boil until soft. Mix hot potato with onion, mint leaves, parsley, cilantro, cumin, turmeric and salt and pepper and mash until soft, but not sloppy. Cool.

6. Punch down dough and divide into 12 equal pieces. Roll each piece into a circle about 6 inches in diameter. Place a large tablespoon of filling in the center of each dough circle and lift both edges of circle to seal. Pinch seam together very well. Allow to rise for 10 minutes then brush with beaten egg and sprinkle with sesame seeds. Bake at 400°F for 15–20 minutes or until golden and crisp.

Serves 4

CHAPATIS

Ingredients

8 oz whole wheat flour

1 teaspoon salt

1 cup water

Method

1. Sift flour and salt into a bowl. Make a well in the center and add water, a little at a time, using your fingers to incorporate the surrounding flour to make a smooth, pliable dough.

2. Knead dough on a lightly floured surface for 5–10 minutes, then place in a bowl, cover with a cloth and leave to rest for 30–60 minutes.

3. Knead dough for 2–3 minutes. Divide into 6 balls of equal size, then flatten each ball into a circle, about 5 inches in diameter.

4. Heat an ungreased griddle or electric frying pan until hot. Place one chapati at a time on hot surface. As soon as bubbles appear on surface of chapati, turn the chapati over. Press down on chapati with a thick cloth so that it cooks evenly.

5. To finish chapati, lift it with a fish slice and hold it carefully over an open gas flame without turning until it puffs up slightly. Alternatively, place the chapati under a hot grill.

6. Repeat with remaining dough circles. Keep cooked chapatis hot in a covered napkin-lined basket.

Makes 15

PITA BREAD

Ingredients

$1\frac{1}{2}$ cups warm water

1 teaspoon superfine sugar

1 tablespoon dried yeast

1 pound all-purpose flour plus

$\frac{1}{2}$ teaspoon salt

oil for greasing

Method

1. Pour half of the warm water into a jug. Stir in sugar and dried yeast. Set aside in a warm place for 10 minutes until frothy.

2. Sift flour and salt into a bowl. Add yeast liquid and enough of remaining warm water to make a firm, but pliable, dough. Knead on a lightly floured surface for 10 minutes until dough is smooth and free from cracks.

3. Form dough into a ball, place in a greased bowl, cover with cling film and leave to stand in a warm place for $1\frac{1}{2}$ hours or until dough has doubled in bulk.

4. Turn dough onto a lightly floured surface and knead for 2–3 minutes, then divide into 8 equal pieces, shaping each piece into a ball. Place on greased baking sheets, cover and leave to prove in a warm place until well risen and spongy. Preheat oven to 450°F.

5. Place two dough balls on each baking sheet, flatten slightly and brush with a little cold water. Bake for 10 minutes. Cool on wire racks.

Makes 8

SIMPLE PILAU RICE

Ingredients

14 oz basmati rice, rinsed

6 cloves

2 inch cinnamon stick, crushed

6 green cardamon pods, crushed

$\frac{1}{2}$ teaspoon ground turmeric

2 oz raisins

1 oz slivered almonds

2 bay leaves

1 tablespoon sugar

salt

7 tablespoons melted ghee or oil

$\frac{1}{2}$ teaspoon cumin seeds

1 tablespoon fresh ginger root, grated

Method

1. Soak rice in cold water for 10 minutes. Drain and spread on a clean cloth to dry.

2. Transfer rice to a platter. Sprinkle over whole cloves, a few pieces of cinnamon stick, the cardamon pods, turmeric, raisins, almonds, bay leaves, sugar and salt.

3. Drizzle over half a teaspoon of melted ghee or oil. Using your hand, mix spices thoroughly into rice. Leave for 15 minutes.

4. Heat remaining ghee or oil in a large saucepan. Add cumin seeds, ginger and rice mixture. Fry gently for 5 minutes until rice is transparent.

5. Add hot water to cover rice by $\frac{1}{3}$ inch. Bring to a boil, lower heat and simmer until all liquid is absorbed and rice is tender. Before serving, turn rice over gently.

Serves 4–6

vegetables

Crunchy, crispy, colorful CONTRASTS

All Indians, young and old, seem to adore vegetables, often preferring them to meat, fish or poultry. A walk through a big, bustling food bazaar is a total sensory experience. It is a riot of brilliant color and abundance. Market-goers bargain for gleaming, smooth-skinned eggplants, tomatoes and chilies, rough-textured potatoes, carrots, turnips, creamy cauliflowers and green vegetables of every hue in the form of beans, peas, okra, cabbages, spinach, zucchini, cucumbers and lettuce, all spilling from humble stalls onto pavements where other vendors sit selling their produce.

The key to the popularity of vegetables in India is that, whether exotic or familiar, they are prepared in so many innovative and appetizing ways. India can easily claim to be the world's leader in vegetable and vegetarian cooking.

Millions of Indians are vegetarians, especially in the South, including strict Hindus. A devout Buddhist will not even crack an egg. Vegetables are cooked in a little liquid, which is not discarded and never boiled, so that nutrients are retained. This cooking method is known as wet cooking. Dry cooking is when the vegetables are sliced or shredded and stir-fried with whole spices.

In the South, cauliflower, potatoes, peas, onions and chilies are cooked in a mildly spiced creamy, coconut sauce. In Kashmir, spiced spinach, onions and mushrooms with cream makes a wonderful stir-fried main dish served with lamb, stuffed bread and rice. Spinach is superb as are peas when cooked with paneer (home-made cheese).

Try our exciting salads at home, but be wary of salads when travelling in India as the water in which the ingredients are washed may be unsafe.

GREEN BEAN SALAD WITH CILANTRO AND GINGER

Ingredients
1½ pounds fresh snake beans
1 inch piece fresh ginger
1 tablespoon vegetable oil
1 tablespoon sesame oil
1 teaspoon mustard seeds
2 teaspoons ground cumin
½ teaspoon turmeric
1 fresh green chili, finely minced
5 oz chicken or vegetable bouillon
juice of 2 lemons
1 bunch fresh cilantro leaves, washed, dried then chopped
salt to taste
3 oz peanuts, roasted and chopped and lemon wedges to serve

Method
1. Trim beans to lengths of 3 inches and discard any discolored ends. Peel ginger and cut into fine matchstick-sized pieces.

2. In a wok, heat vegetable and sesame oils and, when hot, add mustard seeds. Allow to cook for a moment or two until seeds start popping. Add ginger and cook for a further minute. Add cumin, turmeric and chili and stir until fragrant, for about 2 minutes.

3. Add beans and toss in flavored oil to coat beans thoroughly. Add bouillon, simmer for 5–8 minutes or until liquid has almost evaporated completely, and beans are tender.

4. Remove lid and add lemon juice, cilantro and salt. Stir thoroughly to combine all ingredients then cool. Serve garnished with roasted chopped peanuts and lemon wedges if desired.

Serves 4

INDIAN CHICKPEA SALAD WITH SPINACH

Ingredients

2 cups dried chickpeas

4 onions

1 teaspoon whole cloves

4 bay leaves

2 oz peanut or olive oil

4 cloves garlic

1 teaspoon turmeric

2 teaspoons cumin

2 teaspoons garam masala

3 tablespoons tomato paste

2 red bell peppers, sliced

4 medium zucchini, sliced on the diagonal

salt and pepper, to taste

2 bunches of spinach or 1 pound baby spinach

Method

1. Pick over chickpeas and remove any that are discolored. Place all remaining chickpeas in a large saucepan and cover with cold water. Peel 2 onions and chop in half. Place in saucepan with chickpeas. Add cloves and bay leaves bring to a boil and simmer for 10 minutes. Remove chickpeas from heat and cover and allow to steep for 2 hours. Strain chickpeas, keeping the water.

2. Chop the remaining 2 onions. Heat oil and sauté the onions and minced garlic. Add all spices and cook briefly to release fragrance. Add chickpeas and 2 cups of the soaking water, tomato paste and the bell pepper.

3. Cover and simmer gently for about 20 minutes until chickpeas soften and liquid evaporates. Add zucchini and salt and pepper and stir well. Remove from heat. Allow to cool slightly then fold through spinach leaves. Cool completely and serve.

Serves 8

CAULIFLOWER AND PEAS IN CHILI SAUCE

Ingredients

2 tablespoons oil

1 teaspoon mustard seeds

$^{1}/_{2}$ teaspoon hot chili powder

pinch of asafoetida

1 cauliflower, divided into florets

4 oz fresh or frozen peas (thawed if frozen)

1 potato, cut into $^{1}/_{3}$ inch cubes

2 tomatoes, peeled and finely chopped

$^{1}/_{2}$ teaspoon ground turmeric

$^{1}/_{2}$ teaspoon aadoo mirch spice mix (page 246)

pinch of salt

1 tablespoon chopped fresh cilantro

1 teaspoon molasses

1$^{2}/_{3}$ cups water

Method

1. Heat oil in a heavy-based saucepan over moderately high heat. Add mustard seeds. As soon as seeds pop, stir in chili powder and asafoetida. Shake pan briefly over heat, then add cauliflower florets and peas.

2. Fry, stirring, for a few seconds, then add potato cubes, tomatoes, turmeric, aadoo mirch, salt, cilantro and molasses.

3. Stir well, cover and cook for 3–4 minutes, then add the water, mixing thoroughly. Lower heat, cover and simmer for about 30 minutes or until vegetables are tender and sauce has thickened slightly. Serve hot with chapatis (see page 272).

Serves 4

MOGUL SALAD

(below)

Ingredients

7 oz mung bean sprouts

3 cucumbers, diced

4 teaspoons grated fresh or dried coconut

2 tomatoes, diced

¼ bunch fresh cilantro, chopped

½ bunch fresh mint, chopped

½ bunch fresh basil, chopped

1 bunch scallions, chopped

2 tablespoons lemon juice

salt and freshly ground black pepper

Method

1. Place bean sprouts, cucumbers, coconut, tomatoes, cilantro, mint and basil leaves, scallions, lemon juice, and salt and black pepper in a bowl and toss to combine. Cover and stand at room temperature for 2–3 hours before serving.

Serves 6

ONION BHAJIS

Ingredients

8 oz whole wheat flour

1 tablespoon salt

1 teaspoon garam masala (page 246–247)

2 tablespoons fresh mint, chopped

1 teaspoon fresh cilantro, chopped

4 onions, thinly sliced

oil for deep-frying

Method

1. Sift flour, salt and garam masala into a bowl. Add enough water to make a stiff batter.

2. Stir in mint, cilantro and onions, mixing well.

3. Heat oil for deep-frying. Scoop up about a tablespoon of mixture at a time and use a second spoon to mold it into a roughly round shape. Drop into hot oil. Cook for 3 minutes, then remove with slotted spoon. You can cook several bhajis at once, but take care not to crowd the pan.

4. When oil has heated up again return bhajis to pan for 2–3 minutes more or until dark brown and crisp. Drain on paper towels before serving.

Serves 4

VEGETABLE KORMA

Ingredients

2 tablespoons vegetable oil

2 tablespoons green masala curry paste (page 247)

1 teaspoon chili powder

1 tablespoon fresh ginger, finely grated

2 cloves garlic, crushed

1 onion, chopped

1 pound cauliflower, cut into florets

7 oz green beans

3 baby eggplants

2 carrots, sliced

4 oz button mushrooms

14 oz canned tomatoes, mashed in their juices

1 cup vegetable bouillon

Method

1. Heat oil in a saucepan over medium heat, stir in masala paste and chili powder, and cook for 2 minutes. Add ginger, garlic and onion and cook, stirring, for 3 minutes or until onion is soft. Add cauliflower, beans, eggplant, carrots and mushrooms and cook, stirring, for 5 minutes.

2. Stir in tomatoes and bouillon, and bring to a boil. Reduce heat and simmer, stirring occasionally, for 20 minutes or until vegetables are tender.

Serves 4

POTATO AND PEA BHAJIS

Ingredients

3–4 tablespoons oil

1 onion, thinly sliced

1 teaspoon ground turmeric

1 teaspoon cumin seeds

1/4 teaspoon ground ginger

1 green chili, seeded and chopped

1 pound potatoes, peeled and diced

8 oz fresh or frozen peas (thawed if frozen)

chopped fresh cilantro to garnish

Method

1. Heat oil in a flameproof casserole, add onion and fry for 5–7 minutes, stirring frequently, until browned but not crisp.

2. Stir in turmeric, cumin seeds, ginger and chili, then add potatoes and cook gently for 5 minutes, stirring frequently.

3. Stir in peas. Cover casserole and simmer over very low heat for 15–20 minutes or until potatoes are tender, but retain their shape. Garnish with cilantro and serve.

Serves 4

SPICED PEAS AND CARROTS

Ingredients

8 oz frozen or fresh peas

2 carrots, diced

2 tablespoons vegetable oil

1 teaspoon cumin seeds

2 teaspoons fresh ginger, finely chopped

2 fresh red or green chilies, finely chopped

5–6 tablespoons water

salt to taste

Dry spice mixture

$\frac{1}{2}$ teaspoon ground cumin

$\frac{1}{4}$ teaspoon ground coriander

$\frac{1}{4}$ teaspoon mango powder

$\frac{1}{4}$ teaspoon ground turmeric

Method

1. For spice mixture, place cumin, coriander, mango powder and turmeric in a small bowl. Mix to combine and set aside.

2. Boil or microwave peas and carrots, separately, until just cooked. Drain, refresh under cold running water and set aside. Heat oil in a heavy-based saucepan over low heat, add cumin seeds, ginger and chilies, and cook, stirring, for 2–3 minutes. Add peas and carrots and mix to combine well. Stir in water and salt and simmer for 5 minutes. Add spice mixture and simmer, stirring occasionally, for 5 minutes longer.

To microwave

Place peas, carrots, oil, cumin seeds, ginger, chilies and spice mixture in a microwave-safe dish. Cover and cook on medium, stirring occasionally, for 20 minutes. Season to taste with salt.

Serves 4

poultry
& meat

Marvellous for a
MAHARAJAH

Hindus don't eat beef because for them, the cow is sacred. Some Hindus don't eat any meat at all, just like vegetarian Buddhists. Muslims and Jews are forbidden to eat pork and some Muslims and Jews are so strict that they will not eat if they believe the pot or pan has been previously used to cook pork. But the remaining Indian population who enjoy, and can afford, lamb, beef, pork, goat and chicken (which is especially popular during festivals) make the most of them.

Meat markets in India are eye-openers as conditions cannot be described as hygienic. People buying poultry choose live birds from cages. Chicken is less expensive, more available, and therefore more popular than duck.

The tandoori and rich biryani dishes to follow hail from the North whose cuisine was influenced by the conquering Moghuls and Muslims. Northern dishes are relatively mild. The meat, chicken and other ingredients in these dishes are cooked in ghee. The further south one travels, the hotter the food becomes, with added quantities of chili. Southern food tends to be cooked in oil. Christian Goans have perfected cooking pork. Most dishes containing cashews come from Goa which produces these nuts plentifully.

You may be tempted to use commercial curry powders or pre-mixed curry sauces to flavor your poultry or meat instead of the individual spices generally recommended. But, by using the latter, you can vary quantities–less chili or more coriander–to suit the tastes of family and friends. You can also interchange meats: use beef instead of lamb for the korma or lamb instead of chicken in Kashmiri chicken. Chicken rogan josh can easily become lamb or beef rogan josh. Just alter the cooking times accordingly; poultry takes less time to cook than other meats.

TANDOORI CHICKEN

Ingredients

2 fresh chickens (about 2 pounds each)
3 tablespoons tandoori spice mix (see page 246)
7 oz natural yogurt
2 tablespoons lemon juice
2 tablespoons melted butter
lettuce leaves, onion rings, tomato wedges and
 lemon for serving

Method

1. Rinse chickens inside and out and pat dry with paper towels. Make deep gashes in thighs and on each side of breast. Pin back wings.

2. Mix tandoori spice mix, yogurt, lemon juice and melted butter together. Place chickens in a stainless steel or other non-metal dish and spread mixture all over, rubbing well into gashes. Cover and refrigerate for 12 or more hours.

3. Preheat oven to 375°F. Place chickens on a roasting rack in a baking dish and spoon any remaining marinade over chickens. Place in preheated oven and cook for 1 hour. Baste with pan juices during cooking. When cooked, cover with foil and rest for 10 minutes before serving.

4. Arrange crisp lettuce leaves on a large platter and cover with onion rings. Cut chicken into portions and place on the platter. Garnish with tomato wedges and lemon slices and serve immediately.

Serves 4–6

LAMB KORMA

Ingredients

3 pound shoulder of lamb

salt and freshly ground black pepper

2 tablespoons ghee

1 red onion, finely chopped

1 clove garlic, finely chopped

1 tablespoon green masala curry paste (page 246)

$\frac{1}{4}$ teaspoon ground ginger

$\frac{1}{4}$ teaspoon turmeric

$\frac{1}{8}$ teaspoon cayenne pepper

2 tablespoons flour

$1\frac{1}{4}$ cups chicken bouillon

$\frac{3}{4}$ cup golden raisins

5 oz yogurt

1 tablespoon lemon juice

rice and sambals to serve

Method

1. Cut lamb from bone and chop into $1\frac{1}{2}$ inch cubes. Season with salt and pepper.

2. Heat ghee in a large, heavy-based saucepan, add one third of the lamb and brown well on all sides. Remove and brown remainder in 2 batches.

3. Add onion and garlic and sauté until transparent. Stir in curry paste, spices and flour and cook for 1 minute. Add chicken bouillon, golden raisins and lamb. Cover with a lid and simmer gently for 1 hour or until lamb is very tender. Stir occasionally during cooking.

4. Stir in yogurt and lemon juice. Serve with boiled rice and sambals.

Serves 4–6

POULTRY & MEAT

CHICKEN BIRYANI
(opposite, top)

Ingredients

3 tablespoons ghee

3 onions, sliced

3 pounds chicken pieces

2 teaspoons fresh ginger, grated

3 cloves garlic, crushed

$\frac{1}{2}$ teaspoon ground cumin

$\frac{1}{2}$ teaspoon ground cinnamon

$\frac{1}{4}$ teaspoon ground cloves

$\frac{1}{4}$ teaspoon ground cardamon

$\frac{1}{4}$ teaspoon ground nutmeg

$\frac{1}{2}$ teaspoon all-purpose flour

1 cup chicken bouillon

$\frac{1}{2}$ cup natural yogurt

$\frac{1}{2}$ cup cream

Rice pilau

2 tablespoons ghee

$\frac{1}{2}$ teaspoon ground saffron

$\frac{1}{2}$ teaspoon ground cardamon

1 teaspoon salt

7 oz basmati rice, well washed

4 cups chicken bouillon

2 tablespoons golden raisins

Method

1. Heat ghee in a large frying pan and cook onions for 2–3 minutes or until golden brown. Remove from pan and set aside.

2. Add chicken to the pan and cook until well browned on all sides. Remove from pan and set aside.

3. Combine ginger, garlic, cumin, cinnamon, cloves, cardamon, nutmeg and flour. Stir into pan and cook for 1–2 minutes. Add bouillon, yogurt and cream, stirring to lift pan sediment.

4. Return chicken to pan with half the onions. Cover and simmer for 15–20 minutes. Remove from heat and let stand, covered, for 15 minutes.

5. To make rice pilau, heat ghee in a large saucepan. Cook saffron, cardamon, salt and rice for 1–2 minutes. Pour in bouillon and bring to a boil. Add raisins, reduce heat and cook gently for 10–15 minutes or until most of the bouillon is absorbed. Cover and set aside for 10 minutes. Preheat oven to 350°F.

6. Transfer half the rice to a large ovenproof dish, top with chicken pieces, then remaining rice. Drizzle over sauce from chicken, top with remaining onions and cashew nuts. Cover and bake for 20–30 minutes.

Serves 4

MUSTARD CHILI PORK
(opposite, bottom)

Ingredients

$1\frac{1}{2}$ pound pork fillets

2 oz melted butter

1 oz ghee

2 tablespoons peanut oil

3 onions, chopped

1 tablespoon black mustard seeds

2 cloves garlic, crushed

2 red chilies, chopped

$\frac{1}{2}$ teaspoon ground cumin

$\frac{1}{2}$ teaspoon ground turmeric

1 tablespoon brown sugar

1 cup water

1 tablespoon lime juice

8 lime leaves

Method

1. Trim meat of all visible fat, brush with melted butter and bake at 350°F for 25–30 minutes.

2. Heat ghee and oil in a saucepan, cook onions, mustard seeds, garlic and chilies for 2–3 minutes or until onions soften.

3. Stir in cumin, turmeric, brown sugar, water, lime juice and lime leaves. Bring to a boil, then reduce heat and simmer, uncovered, for 10 minutes or until mixture reduces and thickens.

4. Transfer mixture to a food processor or blender. Process until smooth, then return to pan. Slice pork diagonally and add to mustard mixture. Heat through gently and serve.

Serves 4

286

chicken biryani

mustard chili pork

287

TANDOORI LAMB CUTLETS

(below)

Ingredients

8 lamb cutlets

Marinade

4 tablespoons natural yogurt

1 teaspoon fresh ginger, grated

1 clove garlic, crushed

1 tablespoon lime juice

1 teaspoon ground cumin

$\frac{1}{4}$ teaspoon ground cardamon

$\frac{1}{4}$ teaspoon chili powder

$\frac{1}{4}$ teaspoon garam masala (pages 246–247)

few drops red food coloring

Method

1. Trim meat of all visible fat and set aside.

2. To make marinade, combine yogurt, ginger, garlic, lime juice, cumin, cardamon, chili powder and garam masala. Add red food coloring until marinade is pink. Add cutlets, toss to coat and set aside to marinate for 30 minutes.

3. Remove cutlets from marinade. Grill or barbecue for 6–8 minutes, turning and basting with marinade frequently.

Serves 4

KASHMIRI CHICKEN

Ingredients

1 onion, finely chopped

3 tablespoons fresh ginger root, grated

2 cloves garlic, crushed

$\frac{1}{2}$ teaspoon ground coriander

$1\frac{1}{2}$ teaspoon anchovy essence

1 cup almonds or cashew nuts, ground

1 tablespoon oil

4 chicken portions, skinned

1 cup chicken bouillon

1 cup thick coconut milk

2 teaspoons light brown sugar

Method

1. Mix onion, ginger, garlic, coriander and anchovy essence with ground almonds or cashews to form a paste.

2. Heat oil in a large heavy-based saucepan. Add paste and stir over moderate heat for 5 minutes.

3. Add chicken portions and cook for 15 minutes, stirring frequently to coat in spice mixture and seal.

4. Pour in bouillon, stirring to incorporate spice mixture. Bring to a boil, lower heat and simmer for 20 minutes.

5. Stir in coconut milk and brown sugar, turn heat to lowest setting and simmer for 20 minutes more. Serve hot.

Serves 4

CASHEW NUT BUTTER CHICKEN

Ingredients

2 oz ghee or butter

2 cloves garlic, crushed

2 onions, minced

1 tablespoon Madras curry paste (page 247)

1 tablespoon ground coriander

½ teaspoon ground nutmeg

3 pounds boneless chicken thigh or breast fillets, cut into 1 inch cubes

2 oz cashew nuts, roasted and ground

1¼ cups heavy cream

2 tablespoons coconut milk

Method

1. Melt ghee or butter in a saucepan over medium heat, add garlic and onions and cook, stirring, for 3 minutes or until onions are golden.

2. Stir in curry paste, coriander and nutmeg and cook for 2 minutes or until fragrant.

3. Add chicken and cook, stirring, for 5 minutes or until chicken is brown.

4. Add cashews, cream and coconut milk, bring to simmering point and simmer, stirring occasionally, for 40 minutes or until chicken is tender.

Note: To roast cashews, spread nuts over a baking tray and bake at 350°F for 5–10 minutes or until lightly and evenly browned. Toss back and forth occasionally with a spoon to ensure even browning. Alternatively, place nuts under a medium grill and cook, tossing back and forth until roasted.

Serves 6

INDIAN SALAD OF SPICED CHICKEN AND DHAL

Ingredients

6 cups vegetable bouillon

1½ cups dried lentils

juice of 2 lemons

1½ oz vegetable oil

1 tablespoon Madras curry paste (page 247)

1 tablespoon garam masala (page 246–247)

1 teaspoon turmeric

salt and pepper to taste

4 large chicken breast fillets, skin removed

1½ cups vegetable bouillon, extra

1 small cauliflower, cut into florets

1½ cups fresh or frozen peas

2 small tomatoes, seeded and diced

1 cucumber, peeled and diced

2 scallions, sliced

2 tablespoons fresh mint, chopped

2 large bunches watercress, trimmed

fresh mint, extra, for garnish

scallion for garnish

Method

1. Bring 6 cups of vegetable bouillon to a boil and add lentils. Simmer until lentils are tender (about 20 minutes). Drain well then transfer lentils to a large bowl and add lemon juice and 1 tablespoon of oil. Mix well, cover and chill.

2. Combine curry paste, garam masala and turmeric in a plastic bag with salt and pepper, then add chicken breasts to bag. Seal bag and shake vigorously. Heat a grill pan or non-stick frying-pan with remaining oil until smoking. Then add chicken breasts to pan and fry on both sides until golden brown and cooked through (about 5 minutes). Remove chicken and set aside.

3. To the used pan, add extra 1½ cups of bouillon and bring to a boil. Add cauliflower and peas and cook over high heat until vegetables are crisp-tender and most of liquid has evaporated (about 5 minutes). Add vegetable mixture to lentils and mix well. Add tomatoes, cucumber, scallions and fresh mint and mix well, adding salt and pepper to taste.

4. Slice chicken into diagonal strips then gently mix into salad. Arrange watercress on a platter and top with salad mixture, arranging so that there is plenty of chicken visible. Garnish with fresh mint and scallion.

Serves 4

INDIAN MEATBALLS IN TOMATO SAUCE

Ingredients

1 pound ground lamb

5 tablespoons natural yogurt

2 inch piece fresh ginger root, finely chopped

1 green chili, seeded and finely chopped

3 tablespoons fresh cilantro, chopped

2 teaspoons ground cumin

2 teaspoons ground coriander

salt and black pepper

2 tablespoons vegetable oil

1 onion, chopped

2 cloves garlic, chopped

½ teaspoon turmeric

1 teaspoon garam masala

14 oz can chopped tomatoes

Method

1. Mix together lamb, 1 tablespoon of yogurt, ginger, chili, 2 tablespoons of cilantro, cumin and ground coriander and season with salt and pepper. Shape the mixture into 16 meatballs.

2. Heat 1 tablespoon of oil in a large saucepan, then fry meatballs for 10 minutes, turning until browned. You may have to cook them in batches. Drain on paper towels and set aside.

3. Heat remaining oil in pan. Add onion and garlic and fry for 5 minutes or until softened, stirring occasionally. Mix turmeric and garam masala with 1 tablespoon of water, then add to onion and garlic. Add remaining yogurt, 1 tablespoon at a time, stirring well each time.

4. Add tomatoes, meatballs and 5 oz of water to mixture, and bring to a boil. Partly cover pan, reduce heat and simmer for 30 minutes, stirring occasionally. Sprinkle rest of the cilantro leaves over to garnish.

Serves 4

ROASTED TANDOORI CHICKEN BREASTS

Ingredients

4 skinless and boneless chicken breasts

Marinade

1 teaspoon salt

2 cloves garlic, chopped

1 inch piece fresh ginger root, chopped

1 tablespoon fresh cilantro, chopped, plus extra
  leaves to garnish

1 tablespoon fresh mint, chopped

1/2 teaspoon turmeric

1/2 teaspoon hot chili powder

2 cardamon pods, husks discarded and seeds
  reserved

4 tablespoons natural yogurt

juice of 1/2 lemon

Method

1. For marinade, grind salt, garlic, ginger, cilantro, mint, turmeric, chili powder and cardamon seeds to a paste, using a mortar and pestle or coffee grinder kept especially for that purpose. Transfer to a large, non-metallic bowl, stir in the yogurt and lemon juice and mix together well.

2. Score each chicken breast 4 times with a sharp knife, then add to bowl and turn to coat thoroughly. Cover and chill for 6 hours or overnight.

3. Preheat oven to 425°F. Place chicken breasts on a rack in a roasting tin and cook for 20–25 minutes until tender and until the juices run clear when pierced with a skewer. Serve with salad and naan bread (page 269).

Serves 4

LAMB AND SPINACH CURRY

Ingredients

2 tablespoons vegetable oil

2 onions, chopped

2 cloves garlic, chopped

1 inch piece fresh root ginger, finely chopped

1 cinnamon stick

1/4 teaspoon cloves, ground

3 cardamon pods

1 1/4 pound diced lamb

1 tablespoon ground cumin

1 tablespoon ground coriander

4 tablespoons natural yogurt

2 tablespoons tomato paste

1 cup beef bouillon

salt and black pepper to taste

1 pound fresh spinach, finely chopped

2 tablespoons roasted flaked almonds

Method

1. Heat oil in a flameproof casserole dish or large heavy-based saucepan. Fry onions, garlic, ginger, cinnamon, cloves and cardamon for 5 minutes to soften onions and garlic, and to release flavor of the spices.

2. Add lamb and fry for 5 minutes, turning, until it begins to color. Mix in cumin and coriander, then add yogurt, 1 tablespoon at a time, stirring well each time.

3. Mix together tomato paste and bouillon and add to the lamb. Season with salt and pepper. Bring to a boil, then reduce heat. Cover and simmer for 30 minutes or until lamb is tender.

4. Stir in spinach, cover and simmer for another 15 minutes or until mixture has reduced. Remove cinnamon stick and cardamon pods and mix in almonds. Serve with steamed rice.

Serves 4

PORK VINDALOO

Ingredients

3 small dried red chilies

1 teaspoon cumin seeds

1½ teaspoon coriander seeds

2 cloves

4–6 black peppercorns

1 inch cinnamon stick

1 inch piece of fresh ginger root, grated

2 cloves garlic, chopped

3 tablespoons vinegar

2 pound lean pork, cubed

pinch of salt

3 tablespoons oil

2 onions, finely chopped

red chilies to garnish

water

Method

1. Dry-fry chilies, cumin seeds, coriander seeds, cloves, peppercorns and cinnamon stick in a frying pan for a few minutes, until mixture starts to crackle. Do not let it burn.

2. Using a mortar and pestle, or a coffee grinder kept especially for the purpose, grind spices along with ginger, garlic and vinegar to a smooth paste.

3. Place pork cubes in a saucepan with salt. Pour in water to cover meat by about 1 inch. Bring to a boil, lower heat and simmer for 45 minutes or until meat is tender.

4. Meanwhile heat oil in a large frying-pan. Fry onions for about 10 minutes, until golden. Stir in spice paste and fry for 2 minutes more, stirring constantly.

5. Drain meat, reserving cooking liquid, and add it to frying-pan. Stir well, cover and cook for 10 minutes over moderate heat.

6. Add about 2 cups of reserved cooking liquid. Stir well, cover and cook for 15–20 minutes more, or until meat is coated in a thick spicy sauce.

7. Serve at once, garnished with red chilies, or tip into a casserole, cool quickly, and refrigerate for reheating next day.

Serves 4

CHICKEN ROGAN JOSH

Ingredients

8 skinless boneless chicken thighs

1 tablespoon vegetable oil

1 small red bell pepper and 1 small green bell
   pepper, seeded and thinly sliced

1 onion, thinly sliced

2 inch piece of fresh root ginger, finely chopped

2 cloves garlic, crushed

2 tablespoons garam masala (pages 246–247)

1 teaspoon of each paprika, turmeric and chili
   powder

4 cardamon pods, crushed

salt

7 oz Greek yogurt

14 oz chopped tomatoes

fresh cilantro to garnish

Method

1. Cut each chicken thigh into 4 pieces. Heat oil in
   a large heavy-based frying-pan and add bell
   peppers, onion, ginger, garlic, spices and a good
   pinch of salt. Fry over low heat for 5 minutes or
   until bell peppers and onion have softened.

2. Add chicken and 2 tablespoons of yogurt. Increase
   heat to medium and cook for 4 minutes or until
   yogurt is absorbed. Repeat with rest of yogurt.

3. Increase heat to high, stir in tomatoes and 7 oz
   of water and bring to a boil.

4. Reduce heat, cover, and simmer for 30 minutes
   or until chicken is tender. Stir occasionally and
   add more water if sauce becomes too dry.

5. Uncover pan, increase heat to high and cook,
   stirring constantly, for 5 minutes or until sauce
   thickens. Garnish with cilantro.

Serves 4

LAMB PILAU WITH YOGURT

Ingredients

1 pound lean boneless leg lamb, cubed

6 cloves

8 black peppercorns

4 green cardamon pods

1 teaspoon cumin seeds

1 inch cinnamon stick

1 tablespoon coriander seeds

2 small red chilies

5 cups water

2 tablespoons ghee or oil

1 onion, finely chopped

2 tablespoons fresh root ginger, grated

2 cloves garlic, crushed

1 pound basmati rice, soaked for 30 minutes in enough water to cover

$\frac{1}{2}$ teaspoon salt

lemon to garnish

yogurt to serve

Method

1. Put lamb cubes in a saucepan. Tie cloves, peppercorns, cardamon pods, cumin seeds, cinnamon, coriander seeds and chilies in a muslin bag and add to pan with the water.

2. Bring to a boil, lower heat and simmer for 40 minutes or until meat is very tender. Strain, reserving lamb cubes and bouillon, but discarding spice bag.

3. Heat ghee or oil in a large frying-pan, add onion, ginger and garlic and fry for 2 minutes, stirring frequently.

4. Add lamb cubes, stirring to coat them in spices. Cook for 10 minutes until golden brown.

5. Meanwhile, drain rice and transfer to a large saucepan. Pour in enough reserved bouillon to cover rice by about 1½ inch. Add salt. Bring to a boil, cover, lower heat and cook for 10–15 minutes or until rice is almost tender and most bouillon has been absorbed.

6. Add rice to meat mixture in pan; fork through lightly. Cover tightly and cook over very low heat until rice is tender, adding more bouillon if necessary. Garnish with lemon and serve with yogurt.

Serves 4–6

MADRAS CURRY

Ingredients

1 oz all-purpose flour

salt and freshly ground black pepper to taste

1 pound stewing steak, cubed

2 oz ghee or 4 tablespoons oil

2 onions, finely chopped

1 teaspoon ground turmeric

1 teaspoon ground coriander

1 teaspoon cayenne pepper

$\frac{1}{2}$ teaspoon ground black mustard seeds

$\frac{1}{2}$ teaspoon ground cumin

2 cloves garlic, crushed

5 oz hot water

2 oz seedless raisins

Method

1. Place flour in a stout polythene bag and season with salt and pepper. Add stewing steak, close bag and shake until evenly coated.

2. Heat ghee or oil in a heavy-based pan, add floured beef cubes and fry for 5 minutes, stirring and turning meat so that all sides are browned.

3. Add onions and cook, stirring occasionally, for 5 minutes longer.

4. Stir in spices and cook for 3 minutes, then add garlic. Cook for 2 minutes.

5. Add the hot water. Bring to a boil and boil briskly, stirring constantly, for 5 minutes.

6. Stir in raisins and add more water, if necessary, to cover meat. Bring to a boil, lower heat and simmer for $2\frac{1}{4}$ hours, adding more water as required. Serve at once or cool swiftly, refrigerate and reheat next day.

Serves 4

MASALA DUCK CURRY

Ingredients

1 tablespoon sesame oil

4 pound duck, cleaned and cut into 8 pieces

1 onion, chopped

2 small fresh red chilies, finely chopped

1 stalk fresh lemongrass, finely chopped or $\frac{1}{2}$
   teaspoon dried lemongrass, soaked in hot water
   until soft

2 tablespoons green masala curry paste
   (pages 246–247)

$1\frac{1}{2}$ cups coconut milk

3 fresh or dried curry leaves

1 tablespoon lime juice

1 tablespoon brown sugar

1 tablespoon fresh cilantro leaves, chopped

1 oz fresh basil leaves

3 fresh green chilies, seeded and sliced

2 fresh red chilies, seeded and sliced

Method

1. Heat oil in a saucepan over medium heat.
   Add duck and cook, turning frequently, for
   10 minutes or until brown on all sides. Remove
   and drain on paper towels.

2. Add onion, chopped red chilies and
   lemongrass to pan and cook, stirring, for
   3 minutes or until onion is golden. Stir in
   masala paste and cook for 2 minutes longer
   or until fragrant.

4. Stir in coconut milk, curry leaves, lime juice
   and sugar and return duck to pan. Bring to a
   boil and simmer, stirring occasionally, for 45
   minutes.

5. Add cilantro, basil and sliced green and red
   chilies and cook for 10 minutes longer or until
   duck is tender.

Serves 4

seafood

Curry flavor
WITH A CATCH

Fishing is a major industry in India. The men harvest at sea while the women await the landing of the distinctive, often colorful boats. In many communities, it is the women who sort and grade the catch and scurry to the bazaar with loaded baskets to sell.

On the West Coast, the people of tropical Goa and Kerala frequently use coconut, from the palms that line their splendid beaches, to add an aromatic delicacy to their fish curries. The Parsis, who mostly settled north on the same coast at former Bombay, enjoy sweet and sour flavors, and have influenced seafood preparation in Maharashtra state. Equally famed for its seafood is the East Coast state of West Bengal, of which Calcutta is the capital. A Bengali meal without fish is rare indeed. Flavors are pungent, with an emphasis on mustard paste, chilies and tamarind. Fish is often baked in banana leaves, a method also favored in Mumbai. Lobster and shrimp are also favorites in this region.

TIKKA SKEWERS

Ingredients

1½ pound firm white fish fillets, cut into 1 inch wide strips
1 lemon, cut into wedges

Spicy yogurt marinade

1 onion, chopped
4 cloves garlic, crushed
2 teaspoons fresh ginger, finely grated
1 tablespoon ground cumin
1 tablespoon garam masala (pages 246–247)
3 cardamon pods, crushed
1 teaspoon ground turmeric
2 teaspoons chili powder
2 teaspoons ground coriander
1 tablespoon tomato paste
1¾ cups natural yogurt

Cucumber raita

1 cucumber, finely chopped
1 tablespoon fresh mint leaves, chopped
1 cup natural yogurt

Method

1. Pierce fish strips several times with a fork and place in a shallow glass or ceramic dish.

2. To make marinade, place onion, garlic, ginger, cumin, garam masala, cardamon, turmeric, chili powder, coriander and tomato paste in a food processor or blender and process until smooth. Add yogurt and mix to combine. Spoon marinade over fish, toss to combine, cover and marinate in refrigerator for 3 hours.

3. Preheat barbecue to medium heat. Drain fish and thread onto lightly oiled skewers. Place skewers on lightly oiled barbecue grill and cook, turning several times, for 5–6 minutes or until fish is cooked.

4. To make raita, place cucumber, mint and yogurt in a bowl and mix to combine. Serve skewers with lemon wedges and raita.

Note: When buying fish fillets look for those that are shiny and firm with a pleasant smell of the sea. Avoid those that are dull, soft, discolored or oozing water when touched.

Serves 6

GOAN-STYLE FISH AND COCONUT CURRY

Ingredients

2 tomatoes

2 cardamon pods, husks discarded and seeds
    reserved

1 teaspoon each of ground coriander,
    cumin, cinnamon and hot chili powder

½ teaspoon ground turmeric

2 tablespoons water

2 tablespoons vegetable oil

1 onion, finely chopped

1 clove garlic, finely chopped

1 inch piece fresh root ginger, finely chopped

14 oz coconut milk

1½ pounds skinless white fish fillet, such cod, cut
    into 1 inch chunks

salt to taste

fresh cilantro to garnish

Method

1. Place tomatoes in a bowl, cover with boiling water and leave to stand for 30 seconds. Peel, then finely dice flesh.

2. Crush cardamon seeds using a mortar and pestle. Add coriander, cumin, cinnamon, chili powder, turmeric and water and mix to a paste. Set aside.

3. Heat oil in a large, heavy-based saucepan. Fry onion, garlic and ginger for 3 minutes or until softened. Add spice paste, mix well and fry for 1 minute, stirring constantly.

4. Pour in coconut milk and bring to a boil, stirring. Reduce heat and simmer for 10 minutes or until liquid has reduced slightly. Add fish, tomatoes and salt. Partly cover pan and simmer, stirring occasionally, for a further 10 minutes or until fish turns opaque and is cooked through. Garnish with cilantro to serve.

Serves 4

BAKED FISH

Ingredients

2 large onions, roughly chopped

1 tablespoon vegetable oil

2 cloves garlic, crushed

2 fresh red or green chilies, finely chopped

2 teaspoons fresh ginger root, finely chopped

1 tablespoon cumin seeds

2 bay leaves

salt to taste

4 large tomatoes, finely chopped

$1/2$ teaspoon ground cumin

$1/2$ teaspoon ground coriander

pinch of ground cloves

pinch of ground cinnamon

pinch of ground cardamon

$1/2$ teaspoon mango powder

$1/4$ teaspoon ground turmeric

3 tablespoons heavy cream

4 firm white fish fillets, such as John Dory or ocean perch

1 bunch fresh basil leaves, finely chopped

Method

1. Place onions in a food processor or blender and process to make a purée.

2. Heat oil in a heavy-based saucepan, add garlic, chilies, ginger, cumin seeds, bay leaves, salt and onion purée. Cook over medium heat until onions are a pinkish color. Add tomatoes, cumin, coriander, cloves, cinnamon, cardamon, mango powder and turmeric and cook, stirring, for 3–4 minutes. Remove pan from heat and stir in cream.

3. Preheat oven to 350°F. Place fish in a baking dish, pour sauce over and bake for 20 minutes or until fish flakes when tested with a fork. Just prior to serving, sprinkle with basil.

Serves 4

SPICY RED SHRIMP

Ingredients

16 large uncooked shrimp, shelled and deveined

3 large tomatoes, peeled, seeded and chopped

1 tablespoon vegetable oil

1 small bunch cilantro leaves, chopped

Marinade

6 cloves garlic, finely chopped

2 teaspoons fresh ginger, finely chopped

8 fresh red or green chilies, finely chopped

3 tablespoons lemon juice

1 tablespoon superfine sugar

salt to taste

Method

1. To make marinade, place garlic, ginger, chilies, lemon juice, sugar and salt in a bowl and mix to combine. Add shrimp and toss to coat with marinade. Cover and marinate in refrigerator for 15–24 hours.

2. Place tomatoes in a food processor or blender and process until smooth.

3. Preheat oven to 325°F.

4. Heat oil in a wok or large frying-pan, reduce heat and add shrimp with marinade and cook, stirring constantly, for 2–3 minutes.

5. Transfer to a casserole dish and add the tomatoes and cilantro, then combine well.

6. Cover and bake in oven for 30 minutes. Serve in casserole dish with side bowls of boiled rice.

Serves 4

CHILI SESAME SHRIMP KEBABS

Ingredients

1 tablespoon vegetable oil

1 tablespoon Madras curry paste (page 247)

2 tablespoons fresh ginger, finely grated

2 cloves garlic, crushed

2 tablespoons lime juice

½ cup natural yogurt

36 uncooked medium shrimp, shelled and
    deveined, tails left on

6 tablespoons sesame seeds, toasted

Green masala onions

1 oz ghee or butter

2 onions, cut into wedges

2 tablespoons green masala curry paste
    (page 247)

Method

1. Place oil, Madras curry paste, ginger, garlic, lime
   juice and yogurt in a bowl and mix to combine.
   Add shrimp and toss to coat. Cover and
   marinate in the refrigerator for 2–3 hours.

2. Drain shrimp and thread 3 shrimp onto an oiled
   skewer. Repeat with remaining shrimp to make
   12 kebabs. Toss kebabs in sesame seeds and
   cook on a lightly oiled, preheated medium
   barbecue or under a grill for 3 minutes on each
   side or until shrimp are cooked.

3. To make masala onions, melt ghee or butter in a
   saucepan over medium heat. Add onions and
   cook, stirring, for 5 minutes or until soft. Stir in
   green masala paste and cook for 2 minutes
   longer or until heated through. Serve with the
   kebabs.

Serves 6

desserts

Golden to
SILVER TASTES

Indian dessert is usually not served with a family meal. At special festival times and celebrations, such as weddings, Indians indulge their passion for sweet, very sweet foods.

Indian desserts can seem unusual to Westerners. Rice pudding comes in exotic guises. The west has long been acquainted with various nuts and some aromatic spices such as powdered cardamon, cloves, saffron, cinnamon, nutmeg, ginger, vanilla extract and coconut, but not in the combinations used on the subcontinent. In one recipe, green peas form the basis of the dessert!

Milk and yogurt are used extensively in Indian sweets. Real silver leaves, beaten until paper thin and edible, are surprising ingredients available at some specialty stores selling Indian fare.

Ice cream is rarely served in Indian homes, but our mango ice cream makes an appropriate, light finish to a rich dinner. It can also be made with drained, crushed pineapple instead of mango and garnished with mint.

Other Indian desserts include small balls of cream cheese served in rosewater and superfine sugar syrup or balls mixed with almonds, cardamon and a little sweetened condensed milk. And, believe it or not, fritters of banana, pineapple, pear or apple are also common, as they are all over Asia. To make your fritters distinctively Indian, flavor your usual sweet batter mix with cardamon and cinnamon, cut all fruits into big cubes and cook in batches. You can serve each guest little fritters of each fruit, white with sifted confectioner's sugar, and drizzled with rosewater-flavored syrup.

INDIAN RICE PUDDING WITH PISTACHIOS

Ingredients

2 oz basmati rice

2 cups whole milk

14 oz full-cream evaporated milk

butter for greasing

3 cardamon pods, husks discarded and seeds reserved

1 cinnamon stick

2 oz superfine sugar

2 tablespoons flaked almonds, roasted

1 oz shelled pistachios, roughly chopped

Method

1. Preheat oven to 300°F. Place rice, milk and evaporated milk in a small, heavy-based saucepan and bring to a simmer, taking care not to let mixture boil. Simmer, uncovered, for 10 minutes.

2. Butter an ovenproof dish. Transfer rice mixture to dish, then stir in cardamon seeds, cinnamon stick, sugar, almonds and pistachios, reserving 1 tablespoon pistachios to garnish. Bake for 2 hours, or until reduced to a thick consistency, stirring in the skin that will form on top every 30 minutes. Remove cinnamon stick. Serve warm or cold, garnished with reserved pistachios.

Serves 4

ORANGE CARDAMON CAKES

Ingredients

2 cups all-purpose flour

1½ teaspoons baking powder

1 teaspoon baking soda

2 teaspoons ground cardamon

½ cup butter, softened

1 cup sugar

zest and juice of 2 oranges

2 large eggs

⅔ cup yogurt

3 tablespoons marmalade

2 tablespoons boiling water

2 tablespoons sugar, extra

Orange sauce

2 cups sugar

1 cup water

juice of two oranges

2 tablespoons thick cream

4 large oranges, peeled and segmented

Method

1. Preheat oven to 350°F and generously grease twelve 1 cup capacity non-stick muffin tins.

2. In a large bowl, combine flour, baking powder, baking soda and ground cardamon. Set aside.

3. Using an electric mixer, cream butter, sugar and orange zest together until light and fluffy. Add eggs and yogurt and mix on low speed until ingredients are well combined, then fold flour mixture by hand. Do not overmix.

4. Divide batter evenly among the 10–12 muffin tins and bake for 15–18 minutes. Meanwhile, whisk together fresh orange juice, marmalade, boiling water and extra 2 tablespoons sugar.

5. When orange cakes are ready (test with a skewer), remove muffin tins from the oven and spoon orange syrup over cakes. Allow to cool in the tins.

6. Meanwhile, make sauce. Mix together sugar and water and stir until sugar has dissolved. Raise heat and boil vigorously, washing down sides of pan with a pastry brush dipped in cold water. Continue boiling until syrup turns a rich, deep gold then remove pan from heat. Carefully add orange juice to syrup (be careful because it will splatter). Swirl pan to dissolve juice, returning pan to heat if necessary. Once mixture is smooth, remove from heat and set aside to cool. When cool, whisk in the cream then chill.

7. To serve, turn out cakes and place each on a plate. Heap orange segments on top of cakes. then spoon sauce all around.

Serves 6–8

ALMOND BARFI

Ingredients

8 oz blanched almonds

5 oz milk

4 oz sugar

5 oz water

14 oz condensed milk

6 oz butter, diced

Decoration

silver leaf (optional)

2 oz pistachio nuts, shelled and roughly chopped

Method

1. Grease a 10 x 8 inch baking tin. Grind almonds with a little of the milk in a blender or food processor to make a rough paste. Add remaining milk and blend briefly.

2. Put sugar and water in a heavy-based saucepan. Stir over gentle heat until sugar has dissolved. Increase heat and boil rapidly until mixture registers 240°F on a sugar thermometer, the 'soft ball' stage.

3. Stir almond paste and condensed milk into syrup. Add butter and stir until fully dissolved.

4. Bring mixture to a boil again and boil until thermometer again registers 240°F.

5. Pour barfi mixture into prepared tin; spread evenly. Carefully lay silver leaf on top, if using, then sprinkle with pistachio nuts. Cool, then refrigerate overnight to set.

6. Allow barfi to return to room temperature before cutting into squares or diamonds to serve.

Makes about 30 pieces

MANGO ICE CREAM

Ingredients

1¾ pound canned sliced mangoes, drained

4 tablespoons lemon juice

6 oz superfine sugar

2 eggs, separated

10 oz heavy cream, whipped

strawberries for garnish (optional)

Method

1. Set aside a few mango slices for decoration. Purée mango with lemon juice and superfine sugar in a blender or food processor. Transfer to a bowl. Cover and refrigerate.

2. Using an electric mixer, beat egg yolks until pale and creamy. In a separate bowl, beat egg whites until stiff.

3. Fold egg yolks into cream, then fold in mango purée. Finally, fold in stiffly beaten egg whites.

4. Spoon mixture into an ice-cream maker and chill according to instructions. Alternatively, freeze in ice cube trays. When semi-frozen, beat mixture to break up any large ice crystals. Repeat the process once more, then freeze in a suitable container until solid.

5. Soften slightly before serving. Decorate with strawberries and the reserved mango slices.

Makes approx. 4 cups

DESSERTS

GULAB JAMUN

Ingredients

6 oz sugar

2½ cups water

8 green cardamon pods

1 oz self-rising flour

4 oz powdered skim milk

1 oz ghee or butter

1 oz cream cheese

1–2 tablespoons rosewater

2–3 tablespoons milk or natural low fat yogurt

oil for deep-frying

Method

1. Put 5 oz of the sugar with the water in a wide saucepan or deep frying-pan. Stir over gentle heat until sugar has dissolved, then add cardamon pods. Increase heat and boil for 15 minutes to make a light syrup. Reduce heat to lowest setting to keep syrup warm.

2. Combine flour and powdered milk in a bowl. Rub in ghee or butter, then add remaining sugar, cream cheese, rosewater and enough milk or yogurt to form a soft dough. Knead lightly and roll into 18 small balls (jamuns).

3. Heat oil for deep-frying. Cook jamuns in small batches, keeping them moving in the oil until they are golden brown all over.

4. When golden brown, remove jamuns with a slotted spoon and drain on paper towels for 5 minutes. Remove syrup from heat and carefully add jamuns. Allow to cool to room temperature in syrup. To serve, transfer jamuns to individual plates with a slotted spoon, then add 2–3 tablespoons syrup.

Note: These small dumplings in a spicy syrup are a traditional dessert. They are usually made with whole powdered milk. This is not always easy to obtain, so this recipe uses skim milk powder and adds cream cheese.

Serves 6

JALLEBI

Ingredients

Batter

1 pound all-purpose flour

$\frac{1}{2}$ teaspoon salt

1 cup natural low-fat yogurt

2 teaspoons sugar

2 tablespoons easy-blend dried yeast

oil for deep-frying

Syrup

1 pound soft light brown sugar

1 quart water

1 cinnamon stick, broken into short lengths

8 green cardamon pods

4–6 cloves

Method

1. Sift flour and salt into a large bowl, make a well in the center and add yogurt. Stir, gradually incorporating surrounding flour to make a smooth batter. Stir in sugar and yeast, cover and set aside in a warm place for 4–6 hours until batter is well risen.

2. To make syrup, put sugar and water in a heavy-bottomed saucepan. Stir over gentle heat until sugar has dissolved, then add cinnamon, cardamon pods and cloves. Increase heat and boil rapidly until syrup is thick and heavy and has reduced by half. Reduce heat to lowest setting to keep syrup warm while cooking jallebi.

3. Heat oil for deep-frying. Fill a large piping bag, fitted with a narrow nozzle, with jallebi batter. Squeeze batter in spirals into hot oil, stopping the flow when each jallebi measures about 4 inches across. Do not cook too many jallebi at the same time. Remove with a slotted spoon as soon as they are golden brown.

4. Drain jallebi on paper towels, then dip into pan of hot syrup. Dip for up to 5 minutes, depending on how sweet you like your jallebi. Drain off excess syrup and serve.

Note: Jallebi are deep-fried spirals of cooked sweet batter which are dunked–or soaked–in a sweet spicy syrup.

Makes about 20

Agar agar (kanten, Japanese): A vegetarian alternative to gelatin. Often used in desserts. A setting agent not requiring refrigeration. Derived from seaweed and known also as Chinese grass. Gelatin is a possible substitute, but amounts required and texture differs.

Aonoriko (Japanese): Seaweed powder

Baguette: Crusty bread stick introduced to Vietnam by the French.

Bamboo shoots: Savory, crunchy vegetable. Young bamboo plant shoots available fresh, in cans or bottled as pickled, salted or unsalted.

Banana leaves: Flavorless leaves used for wrapping rolls. Use foil if unavailable.

Basil: Herb which has a faint anise seed flavor. Used as an ingredient or garnish.

Bean curd: Known also as tofu. Made from soy beans and available fresh to keep for up to three days in water in the refrigerator. Dried, it needs water softening before use. Use sweet in vegetarian or braised dishes. Red bean curd is strong and pungent and available canned or bottled. Available soft, semi-soft and firm. A versatile meat replacement.

Bean paste: Made from soy beans and sold in jars and cans. Varieties are hot bean paste, salty with chili; soy bean paste of fermented beans, dark and very salty; yellow bean paste from yellow soy beans; and sweet bean paste made from black soy beans, sugar, flour and spices. Refrigerate after opening.

Bean sauce: Salted, mashed soy beans in jars. Keeps indefinitely.

Bean sprouts: Grown from mung beans. Used cooked or uncooked. Mung bean sprouts, raw in salads, also a savory ingredient. Can be grown in cotton wool at home.

Black beans: Salted, canned or bottled. Wash in cold water before use.

Black bean sauce: Fermented soy beans with wheat flour and water.

Bok choy: Chinese leafy vegetable available at most supermarkets and markets. Substitute Savoy cabbage if unavailable.

Butaniku (Japanese): Pork.

Can (Vietnamese): Thin bamboo straw for drinking moonshine of same name. Made from rice.

Cane sugar: Gives sugar explosion when sucked. Cane sugar juice is a popular drink.

Cellophane noodles: Made from green mung bean starch. They need soaking before use in soups or stir-fries.

Chao (Vietnamese): Rice porridge.

Chay (Vietnamese): Vegetarian.

Che (Vietnamese): Sweetmeat of mung beans. Cakes available at dessert shops.

Chili sauce: Chinese bottled chili sauce is hot, but, if imported and made to Malaysian and Singaporean recipes, can be sweet.

Chilies: Red or green, mild to hot ingredient and garnish. A fiery seasoning also available powdered (hot) and flaked.

Chirinabe (Japanese): A boiled fish and vegetable dish, eaten with a soy dipping sauce.

Cinnamon: Native of Sri Lanka. Comes in packets or jars, dried whole or powdered.

Cloud ears: Small, dried mushroom, black or white.

Cloves: Dried or powdered. Useful in roasted, braised and sweet dishes.

Coconut: Flaked, use as dry ingredient or mix with boiling water, cool, squeeze and strain through sieve for coconut cream or add more water for milk. Coconut cream and milk are available in cartons, canned or powdered for reconstitution.

Com (Vietnamese): Means rice; also simple.

Coriander: Fresh herb known also as cilantro indispensable fresh in Vietnamese dishes. Dried coriander is no substitute for fresh, but dried seeds can be used in curry dishes.

Cornflour: Cornstarch; thickening flour.

Curry powder: Often used in Vietnamese dishes, but, is not often mixed at home in Vietnam so use a good quality bought curry powder instead.

Daikon: A long white Japanese radish, about the size of a large carrot. It may be cooked or served raw.

Dango (Japanese): Dumpling.

Dashi (Japanese): A delicately flavored fish soup stock.

Don ganh (Vietnamese): Bamboo pole for carrying goods on shoulders.

Dried shrimp: Uses to make shrimp sauce.

Eggplant: Aka Chinese eggplant, thin and less bitter in Vietnam; rub with salt to draw out bitterness then wash if using plumper variety; also called aubergine.

Enoki mushrooms: Cultivated mushrooms, with long thin stems and small white caps. They have a delicate flavor and crisp texture. May be eaten lightly cooked.

Fish sauce: Nuoc cham (Vietnamese), pungent, salty sauce made from fermented anchovies. An essential ingredient in dipping sauce. Keeps indefinitely if refrigerated.

Five spice powder: Strong Chinese mix of Szechuan peppercorns, star anise, fennel, cloves and cinnamon; use sparingly.

Gari (Japanese): Pickled ginger. This pale pink ginger is used as an accompaniment to sushi and sashimi.

Garlic: Fresh, powdered, flaked (to be soaked before use) or shredded in jars. Adds savory flavor.

Ginger: Has a refreshing scent, reminiscent of citrus, and a pleasant sharp flavor. Fresh, peeled, sliced, crushed, used in many dishes; powdered does not have same strong flavor. Fresh root is essential in most meat and seafood dishes. Powder is not a good substitute.

Ginko nuts (ginnan, Japanese): Small nuts from the Japanese maple tree, icho. They have a milky flavor with a slight bitterness. Ginko nuts are often fried and roasted served as an hors d'oeuvre.

Glutinous rice: Not to be confused with long- or short-grained, it comes packaged dry or in powder for puddings and pastries.

Gohan (Japanese): Rice.

Green mustard: Leafy, bitter vegetable suitable for soup and stir-fries.

Gyuuniku (Japanese): Beef.

Hakusai (Japanese): Chinese cabbage.

Hamaguri (Japanese): Clams.

Hashi (Japanese): Wooden chopsticks.

Hoisin sauce: Has a fragrant aroma with a rich, warm, sweet, yet salty, flavor. Soy bean flour, red beans, ginger, chili, garlic, spices, salt and sugar bottled as a condiment.

Horaku-yaki (Japanese): Salted baked fish and vegetables.

Ikura (Japanese): Salmon roe.

Ise-ebi (Japanese): Lobster.

Jingisukan nabe (Japanese): 'Ghengis Khan pot'; beef or lamb cooked with vegetables in a special pot.

Kabayaki (Japanese): Grilled fillets of veal.

Kaibashira (Japanese): Scallops.

Kaki (Japanese): Oysters.

Kani (Japanese): Crab.

Kare raisu (Japanese): 'Curry rice', curry and rice.

Katsvi-bushi (Japanese): Dried bonito.

Kimi oboro (Japanese): Grated hard-boiled egg yolk.

Kinoko (Japanese): Mushrooms.

Kinome (Japanese): Japanese plum paste.

Konbu (Japanese): Kelp seaweed, used as a flavoring for stocks. Is also eaten as a vegetable.

Kuromitsu sauce: Japanese black sugar syrup.

Kuronerigoma (Japanese): Ground black sesame seeds.

Kuruma-ebi (Japanese): Prawn or shrimp

Lard: This rendered pork fat can be an essential binding ingredient or reduced to make oil. It is still available from butcher shops or supermarkets. Substitute another shortening if necessary.

Lemongrass: Has a distinctive citrus aroma with a intense lemon flavor, and a hint of ginger. Lemony stalk should be bruised after discarding leaves. If fresh is unavailable, use bottled.

Lotus fruit: Firm and crunchy fruit for soup and vegetarian dishes. Available canned.

Lotus leaves: Used as food wraps during cooking to transfer flavors. Dried leaves are sold in packets and should be soaked for 25 minutes in warm water before being used.

Lotus root (renkon, Japanese): The rhizome of a water lily, usually available fresh, canned and also frozen.

Lychees: Sweet fruit, canned or fresh for desserts or sweet and sour dishes.

Maguro (Japanese): Tuna fish.

Makisu (Japanese): Bamboo mat used to roll sushi.

Manju (Japanese): A Japanese cake traditionally eaten with green tea at lunchtime.

Menrui (Japanese): Noodles.

Mint: Fresh ingredient or garnish; when chopped and combined equally with cilantro, resembles *rau ram* (Vietnamese mint) aka polygonum.

Mirin (Japanese): Sweet sticky rice wine, used for cooking.

Miso (Japanese): Fermented soy bean paste. Used for soup or as a seasoning.

Miso-shiru (Japanese): Soup thickened with a red bean paste. Can be obtained from a Japanese grocery.

Mitsuba (Japanese): An aromatic herb used mostly in soups.

Mochi (Japanese): Rice cakes made from mochigome rice (sticky rice).

GLOSSARY

Momiji oroshi (Japanese): Japanese chili paste.

Mushrooms: Black, add flavor, fresh, also dried. Straw most popular in Vietnam, substitute button or canned champignons; also dried wood or tree ear or dried black Chinese mushrooms which need to be soaked; dried not as flavorful as fresh.

Musiyaki (Japanese): Fish cooked in potato.

Nabe-mono (Japanese): 'One-pot cookery'.

Niwatori (Japanese): Chicken.

Nizakana (Japanese): Fish cooked in soy sauce.

Noodles: Dried cellophane or glass, from mung beans; reconstitute in hot water; fresh, wide noodles are used in Vietnamese *pho* soup; rice vermicelli, fresh or dry, doubles in quantity when cooked; dried or fresh Chinese yellow egg noodles are for soups and stir-fries.

Nori (Japanese): Very thin sheets of dried seaweed, dark green to black in color.

Nori-maki (Japanese): A bowl of rice garnished with seaweed.

Nuta (Japanese): A strongly flavored dish of raw fish and vegetables.

O-cha (Japanese): 'Honorable green tea'.

Ogura (Japanese): Paste made out of red beans.

Oils: Can comprise sesame, peanut, canola or vegetable, according to the recipe. Olive oil has too strong a flavor for many Asian dishes.

Oyster sauce: Has a pleasant, fragrant aroma, and has a delicious and delicate flavor. A thick mix of ground oysters, salt, water, cornflour and caramel, mostly used in stir-fries.

Oysters: Dried oysters need water softening. Useful when the fresh product is unavailable. Can be bought bottled at some shops.

Pan (Japanese): Bread.

Papaya: Pawpaw; use green in salads; when a ripe orange color, it's a sweet fruit.

Pho (Vietnamese): Beef noodle soup, a national Vietnamese dish.

Pineapple: Use canned if fresh unavailable.

Plum sauce: Bottled, is used as a condiment, dipping sauce or ingredient. It can be homemade with sweetness added.

Ponzu (soy) sauce: A Japanese sauce made with citrus juice, vinegar and seasonings.

Pork fat: Buy from butcher as its flavor cannot be replaced except by bacon fat.

Rice flour: Basis for rice noodle and sweet dishes; cannot be substituted for glutinous rice; rice paper wrappers made from rice flour, commercially available, are brittle and must be well dampened.

Rice vinegar: A pale, delicately flavored vinegar.

Rice: Asia's staple; long-grain accompanies Vietnamese sit-down meals; sticky rice is glutinous rice, sweeter and used as stuffing and in desserts in Vietnam. Varieties of rice are: **Basmati rice:** a non-glutinous rice that has been cultivated at the foot of the Himalayan mountain ranges for centuries. The rice is an aromatic long grain slender rice from India, scented, with a nutty flavor and when literally translated from Hindi it means 'queen of scents' or 'pearl of scents'. **Jasmine rice:** is an excellent white rice and can be interchanged with white Basmati rice for variety. This rice has a slight jasmine aroma after cooking and cooks to nice firm rice. It is just slightly sticky when compared to Basmati.

Saba (Japanese): Mackerel.

Saikyou miso (Japanese): Lightly flavored pale yellow soy bean paste with a sweet taste.

Sake (Japanese): A traditional rice wine for drinking and cooking. Can be served hot or chilled.

Sansho (Japanese): Ground Japanese mountain pepper.

Sashimi (Japanese): Raw fish sliced thinly, served without rice.

Sesame seeds: Black and white sesame seeds can be used, often available roasted or plain.

Shaoxing rice wine (Chinese): Substitute dry sherry if not available.

Shiitake mushrooms: A very popular mushroom in Japan with brown cap and a white stem. Available dried or fresh.

Shironerigoma (Japanese): Ground white sesame seeds.

Shiso leaves: A Japanese herb with a basil-like flavor. Often used to garnish dishes.

Shoyu (Japanese): Soy sauce.

Shrimp, dried: Needs water soaking and is a strong flavoring agent.

Shrimps: See also dried shrimps; shrimp paste, also known as prawn paste, is also an ingredient used in spicy dips and sauces.

Shungiku (Japanese): The edible leaves and stems of the Japanese chrysanthemum.

Snow peas: Crispy, these pods are decorative, tasty and available seasonally fresh. Also known as mangetout.

Soba (Japanese): Buckwheat noodles.

Somen (Japanese): Very thin white flour noodles. Served cold in summer.

Soy sauce: An absolute, bottled must as a condiment for many dishes. It is fermented soy bean extract, sold as either light and delicate or dark and caramel flavored.

Spring onion: Aka green onion or scallion. Green with white root, salad vegetable, ingredient and garnish.

Star anise: Star-shaped, with anise seed flavour, this eight-pointed spice is available in supermarkets and is also a component of five spice powder.

Starfruit: Tart tropical fruit also used in savory dishes.

Suiji (Japanese): A stock used in soups and stock pots.

Sushi (Japanese): Thin slices of fish, seafood or vegetables arranged over a portion of sushi rice.

Sushi vinegar: Sweetened vinegar used to make sushi rice.

Tai (Japanese): Sea bream.

Takenoko (Japanese): Bamboo shoot.

Tamari (Japanese): Thick soy sauce with a delicate flavor.

Tempura (Japanese): Pieces of seafood and vegetables battered and deep-fried.

Tet: Vietnamese New Year.

Tobiko (Japanese): Flying fish roe.

Tofu: Soy bean curd.

Turmeric: Has a peppery aroma with a hint of wood. It imparts a warm, slightly musky flavor. Yellow ochre colored spice, used in curries and to add color.

Udon (Japanese): White ribbon wheat noodles, available fresh, dried or frozen.

Udonji (Japanese): Udon stock.

Unagi (Japanese): Eel.

Wasabi (Japanese): Very hot green Japanese horseradish. Available in a paste, powder or frozen.

Wonton wrapper: Pastry in which various ingredients are wrapped to make dumplings. Available commercially or home-made.

Yuzu (Japanese): A citrus fruit similar to lime.

INDEX